SOLARO

STUDY GUIDE

Mathematics 6

SOLARO Study Guide is designed to help students achieve success in school. The content in each study guide is 100% curriculum aligned and serves as an excellent source of material for review and practice. To create this book, teachers, curriculum specialists, and assessment experts have worked closely to develop the instructional pieces that explain each of the key concepts for the course. The practice questions and sample tests have detailed solutions that show problem-solving methods, highlight concepts that are likely to be tested, and point out potential sources of errors. **SOLARO Study Guide** is a complete guide to be used by students throughout the school year for reviewing and understanding course content, and to prepare for assessments.

Rao,Gautam,1961 –
SOLARO STUDY GUIDE – Mathematics 6 Ontario

1. Mathematics – Juvenile Literature. I. Title

Castle Rock Research Corp.
2410 Manulife Place
10180 – 101 Street
Edmonton, AB T5J 3S4

1 2 3 PP 15 14 13

Publisher
Gautam Rao

Contributors
Stephanie Coles
Betty Morris
Mary Anne Nissen
Lara Tyler

CASTLE ROCK
RESEARCH CORP

Dedicated to the memory of Dr. V. S. Rao

SOLARO STUDY GUIDE

Each **SOLARO STUDY GUIDE** consists of the following sections:

Key Tips for Being Successful at School gives examples of study and review strategies. It includes information about learning styles, study schedules, and note taking for test preparation.

Class Focus includes a unit on each area of the curriculum. Units are divided into sections, each focusing on one of the specific expectations, or main ideas, that students must learn about in that unit. Examples, definitions, and visuals help to explain each main idea. Practice questions on the main ideas are also included. At the end of each unit is a test on the important ideas covered. The practice questions and unit tests help students identify areas they know and those they need to study more. They can also be used as preparation for tests and quizzes. Most questions are of average difficulty, though some are easy and some are hard—the harder questions are called *Challenger Questions*. Each unit is prefaced by a **Table of Correlations**, which correlates questions in the unit (and in the practice tests at the end of the book) to the specific curriculum expectations. Answers and solutions are found at the end of each unit.

Key Strategies for Success on Tests helps students get ready for tests. It shows students different types of questions they might see, word clues to look for when reading them, and hints for answering them.

Practice Tests includes one to three tests based on the entire course. They are very similar to the format and level of difficulty that students may encounter on final tests. In some regions, these tests may be reprinted versions of official tests, or reflect the same difficulty levels and formats as official versions. This gives students the chance to practice using real-world examples. Answers and complete solutions are provided at the end of the section.

For the complete curriculum document (including specific expectations along with examples and sample problems), visit http://www.edu.gov.on.ca/eng/curriculum/

SOLARO STUDY GUIDE *Study Guides* are available for many courses. Check www.castlerockresearch.com for a complete listing of books available for your area.

For information about any of our resources or services, please call Castle Rock Research at 1.800.840.6224 or visit our website at http://www.castlerockresearch.com.

At Castle Rock Research, we strive to produce an error-free resource. If you should find an error, please contact us so that future editions can be corrected.

CONTENTS

Key Tips for being Successful at School

KEY TIPS FOR BEING SUCCESSFUL AT SCHOOL

KEY FACTORS CONTRIBUTING TO SCHOOL SUCCESS

In addition to learning the content of your courses, there are some other things that you can do to help you do your best at school. You can try some of the following strategies:

- **Keep a positive attitude:** Always reflect on what you can already do and what you already know.

- **Be prepared to learn:** Have the necessary pencils, pens, notebooks, and other required materials for participating in class ready.

- **Complete all of your assignments:** Do your best to finish all of your assignments. Even if you know the material well, practice will reinforce your knowledge. If an assignment or question is difficult for you, work through it as far as you can so that your teacher can see exactly where you are having difficulty.

- **Set small goals for yourself when you are learning new material:** For example, when learning the parts of speech, do not try to learn everything in one night. Work on only one part or section each study session. When you have memorized one particular part of speech and understand it, move on to another one. Continue this process until you have memorized and learned all the parts of speech.

- **Review your classroom work regularly at home:** Review to make sure you understand the material you learned in class.

- **Ask your teacher for help:** Your teacher will help you if you do not understand something or if you are having a difficult time completing your assignments.

- **Get plenty of rest and exercise:** Concentrating in class is hard work. It is important to be well-rested and have time to relax and socialize with your friends. This helps you keep a positive attitude about your schoolwork.

- **Eat healthy meals:** A balanced diet keeps you healthy and gives you the energy you need for studying at school and at home.

HOW TO FIND YOUR LEARNING STYLE

Every student learns differently. The manner in which you learn best is called your learning style. By knowing your learning style, you can increase your success at school. Most students use a combination of learning styles. Do you know what type of learner you are? Read the following descriptions. Which of these common learning styles do you use most often?

- **Linguistic Learner:** You may learn best by saying, hearing, and seeing words. You are probably really good at memorizing things such as dates, places, names, and facts. You may need to write down the steps in a process, a formula, or the actions that lead up to a significant event, and then say them out loud.

- **Spatial Learner:** You may learn best by looking at and working with pictures. You are probably really good at puzzles, imagining things, and reading maps and charts. You may need to use strategies like mind mapping and webbing to organize your information and study notes.

- **Kinesthetic Learner:** You may learn best by touching, moving, and figuring things out using manipulatives. You are probably really good at physical activities and learning through movement. You may need to draw your finger over a diagram to remember it, tap out the steps needed to solve a problem, or feel yourself writing or typing a formula.

SCHEDULING STUDY TIME

You should review your class notes regularly to ensure that you have a clear understanding of all the new material you learned. Reviewing your lessons on a regular basis helps you to learn and remember ideas and concepts. It also reduces the quantity of material that you need to study prior to a test. Establishing a study schedule will help you to make the best use of your time.

Regardless of the type of study schedule you use, you may want to consider the following suggestions to maximize your study time and effort:

- Organize your work so that you begin with the most challenging material first.

- Divide the subject's content into small, manageable chunks.

- Alternate regularly between your different subjects and types of study activities in order to maintain your interest and motivation.

- Make a daily list with headings like "Must Do," "Should Do," and "Could Do."

- Begin each study session by quickly reviewing what you studied the day before.

- Maintain your usual routine of eating, sleeping, and exercising to help you concentrate better for extended periods of time.

CREATING STUDY NOTES

MIND-MAPPING OR WEBBING

Use the key words, ideas, or concepts from your reading or class notes to create a mind map or web (a diagram or visual representation of the given information). A mind map or web is sometimes referred to as a knowledge map. Use the following steps to create a mind map or web:

1. Write the key word, concept, theory, or formula in the centre of your page.

2. Write down related facts, ideas, events, and information, and link them to the central concept with lines.

3. Use coloured markers, underlining, or symbols to emphasize things such as relationships, timelines, and important information.

The following examples of a Frayer Model illustrate how this technique can be used to study vocabulary.

Definition	Notes
• Perimeter is the distance around the outside of a polygon.	• Perimeter is measured in linear units (e.g., metres, centimetres, and so on).

Perimeter

Examples	Non-Examples
• The length of a fence around a yard	• The area of grass covering a lawn
• The distance around a circle (circumference)	• The size of a rug lying on a floor

Definition	Notes
• A cube is a solid 3-D object with six faces.	• A cube is different from other shapes because it has six equally-sized square faces, eight vertices, and twelve equal edges.

Cube

Examples	Non-Examples

INDEX CARDS

To use index cards while studying, follow these steps:

1. Write a key word or question on one side of an index card.

2. On the reverse side, write the definition of the word, answer to the question, or any other important information that you want to remember.

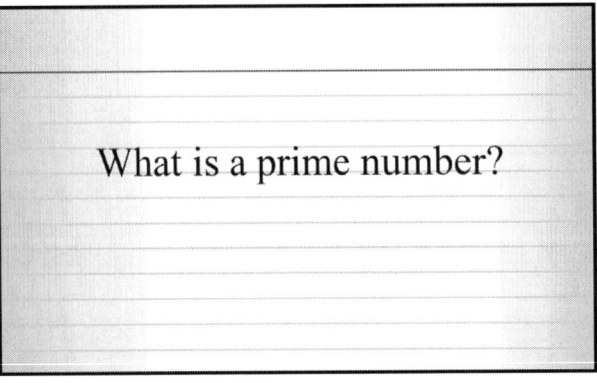

SYMBOLS AND STICKY NOTES—IDENTIFYING IMPORTANT INFORMATION

Use symbols to mark your class notes. The following are some examples:

- An exclamation mark (!) might be used to point out something that must be learned well because it is a very important idea.

- A question mark (?) may highlight something you are not certain about

- A diamond (◊) or asterisk (*) could highlight interesting information that you want to remember.

Sticky notes are useful in the following situations:

- Use sticky notes when you are not allowed to put marks in books.

- Use sticky notes to mark a page in a book that contains an important diagram, formula, explanation, or other information.

- Use sticky notes to mark important facts in research books.

MEMORIZATION TECHNIQUES

- **Association** relates new learning to something you already know. For example, to remember the spelling difference between dessert and desert, recall that the word *sand* has only one *s*. So, because there is sand in a desert, the word *desert* has only one *s*.

- **Mnemonic** devices are sentences that you create to remember a list or group of items. For example, the first letter of each word in the phrase "Every Good Boy Deserves Fudge" helps you to remember the names of the lines on the treble-clef staff (E, G, B, D, and F) in music.

- **Acronyms** are words that are formed from the first letters or parts of the words in a group. For example, RADAR is actually an acronym for Radio Detecting and Ranging, and MASH is an acronym for Mobile Army Surgical Hospital. HOMES helps you to remember the names of the five Great Lakes (Huron, Ontario, Michigan, Erie, and Superior).

- **Visualizing** requires you to use your mind's eye to "see" a chart, list, map, diagram, or sentence as it is in your textbook or notes, on the chalkboard or computer screen, or in a display.

- **Initialisms** are abbreviations that are formed from the first letters or parts of the words in a group. Unlike acronyms, an initialism cannot be pronounced as a word itself. For example, GCF is an initialism for **G**reatest **C**ommon **F**actor.

KEY STRATEGIES FOR REVIEWING

Reviewing textbook material, class notes, and handouts should be an ongoing activity. Spending time reviewing becomes more critical when you are preparing for a test. You may find some of the following review strategies useful when studying during your scheduled study time:

- Before reading a selection, preview it by noting the headings, charts, graphs, and chapter questions.

- Before reviewing a unit, note the headings, charts, graphs, and chapter questions.

- Highlight key concepts, vocabulary, definitions, and formulas.

- Skim the paragraph, and note the key words, phrases, and information.

- Carefully read over each step in a procedure.

- Draw a picture or diagram to help make the concept clearer.

KEY STRATEGIES FOR SUCCESS: A CHECKLIST

Reviewing is a huge part of doing well at school and preparing for tests. Here is a checklist for you to keep track of how many suggested strategies for success you are using. Read each question, and put a check mark (✓) in the correct column. Look at the questions where you have checked the "No" column. Think about how you might try using some of these strategies to help you do your best at school.

Key Strategies for Success	Yes	No
Do you attend school regularly?		
Do you know your personal learning style—how you learn best?		
Do you spend 15 to 30 minutes a day reviewing your notes?		
Do you study in a quiet place at home?		
Do you clearly mark the most important ideas in your study notes?		
Do you use sticky notes to mark texts and research books?		
Do you practise answering multiple-choice and written-response questions?		
Do you ask your teacher for help when you need it?		
Are you maintaining a healthy diet and sleep routine?		
Are you participating in regular physical activity?		

Number Sense and Numeration

NUMBER SENSE AND NUMERATION

Table of Correlations

Specific Expectation		Practice Questions	Unit Test Questions	Practice Test 1	Practice Test 2
6m8	Quantity Relationships				
6m11	represent, compare, and order whole numbers and decimal numbers from 0.001 to 1 000 000, using a variety of tools	1, 2	5	26	
6m12	demonstrate an understanding of place value in whole numbers and decimal numbers from 0.001 to 1 000 000, using a variety of tools and strategies	3, 4	6		25
6m13	read and print in words whole numbers to one hundred thousand, using meaningful contexts	5	7		
6m14	represent, compare, and order fractional amounts with unlike denominators, including proper and improper fractions and mixed numbers, using a variety of tools and using standard fractional notation	6, 7	8		26, 27
6m15	estimate quantities using benchmarks of 10%, 25%, 50%, 75%, and 100%	8	9		
6m16	solve problems that arise from real-life situations and that relate to the magnitude of whole numbers up to 1 000 000	9, 10	10, 11	27	
6m17	identify composite numbers and prime numbers, and explain the relationship between them (i.e., any composite number can be factored into prime factors)	11, 12	12, 13	28	
6m9	Operational Sense				
6m18	use a variety of mental strategies to solve addition, subtraction, multiplication, and division problems involving whole numbers	13, 14	14	29	
6m19	solve problems involving the multiplication and division of whole numbers (four digit by two digit), using a variety of tools and strategies	15, 16	15, 16	30	
6m20	add and subtract decimal numbers to thousandths, using concrete materials, estimation, algorithms, and calculators	17	17	31	
6m21	multiply and divide decimal numbers to tenths by whole numbers, using concrete materials, estimation, algorithms, and calculators	18, 19	18		28
6m22	multiply whole numbers by 0.1, 0.01, and 0.001 using mental strategies	20	19		
6m23	multiply and divide decimal numbers by 10, 100, 1 000, and 10 000 using mental strategies	21	20		
6m24	use estimation when solving problems involving the addition and subtraction of whole numbers and decimals, to help judge the reasonableness of a solution	22	21		29
6m25	explain the need for a standard order for performing operations, by investigating the impact that changing the order has when performing a series of operations	23, 24	22		30
6m10	Proportional Relationships				
6m26	represent ratios found in real-life contexts, using concrete materials, drawings, and standard fractional notation	25	1		12

6m27	determine and explain, through investigation using concrete materials, drawings, and calculators, the relationships among fractions (i.e., with denominators of 2, 4, 5, 10, 20, 25, 50, and 100), decimal numbers, and percents	26, 27, 28	2, 3	13, 14	
6m28	represent relationships using unit rates	29	4		13

6m11 represent, compare, and order whole numbers and decimal numbers from 0.001 to 1 000 000, using a variety of tools

REPRESENTING, COMPARING, AND ORDERING WHOLE NUMBERS AND DECIMAL NUMBERS

REPRESENTING WHOLE NUMBERS

Whole numbers can be represented using symbols, words, **place value charts, number lines,** and **base ten materials**. An example of a whole number, such as 130 000, is represented in the place value chart shown below.

Millions			Thousands			Ones		
H	T	O	H	T	O	H	T	O
			1	3	0	0	0	0
H – Hundreds, T – Tens, O – Ones								

BASE TEN BLOCKS

When representing whole numbers using base ten blocks, the large **cube** represents 1 000, the flat represents 100, the rod represents 10, and the small cube represents 1. For example, the number 1 238 can be represented with base ten blocks.

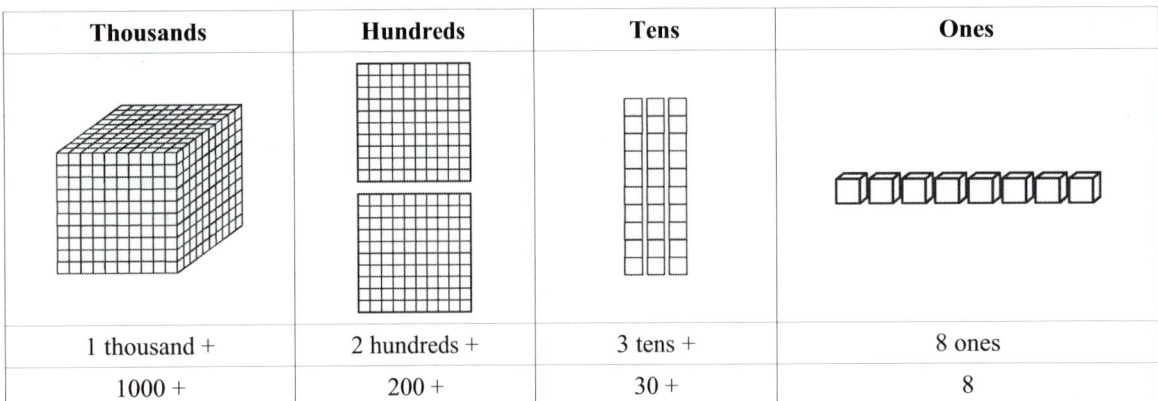

Thousands	Hundreds	Tens	Ones
1 thousand +	2 hundreds +	3 tens +	8 ones
1000 +	200 +	30 +	8

Representing 1 238 as 1 000 + 200 + 30 + 8 is called **expanded notation**.

COMPARING AND ORDERING WHOLE NUMBERS

When you compare and order whole numbers, you place two or more numbers from least to greatest or from greatest to least. An example of numbers ordered from least to greatest is 99, 179, and 304.

ORDER WHOLE NUMBERS TO 1 000 000

To order the whole numbers 36 489, 985, 8 567, and 897 551, you can place the numbers in a place value chart as shown below.

Thousands			Ones		
Hundred thousands	Ten thousands	Thousands	Hundreds	Tens	Ones
	3	6	4	8	9
			9	8	5
		8	5	6	7
8	9	7	5	5	1

To order these numbers from least to greatest, look for the number with its first non-zero digit in the lowest place value position. In this case, 985 is the only number that has no digits in the thousands place, so it is the least number. It is also the number with the least number of digits. The next number is 8 567 because it is the only one of the remaining numbers that has no digits in the ten thousands place. The number 36 489 has a digit in the ten thousands place, but no digit in the hundred thousands place. So, the number 36 489 is the next number, followed by 897 551. The order is 985, 8 567, 36 489, and 897 551.

REPRESENTING DECIMAL NUMBERS

As with whole numbers, **decimal numbers** can also be represented by using a place value chart. The number 3 250.15 is shown in the place value chart below.

Thousands			Ones			.	Parts of a Whole		
H	T	O	H	T	O	.	Tenths	Hundredths	Thousandths
		3	2	5	0	.	1	5	

When decimal numbers are represented with base ten materials, the same base ten materials that are used to represent whole numbers are also used to represent decimal numbers, but they are renamed as shown below. The large cube is 1, the flat is 0.1, the rod is 0.01, and the small cube is 0.001. For example, the number 1.234 is shown below using base ten blocks.

Ones	.	Tenths	Hundredths	Thousandths
1 ones +	.	2 tenths +	3 hundredths +	4 thousandths
1 +		0.2 +	0.3+	0.004

ORDER DECIMALS TO 1000THS

To order decimal numbers from least to greatest, you can use a number line.

NUMBER LINE

The decimal numbers 1.461, 0.986, 0.76, and 0.41 are placed on a number line as shown below.

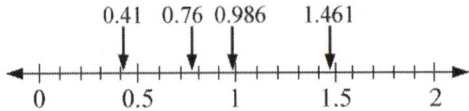

By placing the numbers in the correct place on the number line, they are in order from least to greatest.

Remember that the digits in the thousandths place are less than the digits in the hundredths, the hundredths are less than the tenths, and the tenths are less than the ones.

 1. Which of the following numbers is greater than 931 475 and less than 962 310?
   A. 913 680   B. 929 395
   C. 957 202   D. 985 000

Use the following information to answer the next question.

> Sarah, Yolanda, Jane, and Kevin raced their pet snails. The following table shows the distance that the snails travelled in one minute.
>
> | Snail | Distance Travelled (m) |
> |---|---|
> | Jane's snail | 0.20 |
> | Kevin's snail | 0.12 |
> | Sarah's snail | 0.16 |
> | Yolanda's snail | 0.10 |

2. Listed in order from the child with the fastest snail to the child with the slowest snail, the children are
   A. Sarah, Yolanda, Kevin, and Jane   B. Sarah, Yolanda, Jane, and Kevin
   C. Yolanda, Jane, Sarah, and Kevin   D. Yolanda, Sarah, Kevin, and Jane

6m12 demonstrate an understanding of place value in whole numbers and decimal numbers from 0.001 to 1 000 000, using a variety of tools and strategies

PLACE VALUE IN WHOLE AND DECIMAL NUMBERS

PLACE VALUE IN WHOLE NUMBERS

The relationship between place values can be explained by using a place value chart and base ten blocks. Note that in the chart below, the same base ten material can be used for more than one place value. The small cube can represent 1 in the ones **period** and it can also represent 1 000 in the thousands period. The ten rod can represent 10 in the ones period and 10 000 in the thousands period. The hundred flat can represent 100 in the ones period and 100 000 in the thousands period.

Thousands			Ones		
Hundreds	Tens	Ones	Hundreds	Tens	Ones
100 000	10 000	1 000	100	10	1

x 10   x 10   x 10   x 10   x 10   x 10

As you move from right to left in the place value chart, multiply the place value on the right by 10 to get the next place value immediately to the left. For example, 10 ones make 1 ten, 10 tens make 1 hundred, 10 hundreds make 1 thousand, and so on.

Another method for showing the place values of the digits of a number is to use a place value chart with numbers.

Example
Show the number 952 834 in a place value chart.

Solution

Millions			Thousands			Ones		
H	T	O	H	T	O	H	T	O
			9	5	2	8	3	4

The digit 9 is in the hundred thousands place. The value is 9 × 100 000, or 900 000.
The digit 5 is in the ten thousands place. The value is 5 × 10 000, or 50 000.
The digit 2 is in the thousands place. The value is 2 × 1 000, or 2 000.
The digit 8 is in the hundreds place. The value is 8 × 100, or 800.
The digit 3 is in the tens place. The value is 3 × 10, or 30.
The digit 4 is in the ones place. The value is 4 × 1, or 4.

This can also be written in expanded form as
(9 × 100 000) + (5 × 10 000) + (2 × 1 000) + (8 × 100) + (3 × 10) + (4 × 1),
or 900 000 + 50 000 + 2 000 + 800 + 30 + 4, which is equal to 952 834.

PLACE VALUE IN DECIMAL NUMBERS

The pattern showing the relationship among place values is the same in decimal numbers as it is in whole numbers. As you move from right to left in the place value chart, multiply the place value on the right by 10 to get the place value immediately to the left. For example, 10 thousandths make 1 hundredth, 10 hundredths make 1 tenth, and 10 tenths make 1 whole.

Place value position	Ones	•	Tenths	Hundredths	Thousandths
Base ten block		•			
Value	1	•	0.1	0.01	0.001
Shape	Large cube	•	Flat	Rod	Small cube

×10   ×10   ×10

Example

Describe the place value of each digit in the number 1.438 using base ten materials.

Solution

Ones	•	Tenths	Hundredths	Thousandths
	•			
1	•	0.1	0.01	0.001
1 one	•	4 tenths	3 hundredths	8 thousandths

First, remember that the decimal place is in between the ones and the tenths place.
The digit 1 is in the ones place. The value is 1×1, or 1.
The digit 4 is in the tenths place. The value is 4×0.1, or 0.4.
The digit 3 is in the hundredths place. The value is 3×0.01, or 0.03.
The digit 8 is in the thousandths place. The value is 8×0.001, or 0.008.
Therefore, $1 + 0.4 + 0.03 + 0.008 = 1.438$

3.   What is the expanded form of the number 2 016?
   A. $200 + 10 + 6$ B. $2\ 000 + 1 + 6$
   C. $2\ 000 + 10 + 6$ D. $2\ 000 + 100 + 6$

4.   In the number 1 864, what is the place value position of the digit 6?
   A. Ones   B. Tens
   C. Hundreds   D. Thousands

6m13 read and print in words whole numbers to one hundred thousand, using meaningful contexts

READING AND PRINTING WHOLE NUMBERS

To read and write out whole numbers up to one hundred thousand, it is important to know the place value of each digit. Place values are arranged in groups of three called periods as shown in the place value chart below.

Periods

Thousands			Ones		
Hundred Thousands	Ten Thousands	Thousands	Hundreds	Tens	Ones

When you read whole numbers, read each period separately. After the thousands period, include the word thousand before reading the ones period.

Example

The population of Niagara Falls in 2006 was 82 184. Read the number 82 184 and write it using words.

Solution

Start by placing the number in the place value chart as shown.

Thousands			Ones		
H	T	O	H	T	O
	8	2	1	8	4
H – Hundreds T – Tens O – Ones					

First, read the thousands period containing 8 tens and 2 ones. This is written in words as eighty-two followed by thousand because it is in the thousands period. Therefore, you would read this as eighty-two thousand.

Next, write the number that is in the ones period. It contains 1 hundred, 8 tens, and 4 ones, which is one hundred eighty-four. Therefore, this number is read and written as eighty-two thousand one hundred eighty-four.

Note: You should not use the word *and* when reading and printing whole numbers. The word *and* is only used when you are reading and writing decimal numbers. For example, the number 23.6 is read and written as twenty-three and six-tenths.

5. For an election campaign, five hundred eighty-seven thousand five hundred pamphlets were printed. The number of pamphlets printed, written in number form, is

   A. 515 875   **B.** 500 587

   C. 587 500   **D.** 875 500

6m14 represent, compare, and order fractional amounts with unlike denominators, including proper and improper fractions and mixed numbers, using a variety of tools and using standard fractional notation

REPRESENTING, COMPARING, AND ORDERING FRACTIONS

REPRESENTING FRACTIONS

Fractions are used to show parts of a set or parts of a whole.

A proper fraction is a fraction in which the **numerator** is less than the **denominator**. Examples of proper fractions are $\dfrac{3}{4}, \dfrac{4}{6}, \dfrac{12}{35}$, and $\dfrac{65}{100}$.

An improper fraction is a fraction in which the numerator is greater than or equal to the denominator. An improper fraction always has a value greater than or equal to one. Examples of improper fractions are $\dfrac{4}{3}, \dfrac{6}{4}, \dfrac{35}{12}$, and $\dfrac{100}{100}$.

A mixed number is a number expressed as a sum of a whole number and a proper fraction. Examples of mixed fractions are $1\dfrac{1}{3}, 3\dfrac{4}{5}$, and $12\dfrac{2}{17}$.

ORDER FRACTIONS WITH UNLIKE DENOMINATORS

Placing fractions in order from least to greatest or greatest to least can be done by using **equivalent fractions** or a number line.

Example
Order the following fractions from least to greatest.

$$1\dfrac{3}{4}, \dfrac{9}{10}, \dfrac{3}{2}, \dfrac{2}{5}$$

Solution

Method One–Using Equivalent Fractions

Since the fractions are a combination of proper fractions, improper fractions, and mixed numbers, you have to change them all to equivalent fractions with the same denominator.

First, change the mixed number into an improper fraction:

$1\dfrac{3}{4}$

4(the denominator) × 1(the whole number) = 4

4 + 3(the numerator) = 7

$1\dfrac{3}{4} = \dfrac{7}{4}$

Next, find a common denominator and change each fraction into an equivalent fraction:

20 is the **lowest common denominator** (LCD) for the numbers 4, 10, 2, and 5.

$$\dfrac{7(\times 5)}{4(\times 5)} = \dfrac{35}{20}, \dfrac{9(\times 2)}{10(\times 2)} = \dfrac{18}{20}, \dfrac{3(\times 10)}{2(\times 10)} = \dfrac{30}{20}, \dfrac{2(\times 4)}{5(\times 4)} = \dfrac{8}{20}$$

Next, order the fractions from least to greatest, in their original form:

$$\frac{8}{20}, \frac{18}{20}, \frac{30}{20}, \frac{35}{20}$$

Therefore, the fractions ordered from least to greatest are $\frac{2}{5}, \frac{9}{10}, \frac{3}{2}, 1\frac{3}{4}$.

Method Two–Using a Number Line

$$1\frac{3}{4}, \frac{9}{10}, \frac{3}{2}, \frac{2}{5}$$

Place all the fractions on a number line. Then, the fractions will be ordered from least to greatest. The fractions are shown on the following number line.

The proper fractions $\frac{2}{5}$ and $\frac{9}{10}$ are less than 1 and are shown with a number line divided into tenths. The fractions greater than 1 are shown with a number line divided into quarters.

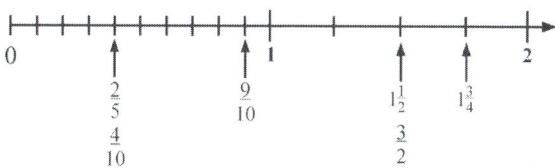

The fractions ordered from least to greatest are $\frac{2}{5}, \frac{9}{10}, \frac{3}{2}, 1\frac{3}{4}$.

Use the following information to answer the next question.

Antoinette is making a batch of chocolate caramel bars. The ingredients are

- $\frac{7}{3}$ litres of caramel

- $\frac{5}{6}$ litres of evaporated milk

- $\frac{3}{4}$ litres of butter

- $\frac{73}{24}$ litres of chocolate cake mix

- 2 litres of semisweet chocolate chips.

6. Which of the following sets lists the ingredients from greatest quantity to least quantity?
   A. Butter, evaporated milk, chocolate chips, caramel, and chocolate cake mix

   B. Chocolate cake mix, caramel, chocolate chips, evaporated milk, and butter

   C. Chocolate cake mix, caramel, evaporated milk, butter, and chocolate chips

   D. Chocolate chips, butter, evaporated milk, caramel, and chocolate cake mix

Use the following information to answer the next question.

Mary Lynn needs at least $5\frac{1}{2}$ m of fabric to make a quilt. She finds a piece of blue fabric that is $\frac{27}{5}$ m long and a piece of red fabric that is $\frac{23}{4}$ m long.

Open Response

7. Which colour fabric should Mary Lynn buy to ensure that she has enough fabric to make the quilt?

Explain your answer.

6m15 estimate quantities using benchmarks of 10%, 25%, 50%, 75%, and 100%

ESTIMATE QUANTITIES USING PERCENT BENCHMARKS

Estimation is an approximation of a quantity, calculation, value, or measurement. Estimation is often used to check the reasonableness of an approximate answer when an exact answer is not required.

For example, if there are 60 students in a school choir and 32 of them are girls, about $\frac{1}{2}$ or 50% of the students in the choir are girls.

A benchmark is something that serves as a reference with which something else may be compared. The benchmark or reference is usually something with which you are familiar. The most common use for benchmarks is in estimation. In mathematics, certain numbers act as benchmarks. Several benchmark numbers exist in percentages and fractions. Percentages and the equivalent fractions with which you should be familiar are

$25\% \left(\dfrac{1}{4} \right)$, $50\% \left(\dfrac{1}{2} \right)$, $75\% \left(\dfrac{3}{4} \right)$ and $100\% \left(\dfrac{1}{1} \right)$.

Example

Estimate what percentage of the glass is full of juice, using percentages as benchmarks.

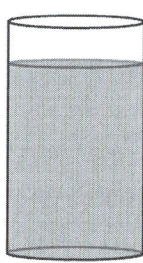

Solution

To estimate the percentage of the glass that contains juice, use the benchmarks 25%, 50%, 75%, and 100%. Mark the glass to show these benchmarks, as shown below.

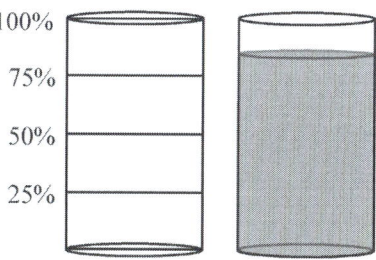

From this diagram, you can see that the glass is more than 75% full of juice. A reasonable estimate is that the glass is about 85% full of juice.

Use the following information to answer the next question.

Before Nigel watered his garden, his rain barrel was full of water. The rain barrel below shows how much water was left after Nigel watered his garden.

8. About how much water is left in the barrel after Nigel waters his garden?
   A. 25%   B. 50%
   C. 75%   D. 100%

6m16 solve problems that arise from real-life situations and that relate to the magnitude of whole numbers up to 1 000 000

SOLVING PROBLEMS WITH LARGE NUMBERS

When solving problems using large numbers (up to 1 000 000), it is efficient to use a calculator to do the calculations.

Example
How much time does it take to count out loud to 1 million? Explain a **strategy** that can be used to arrive at a possible answer.

Solution
Suppose it takes 1 second to count out loud each number to 1 million. The smaller numbers will take a little less than 1 second, and the larger numbers will take a little longer. Since there are 60 seconds in one minute and 60 minutes in one hour, there are 3 600 seconds in one hour ($60 \times 60 = 3\ 600$). Using a calculator, find the number of hours by finding the following **quotient**: $1\ 000\ 000 \div 3\ 600 = 277.78$.

To convert 277.78 hours into days, divide 277.78 by 24 (24 hours in one day) to get 11.57 days. It would take a little less than 12 days to count out loud from 1 to 1 000 000.

Example

A man gets a job planting trees. He gets faster every day he plants, and so each day he gets paid twice as much as he did the day before. He earns $1 the first day, $2 the second day, $4 the third day, and so on. Calculate how much money he will earn in 10 days if his pay keeps doubling.

Solution

To solve this problem using **patterns**, one strategy is to put the information in a table.

Day	Daily Pay ($)	Calculations	Total Earnings ($)
1	1	1	1
2	2	$1 + 2$	3
3	4	$3 + 4$	7
4	8	$7 + 8$	15
5	16	$15 + 16$	31
6	32	$31 + 32$	63
7	64	$63 + 64$	127
8	128	$127 + 128$	255
9	256	$255 + 256$	511
10	512	$511 + 512$	1 023

Therefore, the amount of money he will earn in 10 days is $1 023.

9. If Yuri were to put $5.00 in a piggy bank every day, about how much money would he have saved in 50 years?

   A. $1 825.00

   B. $91 250.00

   C. $250 000.00

   D. $1 000 000.00

Open Response

10. Earth's circumference is about 40 000 km. If the average Grade 6 student walks 4 km/h, about how many years would it take to walk around Earth without stopping?

Show your work.

6m17 identify composite numbers and prime numbers, and explain the relationship between them (i.e., any composite number can be factored into prime factors)

PRIME AND COMPOSITE NUMBERS

A factor is a natural number that divides evenly into another natural number.

A prime number is a natural number that has exactly two factors: one and itself. An example of a prime number is 5 because it has exactly two factors: 1 and 5.

$5 \rightarrow 1 \times 5$
The factors are 1 and 5.

Note that the number 1 is neither a prime nor a composite number.

A composite number is a natural number that has three or more factors. An example of a composite number is 4 because it has three factors: 1, 2, and 4.

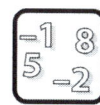

$4 \rightarrow 1 \times 4$

$4 \rightarrow 2 \times 2$

The factors are 1, 2, and 4.

Any composite number can be factored into prime factors. This is called **prime factorization**.

You can determine the prime factors of a composite number by using a tree diagram. Decompose the composite factors into prime factors.

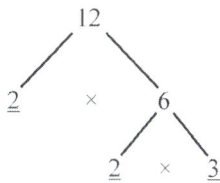

OR

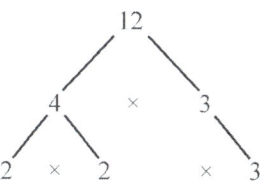

The prime factors of 12 are 2, 2, and 3. The prime factorization is $2 \times 2 \times 3 = 12$.

Example

Use a hundreds chart to find out how many prime numbers there are between 1 and 100.

Solution

On the hundreds chart, circle the prime numbers and shade the composite numbers.

Step 1: Cross out the number 1 because it is neither prime nor composite.

Step 2: Circle 2 because it is prime and shade all the numbers divisible by 2 because they are composite.

1	2	3	4	5	6	7	8	9	10
11	12	13	14	15	16	17	18	19	20
21	22	23	24	25	26	27	28	29	30
31	32	33	34	35	36	37	38	39	40
41	42	43	44	45	46	47	48	49	50
51	52	53	54	55	56	57	58	59	60
61	62	63	64	65	66	67	68	69	70
71	72	73	74	75	76	77	78	79	80
81	82	83	84	85	86	87	88	89	90
91	92	93	94	95	96	97	98	99	100

Step 3: Circle 3 because it is prime and shade all the numbers divisible by 3 because they are also composite.

Continue circling the prime numbers and shading the numbers that are divisible by the prime number circled.

There are 25 prime numbers on the hundreds chart.

---

11. Which of the following sets of numbers lists all the factors of 40?

    A. 2, 20   **B.** 1, 2, 20, 40

    C. 1, 2, 3, 15, 20, 40   **D.** 1, 2, 4, 5, 8, 10, 20, 40

12. Which of the following sets of numbers contains four prime numbers?

    A. 3, 5, 7, and 19   **B.** 4, 5, 11, and 19

    C. 5, 7, 19, and 21   **D.** 17, 18, 19, and 23

6m18 use a variety of mental strategies to solve addition, subtraction, multiplication, and division problems involving whole numbers

USING MENTAL STRATEGIES TO SOLVE PROBLEMS

COMMUTATIVE PROPERTY

If the order of numbers in an operation does not affect the answer, then the operation is said to be **commutative**. In other words, if you can switch the numbers in an operation and get the same answer, then it is commutative. Multiplication and addition are commutative, but subtraction and division are not.

A multiplication example is $5 \times 8 = 40$ and $8 \times 5 = 40$. Both 8×5 and 5×8 have a product of 40. You can use the commutative property to make multiplying or adding a group of numbers easier.

Example
What is the product of $2 \times 67 \times 5$?

Solution
Because both signs are multiplication, you can use the commutative property to arrange the numbers to make it easier to multiply.
Arrange the numbers so that you have $2 \times 5 \times 67$
$10 \times 67 = 670$

DISTRIBUTIVE PROPERTY

The **distributive property** of multiplication over addition is used when you need to multiply a set of numbers that are being added.

Example
Your neighbour pays you $4 every time you shovel the snow on his driveway. In December, you shovelled his driveway 11 times. In January, you shovelled his driveway 5 times. Calculate how much money you have earned using the distributive property.

Solution
$4(11 + 5)$
First, multiply the $4 you earn each time you shovel the driveway by the number of times you shovelled in December. Then, do the same operation for January.
$= (\$4 \times 11) + (\$4 \times 5)$
Now, add the two numbers together.
$= \$44 + \$20$
$= \$64$
For the months of December and January, your neighbour owes you $64.

The distributive property of division over addition is used when you need to divide a set of numbers that are being added.

Example
Suppose that 4 of your friends need to put posters up around the school for an upcoming dance. There are 36 posters to put up inside the school and 12 posters to put up outside the school. If each person gets the same number of posters, how many posters will each person have to put up? Use the distributive property of division over addition.

Solution
$(36 + 12) \div 4$
$(36 \div 4) + (12 \div 4)$
$9 + 3 = 12$

Each person will have to put up 12 posters.

MENTAL STRATEGIES

Mental strategies in math are strategies that you teach yourself to help you solve problems without the help of a calculator or a pencil and paper. Examples of different mental strategies you can use are estimation by rounding, finding compatible numbers, and **compensation**.

Estimation by **rounding** is a method of finding numbers that are close to the actual numbers, but are easier to mentally add, subtract, multiply, or divide. These numbers are called **compatible numbers**. When using estimation to approximate a calculation, you can replace actual numbers with compatible numbers.

Example
Estimate the product of 89 and 3 789.

Solution
You can estimate the product of $89 \times 3\ 789$ by using compatible numbers. In this case, round to the highest place value position.

$89\ \to 90$

$3\ 789\ \to 4\ 000$

Now, multiply the two estimated numbers.
$90 \times 4\ 000 = 360\ 000$

Because both of your estimated numbers are higher than the original numbers, you need to compensate in the answer by estimating a little lower, possibly to 340 000.

Use the following information to answer the next question.

By late summer, Riverdale School had 1 000 students registered. Just before school started, 100 more students were admitted from another district.

13. If all of the students at Riverdale are divided into groups of 10 for the annual Fall Sports Day, which of the following expressions could be used to calculate how many groups there will be?

A. $(100 + 10) \div 1\ 000$

B. $(1\ 000 + 10) \div 100$

C. $(1\ 000 + 100) \div 10$

D. $1\ 000 \div (100 + 10)$

14. What is an equivalent expression of $(12 + 9) \div 3$?

    A. $(12 + 9) \div (12 \div 9)$ **B.** $(12 + 3) \div (9 + 3)$

    C. $(12 \div 3) + (9 \div 3)$ **D.** $(12 \div 9) - (9 \div 3)$

6m19 solve problems involving the multiplication and division of whole numbers (four digit by two digit), using a variety of tools and strategies

SOLVING MULTIPLICATION AND DIVISION PROBLEMS

One strategy you can use to solve problems is to use an algorithm. An **algorithm** is a set of steps for calculating a solution to a problem.

MULTIPLICATION OF WHOLE NUMBERS

The first step for solving multiplication problems is to begin with estimation. This will give you an idea as to whether your final answer is reasonable or not.

Example

A company produces 2 952 boxes of pencil crayons. Each box contains 24 pencil crayons. How many pencil crayons does the company produce in total?

Solution

Begin by estimating the solution. Do this by rounding each number to the largest place value.

Round 2 952 up to 3 000 and round 24 down to 20.
3 000 × 20 = 60 000

You can use this estimate to determine the reasonableness of your calculation.

Next, use the following steps to calculate the actual product using an algorithm.

1. Multiply 4 by 2 to get 8. Write 8 in the ones place.

    2 952
    × 24
    ―――
       8

2. Multiply 4 by 5 tens to get 20 tens, or 200. Write the 0 in the tens place and regroup the 2 hundreds to the hundreds column.

      2
    2 952
    × 24
    ―――
      08

3. Multiply 4 by 9 hundreds to get 36 hundred, or 3 600 and add the 2 hundreds(3 600 + 200 = 3 800). Write 8 in the hundreds place and regroup the 3 thousands to the thousands column.

    3 2
    2 952
    × 24
    ―――
     808

4. Multiply 4 by 2 thousands to get 8 thousands and add the
   3 thousands(8 000 + 3 000 = 11 000). Write 11 in the thousands place.

$$\begin{array}{r} \overset{3\ 2}{2\ 952} \\ \times\quad 24 \\ \hline 11\ 808 \end{array}$$

5. Now, multiply 2 tens (20) by 2 to get 40. Write 40 below 11 808, lining up the **digits** correctly.

$$\begin{array}{r} 2\ 952 \\ \times\quad 24 \\ \hline 11\ 808 \\ 40 \end{array}$$

6. Multiply 2 tens by 5 tens to get 10 hundreds, or 1 000. Write 0 in the hundreds place and
   regroup the 1 thousand to the hundreds column.

$$\begin{array}{r} \overset{1}{2\ 952} \\ \times\quad 24 \\ \hline 11\ 808 \\ 40 \end{array}$$

7. Multiply 2 tens by 9 hundreds to get 18 thousands and add the
   1 thousand(18 000 + 1 000 = 19 000). Write 9 in the thousands place and regroup the
   10 thousands to the thousands column.

$$\begin{array}{r} \overset{1\ 1}{2\ 952} \\ \times\quad 24 \\ \hline 11\ 808 \\ 9\ 040 \end{array}$$

8. Multiply 2 tens by 2 thousands to get 40 thousands and add the
   10 thousand(40 000 + 10 000 = 50 000). Write 5 in the ten thousands place. Add the products
   to get the final answer as shown.

$$\begin{array}{r} \overset{1\ 1}{2952} \\ \times\quad 24 \\ \hline \overset{1}{11}\ 808 \\ +59\ 040 \\ \hline 70\ 848 \end{array}$$

You can determine that your calculation of 70 848 is reasonable since it is close to your estimate
of 60 000.

DIVISION OF WHOLE NUMBERS

As in multiplication, the best step to begin with when dividing large whole numbers is estimation.

Example

Calculate the quotient to 6 337 ÷ 30.

Solution

Begin by estimating the solution. Round each number to the highest place value. To estimate 6 337 ÷ 30, round 6 337 down to 6 000.

6 000 ÷ 30 = 200

Use the following steps to calculate the quotient of 6 337 ÷ 30.

1. There are about 200 groups of 30 in 6 000, so multiply 200 by 30 and subtract this product from 6 337 as shown. The **remainder** from this step is 337.

$$
\begin{array}{r|l}
30\,\overline{)6\ 337} & \\
-6\ 000 & 200 \\
\hline
337 &
\end{array}
$$

2. There are about 10 groups of 30 in 337, so multiply 10 × 30 and subtract this product from 337 as shown. The remainder from this step is 37.

$$
\begin{array}{r|l}
30\,\overline{)6\ 337} & \\
-6\ 000 & 200 \\
\hline
337 & \\
-300 & 10 \\
\hline
37 &
\end{array}
$$

3. There is 1 group of 30 in 37, so multiply 1 × 30 and subtract this product from 37. There is still 7 remaining, but since 7 is less than 30, 7 is the remainder. Add the numbers down the side of your calculation. The calculated quotient is 211 with a remainder of 7.

$$
\begin{array}{r|l}
30\,\overline{)6\ 337} & \\
-6\ 000 & 200 \\
\hline
337 & \\
-300 & 10 \\
\hline
37 & \\
-30 & 1 \\
\hline
7 &
\end{array}
$$

Alternate Solution:

$63 \div 30 = 2$ with a remainder of 3
$33 \div 30 = 1$ with a remainder of 3
$37 \div 30 = 1$ with a remainder of 7

Therefore, the calculated quotient is 211 with a remainder of 7.

$$
\begin{array}{r}
211 \\
30\overline{)6\,337} \\
-6\,0 \\
\hline
33 \\
-30 \\
\hline
37 \\
-30 \\
\hline
7
\end{array}
$$

This calculation of 211 is reasonable because it is very close to your estimate of 200.

Use the following information to answer the next question.

At the candy factory, 3 456 jelly beans are put into 48 boxes.

15. About how many jelly beans are in each box?

    A. 30   **B.** 50

    C. 70   **D.** 100

Use the following information to answer the next question.

Lin makes jewellery out of beads. The following table lists the colours and sizes of beads she uses.

Colour of Bead	Length of Bead (cm)
Teal	2.37
Pink	1.23
Purple	2.89
Silver	0.86

16. Lin made one necklace using 3 teal beads, 5 purple beads, and 8 silver beads. Approximately how long was the necklace?

    A. 20 cm   **B.** 23 cm

    C. 26 cm   **D.** 29 cm

6m20 add and subtract decimal numbers to thousandths, using concrete materials, estimation, algorithms, and calculators

ADDING AND SUBTRACTING DECIMAL NUMBERS

ADDING DECIMAL NUMBERS

Adding decimal numbers is similar to adding whole numbers. In both cases, place value is important and only the digits in the same place value position can be added together. You can use different methods to add decimal numbers together: base ten materials, an algorithm, or a calculator.

Example
Add 3.780 + 2.134.

Solution
You can use base ten blocks and an algorithm to add decimal numbers.

To start, create each number using base ten blocks. Then, add the groups of base ten blocks together starting from the right.
0 thousandths + 4 thousandths = 4 thousandths
8 hundredths + 3 hundredths = 11 hundredths
For the hundredths, you need to trade 10 hundredths for 1 tenth.
7 tenths + 1 tenth + 1 tenth = 9 tenths
3 ones + 2 ones = 5 ones

You have a total of 5 ones, 9 tenths, 1 hundredth, and 4 thousandths. The sum is 5.914.

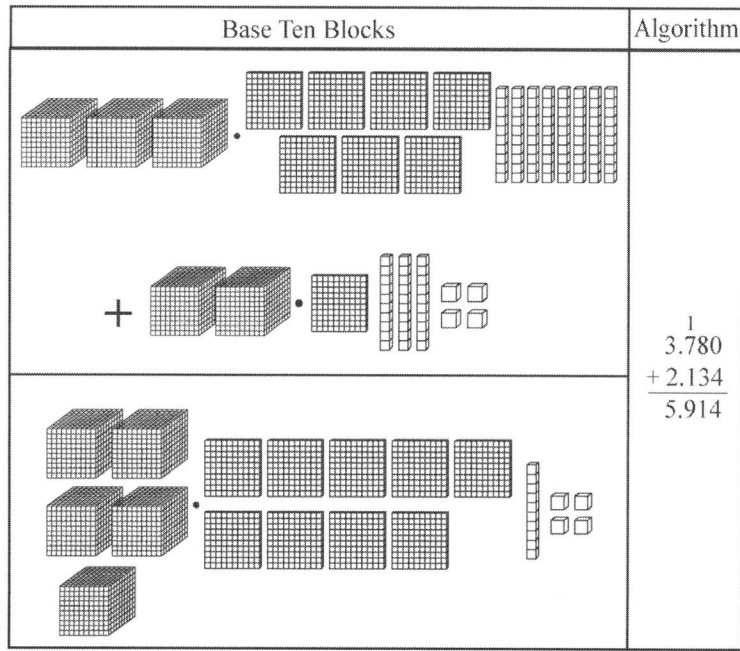

SUBTRACTING DECIMAL NUMBERS

Subtracting decimal numbers is similar to adding decimal numbers because place value is still important. The methods for adding decimal numbers that use an algorithm and a calculator can also be followed for subtraction.

SUBTRACTING USING AN ALGORITHM

Example
Calculate 3.780 – 2.134

Solution

Start on the right side to subtract. In order to subtract 4 thousandths from 0 thousandths, you must take 1 hundredth from the next column. Subtract 10 – 4.

Write 6 below.

$$\begin{array}{r} {\scriptstyle 7\ 10} \\ 3.7\cancel{8}\cancel{0} \\ -2.134 \\ \hline 6 \end{array}$$

Subtract 7 – 3. Write 4 below.

$$\begin{array}{r} {\scriptstyle 7\ 10} \\ 3.7\cancel{8}\cancel{0} \\ -2.134 \\ \hline 46 \end{array}$$

Subtract 7 – 1. Write 6 below.

$$\begin{array}{r} {\scriptstyle 7\ 10} \\ 3.7\cancel{8}\cancel{0} \\ -2.134 \\ \hline 646 \end{array}$$

Write the decimal. Subtract 3 – 2. Write 1 below.

$$\begin{array}{r} {\scriptstyle 7\ 10} \\ 3.7\cancel{8}\cancel{0} \\ -2.134 \\ \hline 1.646 \end{array}$$

The answer is 1.646.

Use the following information to answer the next question.

Jay, Stacey, and Carol each take a different school bus. Each day, Jay travels a total of 5.85 km, Stacey travels a total of 8.13 km, and Carol travels a total of 12.28 km.

17. About how far do Jay, Stacey, and Carol travel in total?

    A. 20 km   **B.** 24 km

    C. 26 km   **D.** 30 km

6m21 multiply and divide decimal numbers to tenths by whole numbers, using concrete materials, estimation, algorithms, and calculators

MULTIPLYING AND DIVIDING WHOLE AND DECIMAL NUMBERS

MULTIPLYING BY ESTIMATION

Estimating the products of decimal numbers multiplied by whole numbers is similar to estimating the products of whole numbers multiplied by whole numbers. To estimate a product, focus on the digits in the highest place value positions, rounding them if necessary. For example, to estimate the product of 3×1.7, round 1.7 up to 2. The expression then becomes $3 \times 2 = 6$

The actual product will be a number slightly less than 6 because you rounded up. You can use the actual product to determine the reasonableness of your estimate.

MULTIPLYING USING ADDITION

Multiplying decimal numbers by whole numbers is similar to adding decimal numbers. This is because multiplication is like adding equal groups. For example, 3×1.7 means 3 groups of 1.7. This can also be written as $1.7 + 1.7 + 1.7$.

When you multiply a decimal number by a whole number, you must remember that you will have a decimal in your answer.

MULTIPLYING USING AN ALGORITHM

Multiplying decimal numbers by whole numbers is similar to multiplying whole numbers by whole numbers.

Example
Multiply 3×7 tenths. Write the digit 1 below the line and regroup the 2 ones above the 1.

$$\begin{array}{r} \overset{2}{} \\ 1.7 \\ \times\ 3 \\ \hline 1 \end{array}$$

Multiply 3×1 and add the 2. Write 5 below the line. Because there is one digit after the decimal in the question, there must be one digit after the decimal in the product. Therefore, $3 \times 1.7 = 5.1$

$$\begin{array}{r} \overset{2}{} \\ 1.7 \\ \times\ 3 \\ \hline 5.1 \end{array}$$

DIVIDING DECIMAL NUMBERS BY WHOLE NUMBERS

Dividing decimal numbers by whole numbers is similar to dividing a whole number by a whole number. The only difference is that when you divide a decimal number by a whole number, you have a decimal in your answer.

DIVIDING USING ESTIMATION

To estimate the quotient of a decimal divided by a whole number, round the decimal number either up or down to get a whole number. For example, to estimate the quotient of 4.2 ÷ 3, round 4.2 down to the whole number 4. Since 4 ÷ 3 is 1.33, the estimate is 1.33.

DIVIDING USING EQUAL SHARING

Division can also mean the equal sharing of a given amount.
The expression 4.2 ÷ 3 can be understood as equally sharing 4.2 among 3 separate groups.

The 4 ones are equally shared into 3 groups of 1 whole. The 1 whole is placed directly above the ones place and the decimal point is placed directly above the decimal point in 4.2.

```
      1.
 3)4.2
  - 3
    12
```

The 12 tenths are equally shared into 3 groups of 4 tenths. The 4 is placed directly above the tenths place in 4.2 to complete the division.

```
      1.4
 3)4.2
  - 3
    12
  - 12
     0
```

The answer is 1.4.
4.2 ÷ 3 = 1.4

To check your division, multiply the quotient by the **divisor**. Your answer should be the **dividend**.
3 × 1.4 = 4.2

18. Jackie has 68 straws. Each straw is 21.1 cm long. If Jackie places all the straws in a straight line, about how long will the line of straws be?

   A. 1 000 cm

   B. 1 300 cm

   C. 1 400 cm

   D. 1 600 cm

19. If 3 ropes of equal length are laid end to end to form a rope that is 9.75 m long, then how long are each of the ropes?

   A. 3.25 m

   B. 3.50 m

   C. 3.75 m

   D. 4.25 m

6m22 multiply whole numbers by 0.1, 0.01, and 0.001 using mental strategies

To make problem solving easier, it is useful to find a general rule or mental strategy instead of always relying on a calculator. A pattern based on the multiplication of any whole number by 0.1, 0.01, or 0.001 gives one such rule.

The rule states that you first count the number of decimal places that the decimal number has. Then, you move the decimal point of the whole number this number of places to the left. For example, 0.1 has one decimal place after the decimal. So, when you multiply a whole number by 0.1, you move the decimal point behind the whole number one place to the left.

51 × 0.1 becomes 5.1

When you multiply any whole number by a decimal number, such as 0.1, 0.01, or 0.001, your answer will always be less than the whole number being multiplied. A pattern can be seen when you multiply 51 by 0.1, 0.01, or 0.001.

51 × 0.1 = 5.1
51 × 0.01 = 0.51
51 × 0.001 = 0.051

This pattern clearly shows the given mental strategy: the number of decimal places in the decimal number that you are multiplying is the number of places you move the decimal point to the left in the product.

Multiplying a whole number by 0.1 is the same as dividing that number by 10.
Multiplying a whole number by 0.01 is the same as dividing that number by 100.
Multiplying a whole number by 0.001 is the same as dividing that number by 1 000.

20. Ava made a square quilt by sewing together a total of 16 small quilt squares. If each small quilt square has an area of 0.01 m^2, what is the area of the whole quilt?

A. 0.016 m^2 B. 0.16 m^2

C. 1.6 m^2 D. 16 m^2

6m23 multiply and divide decimal numbers by 10, 100, 1 000, and 10 000 using mental strategies

MULTIPLYING AND DIVIDING DECIMAL NUMBERS BY MULTIPLES OF 10

MULTIPLYING DECIMAL NUMBERS BY MULTIPLES OF 10

When multiplying a decimal number by a multiple of ten, you will notice that you move the decimal point as many places to the right as there are zeros. This pattern can help you remember a strategy for multiplying any decimal number by 10, 100, 1 000, or any other multiple of 10.

When multiplying any decimal number by 10, move the decimal point in the decimal number one place to the right. For example,

1.42 × 10 becomes 14.2

Notice that there is one zero at the end of the multiple of ten (10). Therefore, the decimal point is moved one place to the right.

When multiplying any decimal number by 100, move the decimal point in the decimal number two places to the right. For example,

1.42 × 100 becomes 142.

Notice that there are two zeroes at the end of the multiple of ten (100). Therefore, the decimal point is moved two places to the right.

If a decimal point ends up being at the end of the number, remember that you do not have to include it in your final result.

When multiplying any decimal number by 1 000, move the decimal point in the decimal number three places to the right. For example,

$$1.42 \times 1\ 000 \text{ becomes } 1.420$$

Notice that there are three zeroes at the end of the multiple of ten (1 000). Therefore, the decimal point is moved three places to the right.

DIVIDING DECIMAL NUMBERS BY MULTIPLES OF 10

When dividing decimal numbers by multiples of 10, the pattern rule is the same only you are moving the decimal point to the left. The following simple statement can help you remember the general rule for dividing any decimal number by 10, 100, 1 000, or 10 000: "Move as many places to the left as there are zeros in the multiple of 10."

When writing numbers with decimals, it is important to follow certain rules. When you need to write a decimal number that only has numbers to the right of the decimal place, make sure to write a zero to the left side of the decimal. For example, the number .234 should be written as 0.234.

When dividing any decimal number by 10, move the decimal point in the decimal number one place to the left because there is one zero in 10. For example,

$$1.42 \div 10 \text{ becomes } 0.142$$

When dividing any decimal number by 100, move the decimal point in the decimal number two places to the left because there are two zeroes in 100. For example,

$$1.42 \div 100 \text{ becomes } 0.0142$$

When dividing any decimal number by 1 000, move the decimal point in the decimal number three places to the left because there are three zeroes in 1 000. For example,

$$1.42 \div 1\ 000 \text{ becomes } 0.001\ 42$$

21. If a loaf of bread costs $3.49, how much would 1 000 loaves of bread cost?
    A. $349.00
    B. $3 490.00
    C. $34 900.00
    D. $349 000.00

6m24 use estimation when solving problems involving the addition and subtraction of whole numbers and decimals, to help judge the reasonableness of a solution

ESTIMATING SUMS AND DIFFERENCES OF WHOLE NUMBERS AND DECIMALS

ESTIMATING SUMS AND DIFFERENCES OF WHOLE NUMBERS

It is important to learn how to perform operations without the use of a calculator or a pencil and paper. When making an estimate, you need to be able to use numbers that are easy to add and subtract. In previous lessons, you learned how to round numbers up or down. Estimation by **rounding** is a method of finding numbers that are close to the actual numbers, but are easier to add or subtract. Estimating a calculation will help you to know if the actual solution is reasonable.

Example
The given chart shows the number of people that were living in different cities in Ontario in 2006.

City	Population
Mississauga	668 549
Windsor	216 473
Kitchener	204 668
Oshawa	141 590
Thunder Bay	109 140

How many more people were living in Mississauga than in Oshawa? Estimate the solution and then compare your estimate with the actual answer.

Solution
To find approximately how many more people were living in Mississauga than in Oshawa, estimate the difference between 668 549 and 141 590. As in other estimation questions, round each of the numbers to the highest place value position.
668 549 → 700 000

141 590 → 100 000

Now, perform the subtraction.
700 000 – 100 000 = 600 000

The larger number was rounded up and the lower number was rounded down. Thus, 600 000 is a good estimate. About 600 000 more people were living in Mississauga than in Oshawa in 2006.

To calculate how many more people were living in Mississauga than in Oshawa exactly, subtract the smaller number from the larger number.

$$\begin{array}{r} {\scriptstyle 7\ 4\,14} \\ 66\,8\,5\,4\,9 \\ -\,1\,4\,1\,5\,9\,0 \\ \hline 5\,2\,6\,9\,5\,9 \end{array}$$

There were 526 959 more people living in Mississauga than in Oshawa in 2006.

Because you are calculating with very large numbers, the actual difference of 526 959 is close to the estimated answer of 600 000, so you know that your estimate is reasonable.

ESTIMATING SUMS AND DIFFERENCES OF DECIMAL NUMBERS

When estimating with decimal numbers, it is important to focus on the digit with the highest place value. This is the place value that you should round to. This often leads to rounding to the nearest whole number.

Example
Susie delivers 5.356 kg of papers and 1.786 kg of flyers in one day. What is the total weight of the papers and flyers that Susie delivers in one day? Estimate the solution and then compare your estimate with the actual answer.

Solution
To find the approximate total weight of the papers and the flyers delivered in one day, estimate the sum of 5.356 kg and 1.786 kg. Round each number to the nearest whole number.

$5.356 \rightarrow 5$

$1.786 \rightarrow 2$

Now, add the two numbers.
$5 + 2 = 7$ kg

To find the exact total, add the two given numbers.

$$\begin{array}{r} \overset{1\ 11}{5.356} \\ +1.786 \\ \hline 7.142 \end{array}$$

Susie delivered 7.142 kg of papers and flyers in one day. The actual sum of 7.142 kg is very close to the estimated answer of 7 kg, so you know that your estimate is reasonable.

---

22. Graham had a piece of licorice that was 25.3 cm long, but he gave a 12.1 cm piece to Tori. About what length of licorice does Graham have left?

   A. 11 cm   **B.** 12 cm

   C. 13 cm   **D.** 37 cm

6m25 explain the need for a standard order for performing operations, by investigating the impact that changing the order has when performing a series of operations

ORDER OF OPERATIONS

It is very important for all students learning math to learn the same rules. These rules help to ensure that math problems always result in the same answer, no matter who solves the problem. One of these rules focuses on the order in which the operations of addition, subtraction, multiplication, and division are carried out.

- First, perform multiplication and division in the order that they appear in the expression from left to right.
- Then, perform addition and subtraction in the order that they appear in the expression from left to right.

The following example can help you understand some of the reasons that there are rules for following the correct order when performing a series of operations.

Example

Calculate and compare the answers to the expression $12 - 6 \div 2$ using a basic four-function calculator and using a scientific calculator.

Solution

Using a basic four-function calculator, input $12 - 6 \div 2 =$. This type of calculator performs the operations from left to right in the order that you press the keys.
$12 - 6 = 6$, then $6 \div 2 = 3$

The answer on the calculator screen should be 3.

Using a scientific calculator, input $12 - 6 \div 2 =$. A scientific calculator is type of a calculator that has more features than a basic four-function calculator. It performs the operations using the correct order of operations.
A scientific calculator performs the division first: $6 \div 2 =$.

Then, the subtraction is done using the answer obtained from the division:
$12 - 3 = 9$.

The correct answer to $12 - 6 \div 2$ is 9.

The answer obtained using a basic four-function calculator is 3, but the answer obtained using a scientific calculator is 9.

You can see that the two calculators perform the operations in a different order, so they each produce a different answer. This tells you that it is very important to follow the rules for order of operations when doing calculations.

If you are using a basic four-function calculator to do math, remember to input the multiplication and division in the correct left-to-right order. Then, correctly input the addition and subtraction operations from left to right.

Example

Find the correct answer to the expression $4 \times 3 + 15 \div 5$. Use the order of operation rules as a sequence of steps that you would follow to calculate the answer.

Solution

Follow the order of operation rules:

1. $4 \times 3 + 15 \div 5 = 4 \times 3 = 12$
2. $12 + 15 \div 5 = 15 \div 5 = 3$
3. $12 + 3 = 15$

The correct answer to $4 \times 3 + 15 \div 5$ is 15.

---

23. What is the value of the equation $3 \times 4 + 8 \div 4$?

    A. 4   **B.** 5

    C. 10   **D.** 14

| Open Response |

24. What is the value of the equation $10 - 3 \times 2 + 5$? Explain your calculation strategy.

6m26 represent ratios found in real-life contexts, using concrete materials, drawings, and standard fractional notation

RATIOS

When you make a container of juice, you may use 1 can of juice and 3 cans of water. The number of cans of juice compared with the number of cans of water is a ratio. A ratio is a comparison of numbers or quantities. A ratio may compare one part with another part. A ratio may also compare one part with the whole.

PART-TO-PART RATIOS

Part-to-part ratios show you the relationship between two parts of a whole. The diagram below shows some groups of cubes. There are 2 grey cubes and 3 white cubes.

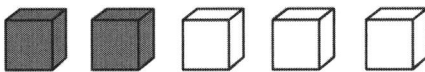

The number of grey cubes can be compared with the number of white cubes by writing a ratio. The ratio of grey cubes to white cubes can be expressed in any one of the following manners.

- The ratio of the number of grey cubes to white cubes is 2 to 3.
- 2 grey cubes to 3 white cubes
- 2 to 3
- The ratio of the number of grey cubes to white cubes is 2:3.
- 2:3

Often a colon (:) is used to separate the numbers in a ratio. It is very important for the numbers in a ratio to be written in the correct order. The first value is written on the left side of the colon, and the second value is written on the right side.

According to the diagram above, the ratio of the number of grape-juice cans to the number of cups of water is 3:5.

The number of cans is written on the left side of the colon and the number of cups is written on the right side of the colon. Just as in the previous example, the ratio can be written as:

- 3:5
- 3 cans of juice:5 cups of water
- 3 to 5

This example also shows that each part of a ratio can have a different unit. In this example, cans of juice are compared with pitchers of water.

PART-TO-WHOLE RATIOS

Part-to-whole ratios show you the relationship between a part and the whole from which the part comes. A ratio can be used to compare part of a set with the whole set. The given diagram shows a set of cubes.

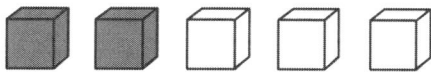

There are 2 grey cubes and 3 white cubes; in the whole set, there are 5 cubes. The ratio that compares the number of grey cubes with the whole set of cubes is 2:5. The ratio that compares the number of white cubes with the whole set of cubes is 3:5.

Example

A sixth grade class consists of 15 girls and 10 boys. The part-to-part ratio of girls to boys is 15:10. The ratio of boys to girls is 10:15. Remember to write the ratio in the correct order. With ratios, order is very important. The part-to-whole ratio of boys to the number of students in the whole class is 10:25.

Use the following information to answer the next question.

A sash of fabric is 10 m long. The first 3 m has embroidery work, and the rest is plain.

25. What is the ratio of the part of the sash with embroidery work to the part that is plain?

    A. 3:7   **B.** 3:10

    C. 7:3   **D.** 10:3

6m27 determine and explain, through investigation using concrete materials, drawings, and calculators, the relationships among fractions (i.e., with denominators of 2, 4, 5, 10, 20, 25, 50, and 100), decimal numbers, and percents

RELATING FRACTIONS, DECIMALS, AND PERCENTAGES

A **percentage** is a ratio that compares a quantity with 100. A percentage always represents a quantity out of 100. The symbol used is %, as in 50 %. This means 50 out of 100, where 50 is the part and 100 is the whole. You can represent 50 % as $\frac{50}{100}$ or 0.50.

Given any one of the three representations, you can always write an equivalent form using the other two representations.

USING A DIAGRAM

Each of the following diagrams represents the same whole region.

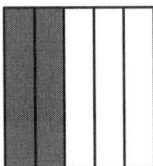

This diagram is $\frac{2}{5}$ shaded. The fraction $\frac{2}{5}$ means that 2 of the 5 equal parts are shaded.

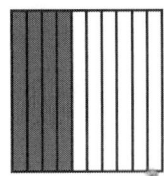

This diagram is $\frac{4}{10}$ shaded. The same amount of this diagram is shaded as the diagram showing $\frac{2}{5}$ shaded. Therefore, $\frac{2}{5} = \frac{4}{10}$. The fraction $\frac{4}{10}$ can also be written as the decimal number 0.4. Therefore, $\frac{2}{5} = 0.4$.

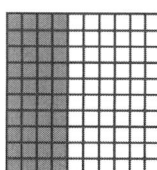

This diagram is $\frac{40}{100}$ shaded. The same amount of this diagram is shaded as the diagrams showing $\frac{2}{5}$ and 0.4. The fraction $\frac{40}{100}$ can also be written as 40 percent(40 %) because it represents 40 out of 100. Therefore, $\frac{2}{5}$ = 40%.

The fraction $\frac{2}{5}$ can be written as a decimal number, 0.4, and as a percentage, 40 %.

26. Which of the following sets of numbers correctly represents an equivalent fraction, decimal, and percentage?

A. $\frac{1}{2}$, 0.2, 20 %　　　　　　　　　**B.** $\frac{1}{3}$, 0.3, 3 %

C. $\frac{6}{10}$, 0.6, 60 %　　　　　　　　　**D.** $\frac{1}{2}$, 0.2, 5 %

Use the following information to answer the next question.

Mario wants to buy a $20 board game, but he only has $8.

27. What percentage of the price of the game does Mario have?
　　A. 4%　　　　　　　　　　　　**B.** 40%
　　C. 60%　　　　　　　　　　　**D.** 80%

Use the following information to answer the next question.

In a basketball game, Henri makes 3 baskets out of every 5 shots. Kate's average of successful shots is 0.67, and Lucas makes baskets 65% of the time.

Open Response

28. Who has the highest percent of successful shots? Show your work.

6m28 represent relationships using unit rates

UNIT RATES

In a **rate,** the two measures being compared are expressed in different units. An example of a rate is 200 km/2 hr, or 200 kilometres in 2 hours. A **unit rate** is a rate in which the second measure is 1. An example is 100 km/hr, or 100 *kilometres* per hour. This is a unit rate because it is 100 kilometres in 1 hour.

Example
If you know that 10 cobs of corn cost $3, you can find the unit rate by finding the cost of 1 cob of corn. The unit rate is the cost of 1 cob of corn.
Since 10 cobs of corn cost $3, divide $3 by 10 to get the cost of 1 cob.

$3.00 ÷ 10 = $0.30

One cob of corn costs $0.30.

Example

In a candy store, the sign above the chocolate fudge reads: $2 per 100 g.
What is the cost of this chocolate fudge per gram?

Solution

Since 100 grams of fudge cost $2, divide $2 by 100 to get the cost of 1 gram.
$2.00 ÷ 100 = $0.02
The cost of 1 gram of chocolate fudge is $ 0.02.

---

29. If a bag of candy costs $3.20 per 100 g, about how much does one gram of candy cost?

    A. $0.02   **B.** $0.03

    C. $0.32   **D.** $3.20

ANSWERS AND SOLUTIONS
NUMBER SENSE AND NUMERATION

1. C	7. OR	13. C	19. A	25. A
2. B	8. C	14. C	20. B	26. C
3. C	9. B	15. C	21. B	27. B
4. B	10. OR	16. D	22. C	28. OR
5. C	11. D	17. C	23. D	29. B
6. B	12. A	18. C	24. OR	

1. C

To determine which number is between 931 475 and 962 310, one method to use is a place value chart, looking at the place values starting from the left in the hundred thousands place.

Thousands			Ones		
H	T	O	H	T	O
9	1	3	6	8	0
9	2	9	3	9	5
9	5	7	2	0	2
9	8	5	0	0	0

Since the digit in the hundred thousands place in each number is the same (9), look at the next place value – the ten thousands place. The answer must have a digit in the ten thousands place that is between 3 and 6.

The digit 1 is in the ten thousands place in 913 680. Therefore, 913 680 is less than 931 475.

The digit 2 is in the ten thousands place in 929 395. Therefore, 929 395 is less than 931 475.

The digit 5 is in the ten thousands place in 957 202. Therefore, 957 202 falls in between 931 475 and 962 310.

The digit 8 is in the ten thousands place in 985 000. Therefore, 985 000 is greater than 962 310.

2. B

The snails' speeds are measured in metres per minute. The fastest snail will have travelled the greatest distance.

One method you can use to find which snail travelled the greatest distance is a place value chart.

Ones	.	Tenths	Hundredths	Thousandths
0	.	0	5	3
0	.	0	9	6
0	.	1		
0	.	1	6	

Compare the ones places: In all four distances, the ones place is zero.

Compare the tenths places: In the numbers 0.16 and 0.1, the tenths place is one, while in the numbers 0.053 and 0.096, the tenths place is zero. Therefore, 0.16 and 0.1 are greater than 0.053 and 0.096.

Note that 0.1 is equivalent to 0.10. Therefore 0.16 is greater than 0.1.
Since 9 > 5, 0.096 is greater than 0.053.

The numbers listed from largest to smallest are 0.16, 0.1, 0.096, and 0.053. This means that the order from the child with the fastest snail to the child with the slowest snail is Sarah, Yolanda, Jane, and Kevin.

3. **C**

Base ten materials can be used to find the expanded form of the number 2 016.

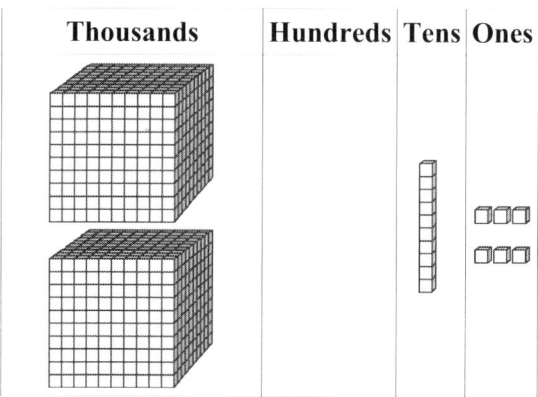

Thousands	Hundreds	Tens	Ones

There are 2 thousands $= 2\ 000$.

There are 0 hundreds $= 0$.

There are 1 tens $= 10$.

There are 6 ones $= 6$.

$2\ 000 + 10 + 6$.

4. **B**

Write the number in a place value chart.

Thousands	Hundreds	Tens	Ones
1	8	6	4

The digit 6 is in the tens position.

5. **C**

To write the numeral for the number five hundred eighty-seven thousand five hundred, you can use a place value chart.

Since there are 587 thousands, write 587 in the thousands period.

Since there are 500 ones, write 500 in the ones period.

Thousands			Ones		
Hundreds	Tens	Ones	Hundreds	Tens	Ones
5	8	7	5	0	0

The numeral in the place value chart is 587 500.

6. **B**

In order to calculate the quantities from greatest to least, the fractions must be converted so that they all have a common denominator.

The lowest common denominator is 24:

$\dfrac{7}{3}$: 3, 6, 9, 12, 15, 18, 21, **24**, 27

$\dfrac{5}{6}$: 6, 12, 18, **24**, 30

$\dfrac{3}{4}$: 4, 8, 12, 16, 20, **24**, 28

$\dfrac{73}{24}$: **24**, 48, 72

Convert all of the fractions:

Caramel: $\dfrac{7}{3} \times \dfrac{8}{8} = \dfrac{56}{24}$

Evaporated milk: $\dfrac{5}{6} \times \dfrac{4}{4} = \dfrac{20}{24}$

Butter: $\dfrac{3}{4} \times \dfrac{6}{6} = \dfrac{18}{24}$

Cake mix: $\dfrac{73}{24}$

Chocolate chips: $\dfrac{2}{1} \times \dfrac{24}{24} = \dfrac{48}{24}$

Arrange the numerators in order from highest to lowest: $\dfrac{73}{24}, \dfrac{56}{24}, \dfrac{48}{24}, \dfrac{20}{24}$, and $\dfrac{18}{24}$

These fractions correspond to chocolate cake mix, caramel, chocolate chips, evaporated milk, and butter respectively.

7. **OR**

Points	Sample Answer
4	Thorough understanding of mixed and improper fractions, how to find equivalent fractions, and how to order fractions.

One method is to first change the two improper fractions into mixed numbers and then compare the fractions.

Points	Sample Answer
	In the fraction $\frac{27}{5}$, $27 \div 5 = 5$, with a remainder of 2. So, as a mixed number, $\frac{27}{5}$ is written as $5\frac{2}{5}$. In the fraction $\frac{23}{4}$, $23 \div 4 = 5$, with a remainder of 3. So, as a mixed number, $\frac{23}{4}$ is written as $5\frac{3}{4}$. Now you must determine if either $5\frac{2}{5}$ or $5\frac{3}{4}$ is greater than $5\frac{1}{2}$. To do this, you can find a common denominator and use equivalent fractions. Since the whole number, 5, is the same for each fraction, you can ignore it and just change the fraction part of the mixed numbers. The lowest common denominator for these fractions is 20. The denominator, 2, must be multiplied by 10 to get the new denominator of 20. Therefore, the numerator must also be multiplied by 10. $\frac{1}{2} \times \frac{10}{10} = \frac{10}{20}$. So, $5\frac{1}{2} = 5\frac{10}{20}$. The denominator, 5, must be multiplied by 4 to get the new denominator of 20. Therefore, the numerator must also be multiplied by 4. $\frac{2}{5} \times \frac{4}{4} = \frac{8}{20}$. So, $5\frac{2}{5} = 5\frac{8}{20}$. The denominator, 4, must be multiplied by 5 to get the new denominator of 20. Therefore, the numerator must also be multiplied by 5. $\frac{3}{4} \times \frac{5}{5} = \frac{15}{20}$. So, $5\frac{3}{4} = 5\frac{15}{20}$. Since Mary Lynn needs at least $5\frac{1}{2}$ m of fabric, she can only use the red fabric, which is $5\frac{3}{4}$, because it is greater than $5\frac{1}{2}$. The fraction $5\frac{2}{5}$ is less than $5\frac{1}{2}$, so Mary Lynn cannot use the blue fabric to make a quilt.

Points	Sample Answer
3	Considerable understanding of mixed and improper fractions, how to find equivalent fractions, and how to order fractions (e.g., changes the improper fractions correctly to mixed numbers but makes an error when calculating the equivalency of one fraction).
2	Some understanding of mixed and improper fractions, how to find equivalent fractions, and how to order fractions (e.g., makes an error when changing an improper fraction to a mixed number or does not show understanding of equivalent fractions).
1	Limited understanding of mixed and improper fractions, how to find equivalent fractions, and how to order fractions (e.g., does not show understanding of improper fractions or equivalent fractions).

8. C

The rain barrel shows that there is more than 50% of the water left in the barrel. There is less than 100% of the water left in the barrel, so there is approximately 75% water left in the barrel.

9. B

If Yuri saved $5/day and there are 365 days in a year, he would have saved $1 825.00 a year:

$5 \times 365 = 1\ 825$

To find how much Yuri would have saved in 50 years, multiply $1 825.00 by 50 years:
$50 \times 1\ 825 = 91\ 250$

Therefore, if Yuri saved for 50 years, he would have $91 250.00.

10. OR

Points	Sample Answer
4	Thorough understanding of large whole numbers and how to convert hours into years.

Points	Sample Answer
	If it takes the average Grade 6 student 1 hour to walk 4 km, then to find out how many hours it would take to walk 40 000 km, you would divide 40 000 by 4. $\dfrac{40\ 000}{4} = 10\ 000$. It would take 10 000 hours of non-stop walking to walk around Earth. To find the number of years it would take, first find out how many days it would take. There are 24 hours in a day, so to find out how many days it would take, divide 10 000 by 24. $\dfrac{100}{24}$ = about 417 days There are 365 days in a year, so to find out how many years it would take, divide 417 by 365. $\dfrac{417}{365}$ = about 1 year Therefore, it would take the average Grade 6 student about 1 year to walk around Earth without stopping.
3	Considerable understanding of large whole numbers and how to convert hours into years (e.g., makes a calculation error when multiplying any step).
2	Some understanding of large whole numbers and how to convert hours into years (e.g., misses a step).
1	Limited understanding of large whole numbers and how to convert hours into years (e.g., does not understand the relationship of multiples).

11. D

Numbers that do not divide evenly into 40 are not factors. Find out which numbers divide evenly by 40.

- Since $40 \div 1 = 40$, 1 and 40 are factors.
- Since $40 \div 2 = 20$, 2 and 20 are factors.
- Since $40 \div 3$ does not divide evenly, 3 is not a factor.
- Since $40 \div 4 = 10$, 4 and 10 are factors.
- Since $40 \div 5 = 8$, 5 and 8 are factors.
- Since $40 \div 6$ does not divide evenly, 6 is not a factor.
- Since $40 \div 7$ does not divide evenly, 7 is not a factor.
- Since $40 \div 8 = 5$, 8 and 5 are factors.

You already know that 8 and 5 are factors because $40 \div 5 = 8$. Do not keep dividing because all the other factors will be repeats. There are no more factors of 40.

The factors of 40 are 1, 2, 4, 5, 8, 10, 20, and 40.

12. A

In A, the numbers 3, 5, 7, and 19 are all prime numbers because each one only has two factors.

In B, the numbers 5, 11, and 19 are prime numbers; however, the number 4 has more than two factors (1, 2, and 4).

In C, the numbers 5, 7, and 19 are prime numbers; however, the number 21 has more than two factors (1, 3, 7, and 21).

In D, the numbers 17, 19, and 23 are prime numbers; however, the number 18 has more than two factors (1, 2, 3, 6, 9, and 18).

13. C

The total number of students in the school
$= 1\ 000 + 100$.
The number of students in each group $= 10$.
Therefore, the number of groups

$$= (1\ 000 + 100) \div 10$$
$$= (1\ 000 \div 10) + (100 \div 10)$$
$$\text{[distributive property]}$$
$$= 100 + 10$$
$$= 110$$

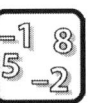

14. C

Using the distributive property, change the order of the expression.

$(12 + 9) \div 3$

$= (12 \div 3) + (9 \div 3)$

$= 4 + 3$

$= 7$

The value of the expression is 7.

15. C

To estimate the number of boxes of jelly beans that can be filled, use compatible numbers that can be divided mentally. $3456 \div 48$ can become $3500 \div 50$.

About 70 jelly beans are in each box.

16. D

Step 1

Round the lengths of the beads used to the nearest whole numbers.

- Teal bead: $2.37 \to 2$ cm because $3 < 5$
- Purple bead: $2.89 \to 3$ cm because $8 > 5$
- Silver bead: $0.86 \to 1$ cm$8 > 5$

Step 2

Calculate the total estimated lengths of each colour of bead used.

- Three teal beads: $2 \times 3 = 6$ cm
- Five purple beads: $5 \times 3 = 15$ cm
- Eight silver beads: $8 \times 1 = 8$ cm

Step 3

Determine the sum of the three lengths. $6 + 15 + 8 = 29$ cm

The necklace Lin made was approximately 29 cm long.

17. C

To estimate how far they all travel, round each trip and add them together.

5.85 is rounded up to 6, 8.13 is rounded down to 8, and 12.28 is rounded down to 12.

$6 + 8 + 12 = 26$ km

Therefore, Jay, Stacey, and Carol travel about 26 km each day.

To calculate how far they all travel, add each trip, making sure that the decimal places line up.

$$\begin{array}{r} {}^{1}{}^{1}\ {}^{1} \\ 5.85 \\ 8.13 \\ +12.28 \\ \hline 26.26 \end{array}$$

18. C

To estimate the length of the line of straws, round the numbers so they can be multiplied mentally.

68 is rounded up to 70, and 21.1 is rounded down to 20.

$70 \times 20 = 1\ 400$.

Therefore, the line of straws will be about 1 400 cm long.

19. A

The length of 3 equal ropes is 9.75 m. The length of a single rope is $9.75 \div 3 = 3.25$ m.

Therefore, the length of a single rope is 3.25 m.

20. B

To find the area of the whole quilt, multiply 0.01 by 16.

Remember, when multiplying a whole number by 0.01, move the decimal two places to the left on the whole number.

$16 \times 0.01 = 0.16$

Therefore, the area of the whole quilt is $0.16\ \text{m}^2$.

21. B

One loaf of bread costs $3.49.

Therefore, 1 000 loaves of bread would cost:

$1 0 \times 3.49 = 3490$

1 000 loaves of bread would cost $3 490.00.

Remember, when multiplying a whole number by 1 000, move the decimal three places to the right.

22. C

To estimate how much licorice Graham has left, round each length and subtract.

25.3 is rounded down to 25, and 12.1 is rounded down to 12.

So, $25 - 12 = 13$.

Therefore, Graham has about 13 cm of licorice left.

23. D

Following the rules for order of operations:

$3 \times 4 + 8 \div 4$

Multiply $3 \times 4 = 12$

Divide $8 \div 4 = 2$.

Add $12 + 2 = 14$

So, $3 \times 4 + 8 \div 4 = 14$.

24. OR

Points	Sample Answer
4	Demonstrates an understanding of order of operations and is able to apply it with a high degree of effectiveness.

Using the rules for order of operations, remember to multiply first and then add and subtract.
$10 - 3 \times 2 + 5$
$= 10 - 6 + 5$
$= 4 + 5$
$= 9$

Points	Sample Answer
3	Demonstrates an understanding of order of operations and is able to apply it with a considerable degree of effectiveness.
2	Demonstrates some understanding of order of operations and is able to apply it with some degree of effectiveness.
1	Demonstrates a limited understanding of order of operations and is able to apply it with a limited degree of effectiveness.

25. A

The sash is 10 m long. To find the plain part of the sash, subtract the part that has embroidery work from the total length of the sash.

$10 - 3 = 7$. The plain part of the sash is 7 m.

Therefore, the ratio of the part of the sash with embroidery work to the part of the sash that is plain is 3:7.

26. C

When looking at decimal numbers, imagine the digit to the right of the decimal as the numerator in a fraction where the denominator is 10. Similarly, you can imagine two digits to the right of the decimal as the numerator in a fraction where the denominator is 100. Any number over 100 is equal to the same percent.

In A, $\frac{1}{2}$ should be equal to 0.50 and 50%.

In B, $\frac{1}{3}$ should be equal to 0.33 and 33%.

In C, $\frac{6}{10}$ is equal to 0.60 and 60%. This is the correct answer.

In D, $\frac{1}{2}$ should be equal to 0.50 and 50%.

27. B

Mario has $8, but the game he wants costs $20.

As a fraction, this is $\frac{8}{20}$. This can also be shown as a decimal.

$8 \div 20 = 0.40$

The decimal 0.40 can be expressed as a percentage by multiplying it by 100.

$0.40 \times 100 = 40\%$

Mario has 40% of the total amount of money he needs.

28. OR

Points	Sample Answer
4	Demonstrates an understanding of fractions and is able to convert fractions into decimals and percents with a high degree of effectiveness.

To determine who has the highest percent of successful shots, you can change each player's shots into percentages.

Henri makes 3 out of every 5 shots, which can be written as $\frac{3}{5}$. To change this into a percentage, divide 3 by 5.

$\frac{3}{5} = 0.60$ or 60%, Henri makes successful shots 60% of the time.

Kate's successful shots are 0.67 or 67%.

Lucas makes successful shots 65% of the time.

Therefore, Kate has the highest percentage of successful shots (67%), followed by Lucas (65%), and then Henri (60%).

3	Demonstrates an understanding of fractions and is able to convert fractions into decimals and percentages with a considerable degree of effectiveness.
2	Demonstrates some understanding of fractions and is able to convert fractions into decimals and percentages with some degree of effectiveness.

Points	Sample Answer
1	Demonstrates a little understanding of fractions and is able to convert fractions into decimals and percentages with a limited degree of effectiveness.

29. B

To find the cost of one gram of candy, divide $3.20 by 100.

Remember, when dividing a decimal by 100, move the decimal two places to the left.

$3.20 \div 100 = \$0.032$

Each gram of candy costs 3.2 cents, but since there is no coin that is worth less than one cent, round this to 3 cents.

Therefore, one gram of candy costs $0.03.

UNIT TEST — NUMBER SENSE AND NUMERATION

Use the following information to answer the next question.

Jennifer uses a diagram to represent all of the cast and crew members for a school play.

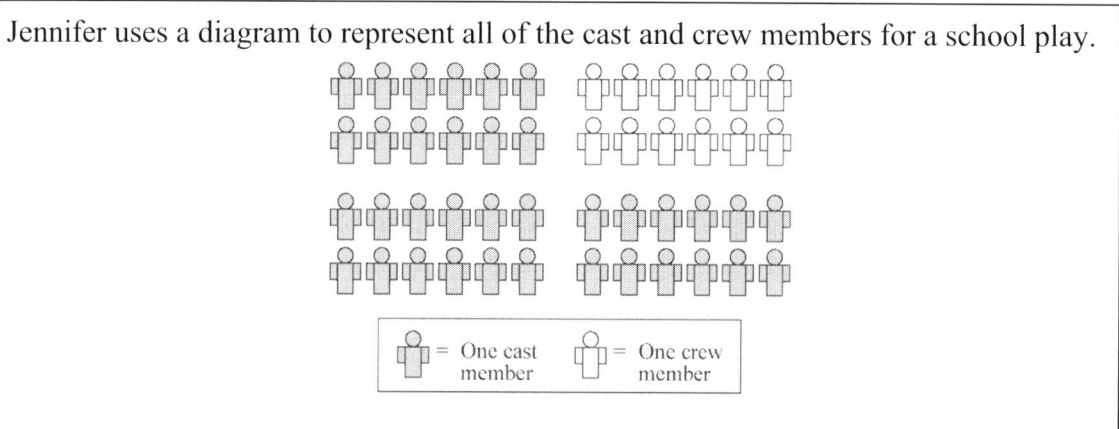

1. What is the ratio of cast members to crew members?

    A. 1 to 3   **B.** 1 to 6

    C. 2 to 4   **D.** 3 to 1

Use the following information to answer the next question.

Jack got 40 questions correct on a math test with a total of 50 questions.

2. What percentage of the questions did Jack **not** answer correctly?

    A. 10%   **B.** 20%

    C. 30%   **D.** 40%

| Open Response |

3. A baseball player hits 8 out of 25 balls pitched to him. What is the percentage of balls he does **not** hit? Show your work.

4. If 7 chocolate bars cost a total of $5.25 and each bar costs the same amount, what is the price of each chocolate bar?

   A. $0.55

   B. $0.75

   C. $0.85

   D. $0.95

5. What is the correct order, from least to greatest, of the numbers 10 011, 11 001, 10 110, and 11 010?

   A. 10 110, 10 011, 11 001, 11 010

   B. 11 001, 10 011, 10 110, 11 010

   C. 10 011, 10 110, 11 001, 11 010

   D. 11 010, 10 011, 10 110, 11 001

6. What is the value of the digit 6 in the number 167 250?

   A. 60

   B. 600

   C. 6 000

   D. 60 000

7. The odometer on Romario's bike has a reading of 3 492. What is this odometer reading written in words?

   A. Three thousand nine hundred forty-two

   B. Three thousand four hundred ninety-two

   C. Four thousand three hundred ninety-two

   D. Four thousand nine hundred forty-two

Use the following information to answer the next question.

> Tanisha has three strips of fabric that she had to sort from longest to shortest. The strips measure $5\frac{1}{3}$ m, $5\frac{7}{15}$ m, and $\frac{27}{5}$ m.

8. What are the lengths of the strips from longest to shortest?

   A. $5\frac{1}{3}, 5\frac{7}{15}, \frac{27}{5}$

   B. $5\frac{7}{15}, 5\frac{1}{3}, \frac{27}{5}$

   C. $5\frac{7}{15}, \frac{27}{5}, 5\frac{1}{3}$

   D. $\frac{27}{5}, 5\frac{1}{3}, 5\frac{7}{15}$

Use the following information to answer the next question.

Four glasses are filled to various heights with chocolate milk.

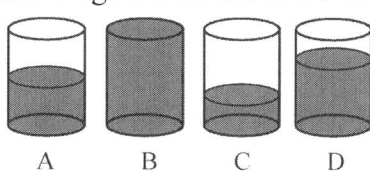

9. Which glass is about 50% filled with chocolate milk?
    A. A   **B.** B
    C. C   **D.** D

Use the following information to answer the next question.

Asher counted the number of toys on a shelf at a toy store. He counted 101 toys on one shelf, and there were ten shelves in one shelf unit.

10. Estimate how many shelf units the toy store would need to hold one million toys.
    A. 800   **B.** 910
    C. 1 000   **D.** 1 100

Open Response

11. How many seconds are in the month of February in a non-leap year? Explain your thinking.

12. Which of the following numbers is a composite number with more than four factors?
    A. 9   **B.** 14
    C. 23   **D.** 32

Use the following information to answer the next question.

> The year that Adela was born is a prime number. The day of the month on which she was born is also a prime number. In the year 2000, her age was a prime number.

13. Which of the following dates could be Adela's birthday?
   A. April 29, 1995   **B.** May 13, 1987

   C. August 21, 1973   **D.** September 19, 1999

14. What is the value of the expression $(300 + 90) \div 3$?
   A. 100   **B.** 103

   C. 130   **D.** 153

15. A box contains 2 907 marbles. Each marble weighs 19 g. What is the total weight of the box?
   A. 47 093 g   **B.** 55 233 g

   C. 61 053 g   **D.** 68 273 g

Use the following information to answer the next question.

> Cais walks to and from school each day. The distance between his home and his school is 644 m. Cais attend school 21 out of 30 days in September.

16. What was the total distance Cais walked between his home and his school in September?
   A. 25 844 m   **B.** 27 048 m

   C. 38 134 m   **D.** 39 918 m

17. If Carl bought a pop for $1.25 and a chocolate bar for $0.85, how much money did he spend in total?
   A. $0.40   **B.** $1.06

   C. $2.00   **D.** $2.10

18. If 1 peanut butter cookie has a mass of 6.72 g, what is the mass of 8 peanut butter cookies?
   A. 19.22 g   **B.** 35.22 g

   C. 53.76 g   **D.** 217.76 g

19. If the value of $2370 \times 0.1 = 237$, what is the value of 2370×0.01?
   A. 2.37   **B.** 23.7

   C. 237   **D.** 237 000

20. When the number 578.542 is divided by 10 000, where does the decimal move?

    A. Four places to the right   **B.** Five places to the right

    C. Four places to the left   **D.** Five places to the left

21. Gillian swam 15 km one day, 20.3 km the next day, and 24.8 km the day after that. About how far did Gillian swim in total?

    A. 19 km   **B.** 24 km

    C. 55 km   **D.** 60 km

22. If $5 \times 7 + 18 = 53$, then what is the value of $5 + 7 \times 18$?

    A. 26   **B.** 53

    C. 131   **D.** 216

ANSWERS AND SOLUTIONS — UNIT TEST

1. D	6. D	11. OR	16. B	21. D
2. B	7. B	12. D	17. D	22. C
3. OR	8. C	13. B	18. C	
4. B	9. A	14. C	19. B	
5. C	10. C	15. B	20. C	

1. D

There are 36 cast members and 12 crew members. As a ratio, this can be written as $36:12$, $\frac{36}{12}$, or 36 to 12.

Since both numbers in the ratio are divisible by 12,

$36:12$

$36 \div 12 = 3$

$12 \div 12 = 1$

$3:1$

Therefore, the ratio of cast members to crew members is 3 to 1.

2. B

Jack got 40 correct answers out of 50 questions. The number of questions that were incorrect is $50 - 40$, or 10.

First, express the ratio as a decimal. Divide 10 by 50.

$\frac{10}{50} = 0.2$

To express the decimal as a percent, multiply by 100 or simply move the decimal point two positions to the right: 0.20 becomes 20%.

So, Jack answered 20% of the questions incorrectly.

3. OR

Points	Sample Answer
4	Demonstrates an understanding of fractions and is able to convert fractions to percents with a high degree of effectiveness.

Points	Sample Answer
	To find the percentage of balls the baseball player did not hit, first find the percentage he did hit. The baseball player hit 8 out of 25 balls, which can be written as $\frac{8}{25}$. To write this as a percentage, you can divide 8 by 25 and then change the decimal into a percent. $\frac{8}{25} = 0.32$ or 32%. Therefore, the baseball player hit 32% of the balls. To find the percentage of balls he did not hit, subtract 32 from 100. $100 - 32 = 68$ Therefore, the baseball player did not hit 68% of the balls pitched to him.
3	Demonstrates an understanding of fractions and is able to convert fractions to percents. (e.g., make a calculation error when converting)
2	Demonstrates some understanding of fractions and is able to convert fractions to percents with some degree of effectiveness.
1	Demonstrates a limited understanding of fractions and is able to convert fractions to percents with a limited degree of effectiveness.

4. B

If the total cost for 7 chocolate bars is $5.25 and each chocolate bar costs the same, the cost of one chocolate bar can be found by dividing the total amount paid by the number of bars bought.

$\$5.25 \div 7 = \$0.75$

Each bar costs $0.75.

5. C

An easy method for comparing and ordering whole numbers is to use a place value chart.

Thousands			Ones		
H	T	O	H	T	O
	1	0	0	1	1
	1	1	0	0	1
	1	0	1	1	0
	1	1	0	1	0

The numbers that have 0 in the thousands place are less than the numbers with 1 in the thousands place.

So, the numbers 10 011 and 10 110 are the two smallest numbers.

Look at the hundreds place to determine which number is less than the other. The number 10 011 has a 0 in the hundreds place, so it is less than 10 110, which has a 1 in the hundreds place.

To determine which number is the biggest, 11 001 or 11 010, look at the digits in the hundreds place.

Both numbers have 0 in the hundreds place, so you must keep looking to the right, at the tens place.

The number 11 001 has a 0 in the tens place and the number 11 010 has a 1 in the tens place, so the number 11 010 is the greatest number.

Therefore, the order of the numbers, from least to greatest, is 10 011, 10 110, 11 001, 11 010.

6. D

Using a place value chart is one way to determine the place value of the digit 6.

Thousands			Ones		
H	T	O	H	T	O
1	6	0	2	5	0

You can see that the digit 6 is in the ten thousands place.

The value of the digit 6 is $6 \times 10\ 000 = 60\ 000$.

7. B

To determine the number written in words, you can use a place value chart.

Thousands	Hundreds	Tens	Ones
3	4	9	2

The digit 3 is in the thousands place, so it is equal to three thousand.

The digit 4 is in the hundreds place, so it is equal to four hundred.

The digit 9 is in the tens place, so it is equal to ninety.

The digit 2 is in the ones place, so it is equal to two.

Therefore, the number 3 492 can be written as three thousand four hundred ninety-two.

8. C

When comparing improper fractions and mixed numbers with unlike denominators, the best strategy is to change all fractions into improper fractions and then find like denominators.

$$5\frac{1}{3} = \frac{16}{3}, \frac{27}{5}, 5\frac{7}{15} = \frac{82}{15}$$

The lowest common multiple is 15 because:

$3 \times 5 = 15$, $5 \times 3 = 15$, and $15 \times 1 = 15$.

$$\frac{16}{3} \times \frac{5}{5} = \frac{80}{15}, \frac{27}{5} \times \frac{3}{3} = \frac{81}{15}, \text{ and } \frac{82}{15}$$

Arranging the strips of fabric from longest to shortest, you get $\frac{82}{15}, \frac{81}{15}, \frac{80}{15}$ or $5\frac{7}{15}, \frac{27}{5}, 5\frac{1}{3}$ respectively.

9. A

Glass A is half full, or about 50% filled with chocolate milk.

Glass B is full, or 100% filled with chocolate milk.

Glass C is less than half full, or about 25% filled with chocolate milk.

Glass D is more than half full, or about 75% filled with chocolate milk.

10. C

To find out how many shelf units it would take to hold a million toys, first estimate how many toys each shelf unit will hold. There are 10 shelves per unit and 101 toys on each shelf. Round 101 to 100 to make for easy multiplication.

$10 \times 100 = 1\ 000$

One unit will hold approximately 1 000 toys.

This number must be divided into 1 million to find out the number of shelf units needed.

$1\ 000\ 000 \div 1\ 000 = 1\ 000$

Therefore, the toy store would need about 1 000 shelf units to hold 1 million toys.

11. OR

Points	Sample Answer
4	Thorough understanding of large whole numbers and how to convert months into seconds.

To determine how many seconds are in the month of February, you must multiply the number of days in February by the number of hours in a day, then multiply the result by the number of minutes in an hour, and then multiply that result by the number of seconds in a minute.

There are 28 days in February. There are 24 hours in a day. So, 28 days × 24 hours = 672 hours.

There are 60 minutes in an hour. So, 672 hours × 60 minutes = 40 320 minutes.

There are 60 seconds in a minute. So, 40320 minutes × 60 seconds = 2 419 200 seconds.

Therefore, there are 2 419 200 seconds in the month of February.

Points	Sample Answer
3	Considerable understanding of large whole numbers and how to convert months into seconds (e.g., makes a calculation error when multiplying in any step).
2	Some understanding of large whole numbers and how to convert months into seconds (e.g., misses a step).

Points	Sample Answer
1	Limited understanding of large whole numbers and how to convert months into seconds (e.g., does not understand the relationship of multiples 28 × 60).

12. D

A composite number is a natural number that has three or more factors.

In A, the number 9 is a composite number, but it only has three factors (1, 3, and 9).

In B, the number 14 is a composite number, but it only has four factors (1, 2, 7, and 14).

In C, the number 23 is a prime number.

In D, the number 32 is a composite number, and it has more than four factors (1, 2, 4, 8, 16, and 32).

13. B

The year 1995 is divisible by 5. Since a prime number is only divisible by 1 and itself, 1995 is not prime. Therefore, A is incorrect.

The date 21 is divisible by 3. Since a prime number is only divisible by 1 and itself, 21 is not prime. Therefore, C is incorrect.

For B and D, find Adela's age in the year 2000.

Year of birth	Date of birth	Adela's age in the year 2000
1987	13	13
1999	19	1

The number 1 is neither prime nor composite. Therefore, D is also incorrect.

By a process of elimination, the correct answer is B The year 1987 is a prime number and the day 13 is a prime number. In the year 2000, Adela would be 13 years old, which is also a prime number.

14. C

Using the distributive property, expand the expression to:

$(300 \div 3) + (90 \div 3)$
$= 100 + 30$
$= 130$

15. B

The number of marbles in the box = 2 907
The weight of one marble is 19 g
The weight of 2 907 marbles is
$2\ 907 \times 719$ g = 55 233 g.

16. B

The distance between Cais's home and school is 644 m. Cais walks to and from school on every school day, which means he walks $644 + 644 = 1\ 288$ m every school day.

Multiply the distance Cais walks everyday by the number of days he walks to school in September.

$$\begin{array}{r} 1\ 288 \\ \times\ 21 \\ \hline 27\ 048 \end{array}$$

So, in 21 days, Cais walked 27 048 m between his home and school.

17. D

To find out how much Carl spent in total, add the amount of the pop and the amount of the chocolate bar.

$$\begin{array}{r} {\scriptstyle 1\ 1} \\ \$1.25 \\ +\$0.85 \\ \hline \$2.10 \end{array}$$

Therefore, Carl spent $2.10 in total.

18. C

To find the mass of 8 cookies, multiply the mass of 1 cookie by 8.

6.72 g $\times 8 = 53.76$ g

Therefore, 8 cookies have a mass of 53.76 g.

19. B

When multiplying 2 370 by 0.01, you are multiplying by $\frac{1}{100}$ or dividing by 100.

The value of $2370 \times 0.01 =$
$2370 \times \frac{1}{100} = \frac{237}{10} = 23.7$

Another way to solve this problem is by moving the decimal point two decimal places to the left. Because there are two decimal places in the question(0.01), you move the decimal point two places to the left of the whole number (2 370). Therefore, $2370 \times 0.01 = 23.7$.

20. C

When a number is divided by 10, the decimal moves one place to the left. When a number is divided by 100, the decimal moves two places to the left. For every additional 0 added to the divisor, the decimal moves one more place to the left.

Therefore, when a number is divided by 10 000, the decimal moves four places to the left.

$578.542 \div 10\ 000 = 0.057\ 8542$

21. D

To estimate how far Gillian swam, round the decimal and add each distance together.

The number 20.3 is rounded down to 20 because the digit 3 is less than 5. The number 24.8 is rounded up to 25 because the digit 8 is greater than 5.

So, $15 + 20 + 25 = 60$.

Therefore, Gillian swam a total of about 60 km.

22. C

In order to solve the equation, you must follow the rules of order of operations. Multiplication must always be done before addition or subtraction.
$5 + 7 \times 18$
$7 \times 18 = 126$
$5 + 126 = 131$

Therefore, the value of $5 + 7 \times 18$ is 131.

NOTES

MEASUREMENT

Specific Expectation	Practice Questions	Unit Test Questions	Practice Test 1	Practice Test 2
Table of Correlations				
6m29 Attributes, Units, and Measurement Sense				
6m31	*demonstrate an understanding of the relationship between estimated and precise measurements, and determine and justify when each kind is appropriate*	1	1		
6m32	*estimate, measure, and record length, area, mass, capacity, and volume, using the metric measurement system*	2, 3, 4	2, 3	2	1
6m30 Measurement Relationships				
6m33	*select and justify the appropriate metric unit (i.e., millimetre, centimetre, decimetre, metre, decametre, kilometre) to measure length or distance in a given real-life situation*	5, 6, 7	4, 5	3	
6m34	*solve problems requiring conversion from larger to smaller metric units*	8, 9, 10	6, 7	4, 5	2
6m35	*construct a rectangle, a square, a triangle, and a parallelogram, using a variety of tools, given the area and/or perimeter*	11, 12	8, 9	6	
6m36	*determine, through investigation using a variety of tools and strategies, the relationship between the area of a rectangle and the areas of parallelograms and triangles, by decomposing and composing*	13, 14	10		3
6m37	*develop the formulas for the area of a parallelogram (i.e., Area of triangle = (base × height)) and the area of a triangle [i.e., Area of triangle = (base × height) ÷ 2], using the area relationships among rectangles, parallelograms, and triangles*	15, 16			4
6m38	*solve problems involving the estimation and calculation of the areas of triangles and the areas of parallelograms*	17, 18	11, 12		5
6m39	*determine, using concrete materials, the relationship between units used to measure area (i.e., square centimetre, square metre), and apply the relationship to solve problems that involve conversions from square metres to square centimetres*	19, 20, 21	13, 14, 15	7	6
6m40	*determine, through investigation using a variety of tools and strategies, the relationship between the height, the area of the base, and the volume of a triangular prism, and generalize to develop the formula (i.e., Volume = area of base × height)*	22	16		
6m41	*determine, through investigation using a variety of tools and strategies, the surface area of rectangular and triangular prisms*	23, 24	17, 18		7
6m42	*solve problems involving the estimation and calculation of the surface area and volume of triangular and rectangular prisms*	25, 26, 27	19, 20	8, 9	8

6m31 demonstrate an understanding of the relationship between estimated and precise measurements, and determine and justify when each kind is appropriate

USING ESTIMATION AND PRECISE MEASUREMENTS

An estimated measure is an approximate value for that measure. For example, your classroom is about 8 metres wide.

A precise measurement is a measure that differs from the true value of the measure by very little.

For example, 2 millilitres of cough syrup is given to a young child every 4 hours as needed. A precise or accurate measure of cough syrup is given to the child. The smaller the unit of measure, the more precise the measurement will be.

For example, the finish times for four participants in a race could be

- 3 minutes 15.2 seconds
- 3 minutes 14.8 seconds
- 3 minutes 15.1 seconds
- 3 minutes 14.7 seconds

There are two finish times recorded at 15 seconds and two recorded at 14 seconds. Therefore, to decide who wins the race and the order in which the race is won, it is necessary to record the time to the nearest tenth of a second. A precise measure of time must be recorded to determine who wins the race.

When determining the distance between two cities, an estimated measure is appropriate. When travelling between the two cities, a precise measurement is not necessary.

1. Ming is exactly 145 cm tall. What is Ming's estimated height in metres?
   A. 0.5 m   **B.** 1.0 m

   C. 1.5 m   **D.** 2.0 m

6m32 estimate, measure, and record length, area, mass, capacity, and volume, using the metric measurement system

ESTIMATING AND MEASURING LENGTH, AREA, MASS, CAPACITY, AND VOLUME

Estimating measures means using a referent to find an approximate measure. For example, you could use a referent for 1 cm, which is about the width of your smallest finger, to approximate the width of your calculator.

Measuring means using an appropriate instrument marked in metric measures to determine the actual measure of length, area, mass, capacity, or volume. For example, to measure the width of your calculator, you would use a ruler marked in centimetres and millimetres.

Length is represented by the number of segments along a line from one end of a figure to another. Length is commonly measured in millimetres (mm), centimetres (cm), metres (m), and kilometres (km). For example, to estimate and measure the length of a crayon, you would use centimetres.

Area is the number of square units needed to cover a region. Area is commonly measured in square metres (m^2), square centimetres (cm^2), square millimetres (mm^2), and square kilometres (km^2). For example, to estimate and measure the area of a floor, you would use square metres.

Mass is a measure of how much matter is present in an object. The common units of mass in the metric system of units include grams (g) and kilograms (kg). For example, to estimate and measure the mass of a cookie, you would use grams. To estimate and measure the mass of a truck, you would use kilograms.

Volume is the amount of space occupied by a solid, liquid, or gas. Volume is commonly measured in cubic millimetres (mm^3), cubic centimetres (cm^3), and cubic metres (m^3). For example, to estimate and measure the volume of a gift box, you would use cubic centimetres.

Capacity is the volume of liquid a container can hold. It is expressed in units such as millilitres(mL) and litres (L). For example, to estimate and measure the capacity of a water bottle, you would use millilitres. To estimate and measure the capacity of a milk jug, you would use litres.

Capacity and volume are closely connected because 1mL (capacity) is equal to $1cm^3$ (volume).

2. What is a precise measurement of the pencil?

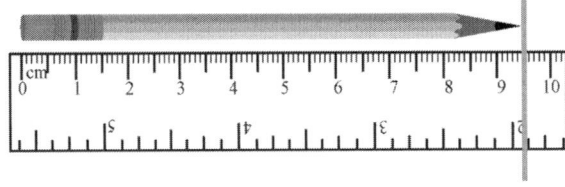

A. 90 mm   **B.** 9 cm

C. 9.5 cm   **D.** 10 cm

Use the following information to answer the next question.

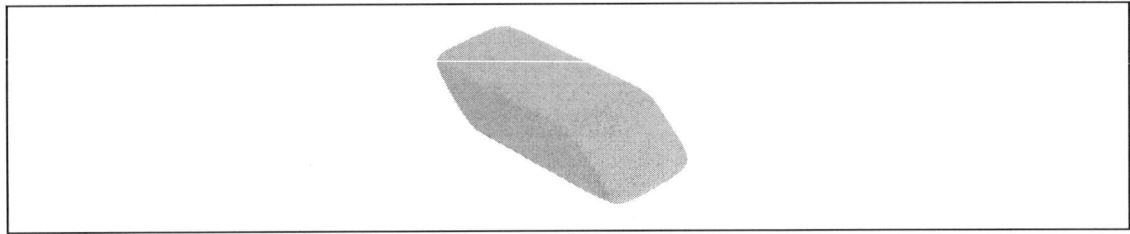

3. Which of the following measures is the **best** estimate of the mass of an eraser?
   A. 0.5 kg   **B.** 5 g

   C. 5 cm   **D.** 25 mL

Use the following information to answer the next question.

Jens has 8 model train track pieces, each measuring 15 cm.

4. If Jens puts all the pieces of train tracks together, how long will the whole train track be?

A. 15 cm   **B.** 120 cm

C. 150 cm   **D.** 120 m

6m33 select and justify the appropriate metric unit (i.e., millimetre, centimetre, decimetre, metre, decametre, kilometre) to measure length or distance in a given real-life situation

SELECTING THE BEST UNIT WHEN MEASURING

When you select a unit of measure to measure a length or distance, you should consider the size of the length or distance. Longer lengths or distances are measured in larger units. The more precise you want the measure to be, the smaller the unit that you should use to measure it.

Example

To determine if a math book will fit into a shelf, you would measure the book using centimetres because this length is relatively short but not short enough to require the use of millimetres. Since you are measuring to determine if the math book will fit into a shelf, precision to the nearest millimetre is not required.

Example

To measure the distance from the front door of your school to your classroom door, you would use metres because this length is longer than what can be easily measured in centimetres.

5. Which of the following units is **most appropriate** for measuring the length of a car?

A. Millimetre   **B.** Centimetre

C. Metre   **D.** Decametre

Use the following information to answer the next question.

Of the five oceans, the Pacific Ocean is the deepest.

6. Which of the following units should be used to measure the depth of the Pacific Ocean?

A. Centimetre   **B.** Decimetre

C. Metre   **D.** Kilometre

7. Which of the following units is **most appropriate** for measuring the length of a book?
   A. Millimetres   **B.** Centimetres

   C. Metres   **D.** Kilometres

6m34 solve problems requiring conversion from larger to smaller metric units

CONVERTING BETWEEN UNITS

The following chart shows the relationship between commonly used metric measures:

Length	Mass	Capacity
1 cm = 10 mm	1 kg = 1 000 g	1 L = 1 000 mL
1 m = 100 cm		1 kL = 1 000 L
1 m = 1 000 mm		
1 km = 1 000 m		

To convert a larger unit of measure into a smaller unit of measure, multiply the number of units in the larger unit of measure by the number of units in the smaller unit of measure that make up one larger unit of measure. For example, to convert 2 kilograms into grams, you must first know that 1 kg is equal to 1 000 g. Then, you would multiply 2 kilograms by 1 000 to get 2 000 grams.

Example

Find out how many packets of peanuts can be filled using a total of 3 kg of peanuts if each packet holds 100 g.

First, you must convert kilograms into grams.

Remember that 1 kg = 1 000 g. Therefore, 3 kg = 1 000 g × 3 or 3 000 g.

Since each packet of peanuts holds 100 g, you must find how many groups of 100 g are in 3 000 g.
3 000 ÷ 100 = 30

Thirty 100 g packets of peanuts can be filled with 3 kg of peanuts.

Solution

---

8. Jean is practicing for a 1 500 m race. If he completes the event 4 times in one practice, how many kilometres would he have run?
   A. 0.6 km   **B.** 6 km

   C. 60 km   **D.** 6 000 km

Use the following information to answer the next question.

Penny and Wayne want to buy some fruit to make a fruit salad to take on a picnic. The prices of four kinds of fruit at the farmer's market are shown below.

Apples: $0.99 per kg

Oranges: $3.95 per 5 kg

Bananas: $0.60 per 500 g

Kiwis: $1.89 per 1 000 g

9. Which of the four fruits is the most expensive by mass?
    A. Apples   B. Oranges
    C. Bananas   D. Kiwi

10. The mass of a bag is 800 g. When 18 metal balls of equal mass are put into the bag, the total mass of the bag becomes 1.7 kg. What is the mass of each metal ball?
    A. 40 g   B. 50 g
    C. 80 g   D. 90 g

6m35 construct a rectangle, a square, a triangle, and a parallelogram, using a variety of tools, given the area and/or perimeter

AREA AND PERIMETER

Perimeter is the distance around a two-dimensional (2-D) figure and is measured in linear units.
Area is the amount of surface that a figure covers and is usually measured in square units.
Congruent figures have the same size and shape, so they will have the same perimeter and area.
Two non-congruent figures may have either the same area or perimeter, but not both.

Example
To construct a rectangle and a parallelogram with an area of 2 square units, you can use grid paper.

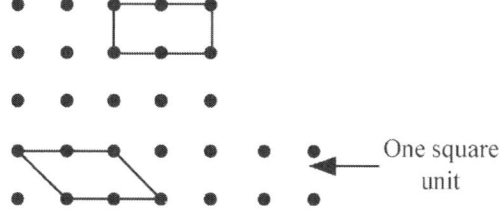

Example

Given an area or perimeter, you can construct different shapes.

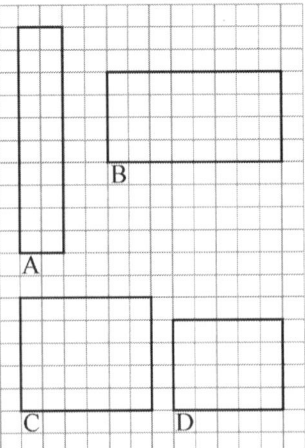

- Rectangle *A* has a perimeter of 24 units and an area of 20 square units.
- Rectangle *B* has a perimeter of 24 units and an area of 32 square units.
- Rectangle *C* has a perimeter of 22 units and an area of 30 square units.
- Rectangle *D* has a perimeter of 18 units and an area of 20 square units.
- Rectangles *A* and *D* have the same area.
- Rectangles *A* and *B* have the same perimeter.

Use the following information to answer the next question.

This square has a perimeter of 12 cm.

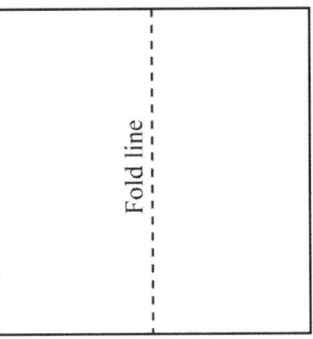

Fold line

11. What is the area of the unfolded piece of paper?

   A. 10 cm^2 **B.** 16 cm^2

   C. 18 cm^2 **D.** 24 cm^2

12. The area and perimeter of a soccer field are 1 125 m^2 and 140 m, respectively. Which of the following dimensions could this field possibly have?

   A. 5 m × 225 m   **B.** 9 m × 125 m

   C. 15 m × 75 m   **D.** 25 m × 45 m

6m36 determine, through investigation using a variety of tools and strategies, the relationship between the area of a rectangle and the areas of parallelograms and triangles, by decomposing and composing

6m37 develop the formulas for the area of a parallelogram (i.e., Area of triangle = (base × height)) and the area of a triangle [i.e., Area of triangle = (base × height) ÷ 2], using the area relationships among rectangles, parallelograms, and triangles

DECOMPOSING 2-D SHAPES AND DEVELOPING AREA FORMULAS

DECOMPOSING A PARALLELOGRAM INTO A RECTANGLE

A parallelogram can be transformed into a rectangle by sliding a triangular section of the parallelogram as shown in the following diagram.

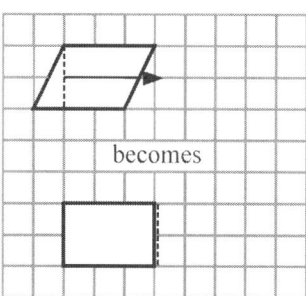

Slide the **triangle** to the right 3 spaces. The rectangle has an area of 6 square units. The rectangle has the same area as the parallelogram for two reasons:

- You can count the number of square units in each figure and see that there are 6 square units in each one.
- The parallelogram was transformed into a rectangle by sliding a triangular section, so the area stays the same.

Therefore, the area of the parallelogram is 6 square units.

The base of the parallelogram is 3 units and the height is 2 units. The base of the rectangle is 3 units and the height is 2 units.

To find the area of a parallelogram, multiply the base by the height.

Area of a Parallelogram = base × height

= 3 units × 2 units

= 6 square units

To find the area of the rectangle, multiply the base by the height.

Area of a Rectangle = base × height

= 3 units × 2 units

= 6 square units

You can see that the area of a parallelogram is the same as the area of a rectangle when the two shapes have the same base and the same height.

DECOMPOSING A RECTANGLE INTO TWO CONGRUENT TRIANGLES

The diagonal of the rectangle cuts the rectangle into two congruent triangles. The area of each of these congruent triangles is half the area of the rectangle. The two triangles have the same area and the two triangles together have the same area as the rectangle.

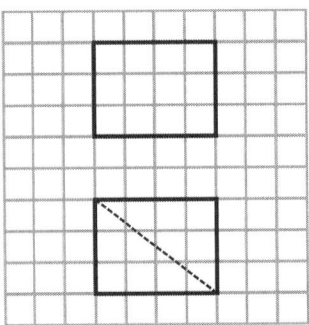

The area of a rectangle is found using the formula.
Area of a Rectangle = base × height

$$= 4 \text{ units} \times 3 \text{ units}$$

$$= 12 \text{ square units}$$

Since one triangle is one-half the area of the rectangle, the area of a triangle is found using the formula.
Area of a Triangle = base × height ÷ 2

$$= 4 \text{ units} \times 3 \text{ units} \div 2$$

$$= 6 \text{ square units}$$

13. If two identical right triangles that are 3 cm high with 4 cm bases are joined, the resulting figure could be a
   A. rectangle with an area 6 cm^2
   B. square with an area 9 cm^2
   C. rectangle with an area 12 cm^2
   D. square with an area 16 cm^2

Two triangles identical to *ABC* are put together to form a parallelogram.

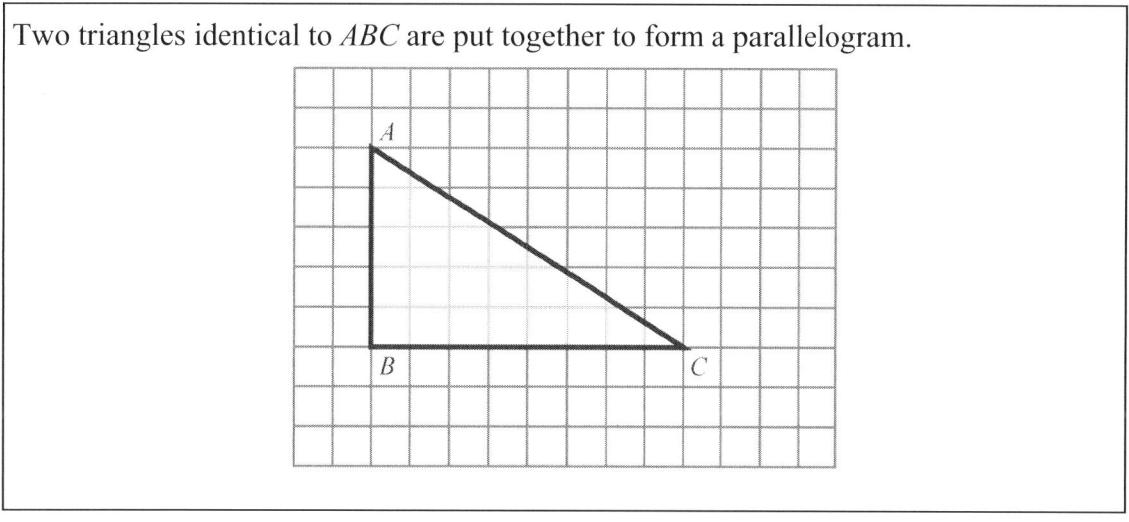

Open Response

14. What would the area of the parallelogram be? Explain your answer.

15. The area of a parallelogram made up of two congruent triangles will be

   A. twice the area of one of the triangles

   B. four times the area of one of the triangles

   C. eight times the area of one of the triangles

   D. the same as the area of one of the triangles

Use the following information to answer the next question.

Mauro is drawing a poster on a piece of paper in the shape of a parallelogram. Naho is drawing two posters on two congruent triangles.

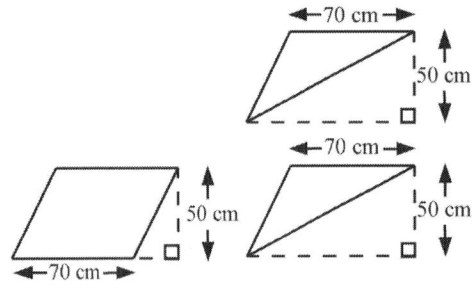

Open Response

16. Does one student require more paper than the other? Explain your answer.

6m38 solve problems involving the estimation and calculation of the areas of triangles and the areas of parallelograms

CALCULATING AREA OF TRIANGLES AND PARALLELOGRAMS

Example
Calculate the area of two triangles that have the same base and the same height.

Solution
The two triangles shown on the grid below have the same base and the same height even though they may look different. The base of each triangle is 3 units and the height of each triangle is 4 units.

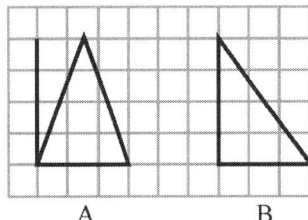

Area of Triangle *A*	Area of Triangle *B*
The base is 3 units and the height is 4 units. $A = \text{base} \times \text{height} \div 2$ $A = 3 \times 4 \div 2$ $A = 12 \div 2$ $A = 6$ The area of Triangle *A* is 6 square units.	The base is 3 units and the height is 4 units. $A = \text{base} \times \text{height} \div 2$ $A = 3 \times 4 \div 2$ $A = 12 \div 2$ $A = 6$ The area of Triangle *B* is 6 square units.

Remember to follow the order of operations when calculating the area. The area of two triangles that have the same base and the same height is the same.

Example

A parallelogram has a base that is 6.25 cm long and a height that is 5 cm.

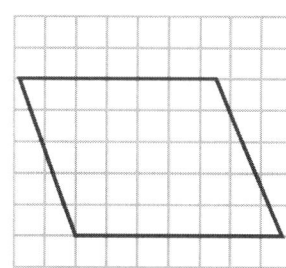

Estimate and then calculate the area of the parallelogram.

Solution

To estimate the area of the parallelogram, round 6.25 to 6, then multiply by 5. $(6 \times 5 - 30)$. Since 6.25 was rounded down to 6, a good estimate would be a little more than 30, about 31. The area of the parallelogram is about 31 cm^2.

To find the area of the parallelogram, use the formula

$A = \text{base} \times \text{height}$

$A = 6.25 \times 5$

$A = 31.25 \text{ cm}^2$

The area of the parallelogram is 31.25 cm^2.

Since the actual area of the parallelogram is very close to the estimated area, you know that the answer is reasonable.

Use the following information to answer the next question.

Martin draws a triangle on grid paper as shown in the figure. Each square on the grid paper has an area of 1 cm². By counting the number of full squares and half squares covered by the triangle, Martin records the area of the triangle.

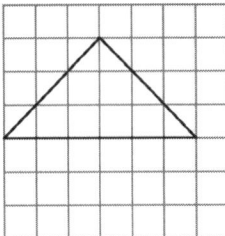

17. Which of the following triangles has the same area as Martin's triangle?

A.
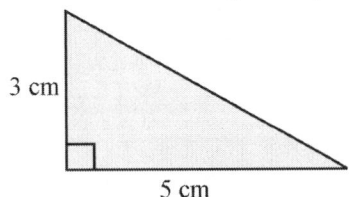
3 cm
5 cm

B.
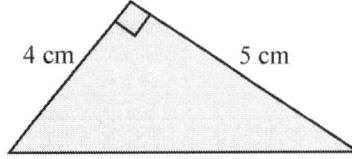
4 cm   5 cm

C.
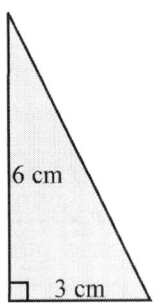
6 cm
3 cm

D.
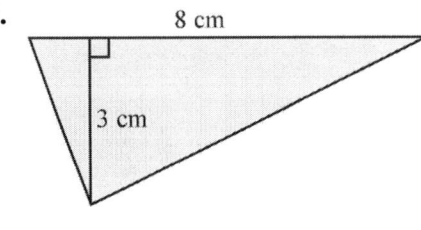
8 cm
3 cm

Use the following information to answer the next question.

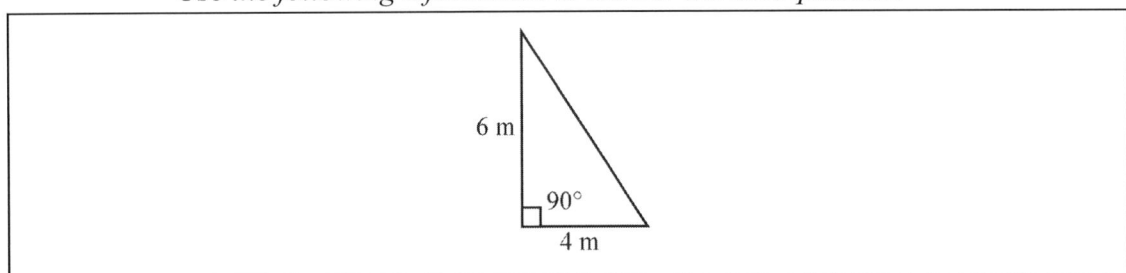
6 m
90°
4 m

18. What is the area of the given triangle?

    A. 4 m²   **B.** 10 m²

    C. 12 m²   **D.** 24 m²

6m39 determine, using concrete materials, the relationship between units used to measure area (i.e., square centimetre, square metre), and apply the relationship to solve problems that involve conversions from square metres to square centimetres

CONVERTING BETWEEN UNITS OF AREA

To measure units of area, square centimetres (cm^2) and square metres (m^2) are two units that are often used.

The relationship between square centimetres and square metres is not the same as the relationship between centimetres and metres. One square metre can be filled in with 100 base ten flats, each of which is 10 cm by 10 cm. The surface area of each flat is 100 cm^2, and there are 100 of these base ten flats.

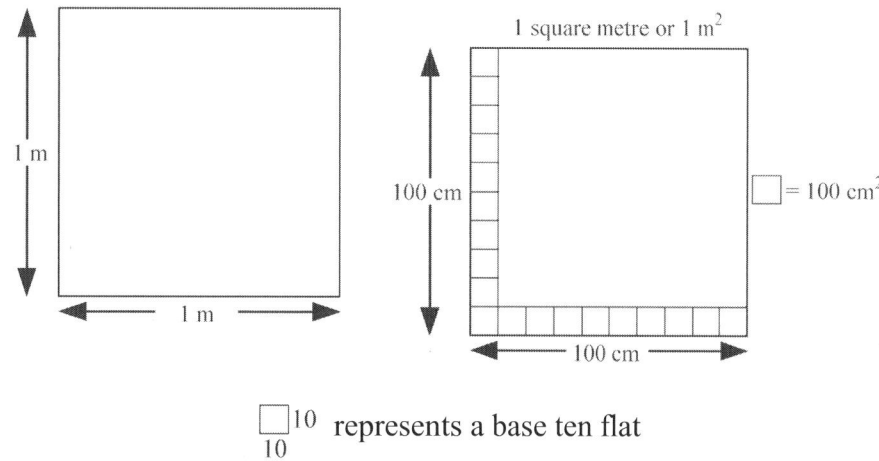

$\square^{10}_{10}$ represents a base ten flat

If one base ten flat is 100 cm^2 and there are 100 base ten flats in one square metre, then there must be 100 × 100 square centimetres in one square metre.

Use the formula for the area of a rectangle, A = base × height, to find the area for each square above.

The base of the first square is 1 m, and the height is 1 m. The base of the second same square is 100 cm, and the height is 100 cm.

Use the formula for the area of a rectangle, $A = \text{base} \times \text{height}$.

$A = \text{base} \times \text{height}$ $A = \text{base} \times \text{height}$

$\quad = 1\text{ m} \times 1\text{ m}$ $= 100\text{ cm} \times 100\text{ cm}$

$\quad = 1\text{ m}^2$ $= 10\ 000\text{ cm}^2$

Therefore, $10\ 000\text{ cm}^2$ is equal to 1 m^2.

Example

Lori has 0.5 m^2 of fabric. She would like to cut this fabric into pieces with each piece measuring 100 cm^2. How many pieces can she cut from this material?

Solution

Since the material is measured in square metres and each piece to be cut is measured in square centimetres, convert the 0.5 m^2 into square centimetres.

$\quad 1\text{ m}^2 = 10\ 000\text{ cm}^2$

$0.5\text{ m}^2 = 10\ 000 \times 0.5\text{ cm}^2$

$0.5\text{ m}^2 = 5\ 000\text{ cm}^2$

Since each piece to be cut is 100 cm^2, divide $5\ 000\text{ cm}^2$ by 100 cm^2 to get the number of pieces.
$5\ 000 \div 100 = 50$

Lori can cut 50 pieces from this material, each measuring 100 cm^2.

---

19. What is the maximum number of tiles measuring $60\text{ cm} \times 50\text{ cm}$ that can be placed on a floor measuring $2.4\text{ m} \times 2.0\text{ m}$?

    A. 16   **B.** 20

    C. 32   **D.** 160

Use the following information to answer the next question.

This rectangle is 40 centimetres wide by 0.6 metres long.

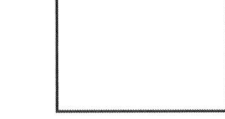

20. What is the area of the rectangle in square centimetres?

    A. 24 cm^2 **B.** 240 cm^2

    C. $2\ 400\text{ cm}^2$ **D.** $2\ 800\text{ cm}^2$

Use the following information to answer the next question.

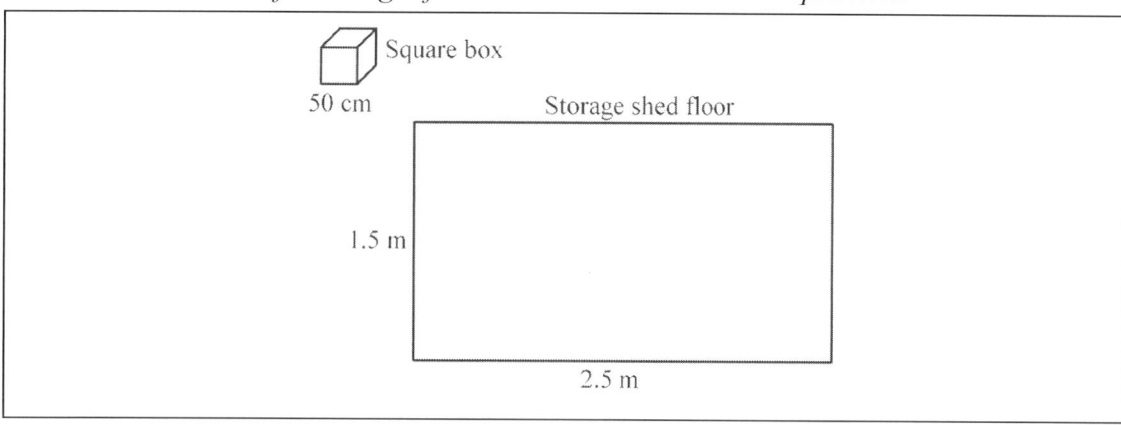

Open Response

21. What is the greatest number of boxes that will fit onto the floor of the storage shed? Show your work.

6m40 determine, through investigation using a variety of tools and strategies, the relationship between the height, the area of the base, and the volume of a triangular prism, and generalize to develop the formula (i.e., Volume = area of base × height)

VOLUME OF A TRIANGULAR PRISM

A rectangular prism has a rectangular base, and a triangular prism has a triangular base.

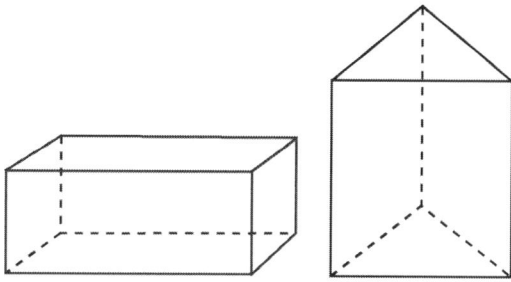

To find the volume of a rectangular prism, take a box in the shape of a rectangular prism and fill the bottom of the box with unit cubes from the base ten materials. A unit cube is 1 cm long, 1 cm wide, and 1 cm high.

To find the volume of the prism, multiply the number of unit cubes in one layer by the number of layers in the box. The number of layers needed is the height of the box in centimetres because each unit cube is 1 cm high.

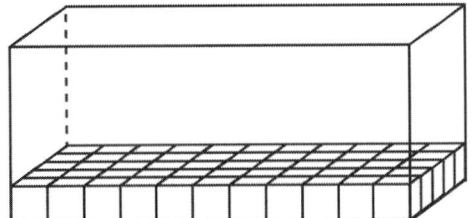 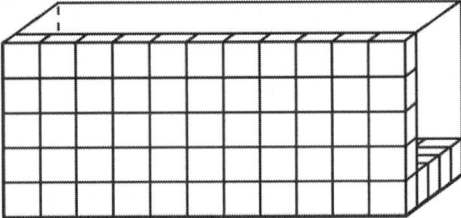

The general formula for the volume of any prism is as follows:
volume = area of the base × height of the prism

Since the area of a rectangle is the length multiplied by the width, the volume of a rectangular prism can also be expressed as follows:
volume = length × width × height

A similar procedure can be used to find the volume of a triangular prism. Just as a triangle is one half of a rectangle cut diagonally, if you split the rectangular prism in half diagonally, you would have two triangular prisms.

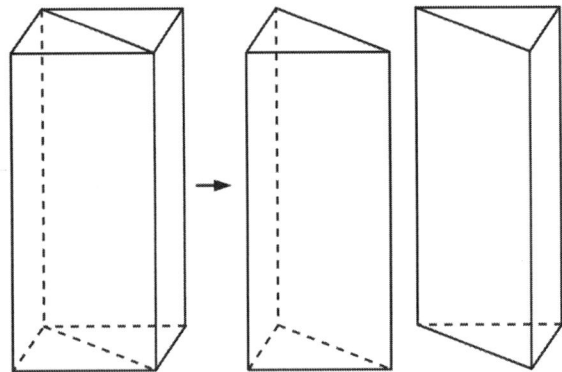

Each triangular prism would be half the volume of the rectangular prism.

You know that the area of a triangle is $\frac{1}{2}$(base × height). The volume of a triangular prism is the area of the base (triangle) multiplied by the height of the prism.

Example
The following table shows the dimensions of two triangular prisms:

	Triangular Prism *A*	Triangular Prism *B*
Base of Triangle (*b*)	5 cm	3 cm
Height of Triangle (*h*)	4 cm	2 cm
Height of Triangular Prism	3 cm	4 cm
Volume of Triangular Prism	30 cm^3	12 cm^3

The process for finding the volume of triangular prisms is summarized in the following tables:

Triangular Prism *A*

Area of Base	Volume of Prism
$A_{triangle} = \dfrac{1}{2}bh$ $= \dfrac{1}{2}(5)(4)$ $= 10 \text{cm}^2$	$V = A_{triangle} \times h_{prism}$ $= A_{triangle} \times 3$ $= 10 \times 3$ $= 30 \text{ cm}^3$

Triangular Prism *B*

Area of Base	Volume of Prism
$A_{triangle} = \dfrac{1}{2}bh$ $= \dfrac{1}{2}(3)(2)$ $= 3 \text{ cm}^2$	$V = A_{triangle} \times h_{prism}$ $= A_{triangle} \times 4$ $= 3 \times 4$ $= 12 \text{ cm}^3$

By looking at the patterns in the tables, you can see that the volume of a triangular prism can be found by multiplying the area of the triangular base by the height of the prism.

Use the following information to answer the next question.

Tom constructs a tent in the shape of a triangular prism.

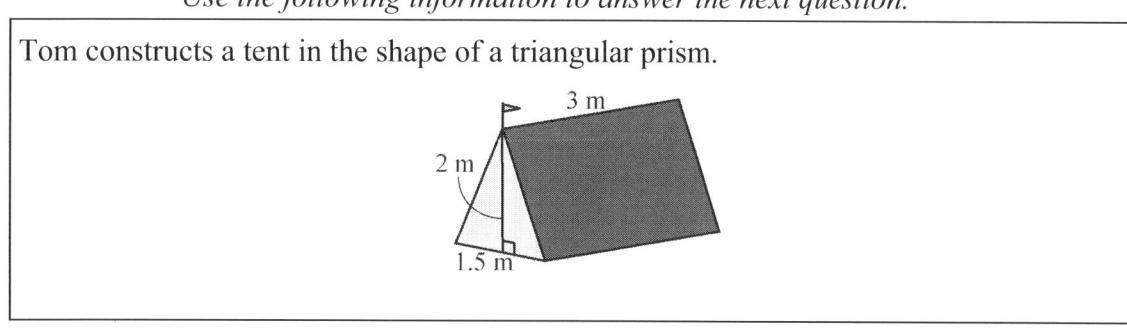

22. What is the volume of space in the tent?

A. 4.5 m³

B. 6.5 m³

C. 9 m³

D. 12 m³

6m41 determine, through investigation using a variety of tools and strategies, the surface area of rectangular and triangular prisms

SURFACE AREA

The **surface area** of a prism is the total area of all the faces, or surfaces, of a prism. The units for surface area are always units^2 or square units.

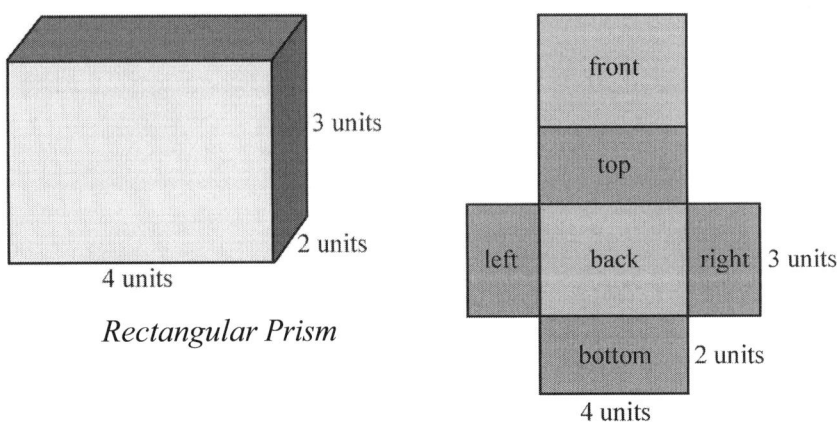

Rectangular Prism

Net of Rectangular Prism

To calculate the surface area of the prism, find the area of each face of the prism and add the six areas.

Example

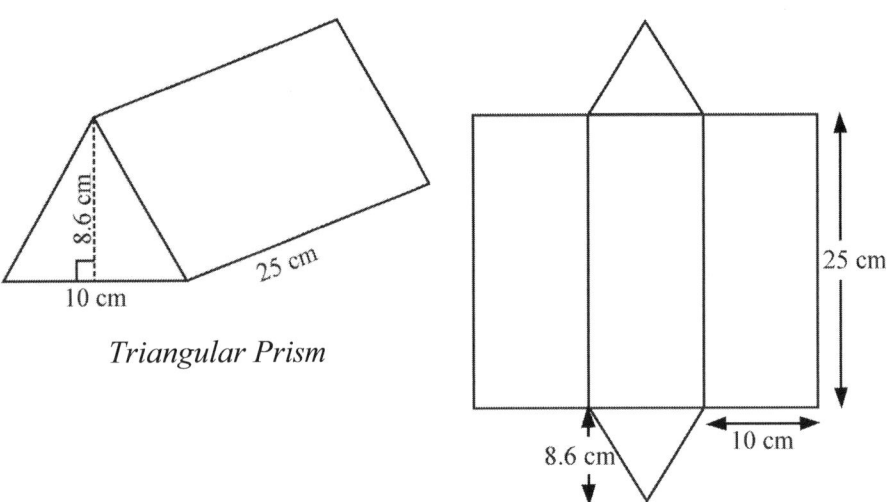

Triangular Prism

Net of Triangular Prism

The surface area of the triangular prism can be found by finding the area of each face and then adding these areas.

Surface Area = area of the triangle + area of the triangle + area of first rectangle + area of second rectangle + area of third rectangle.

Use the following information to answer the next question.

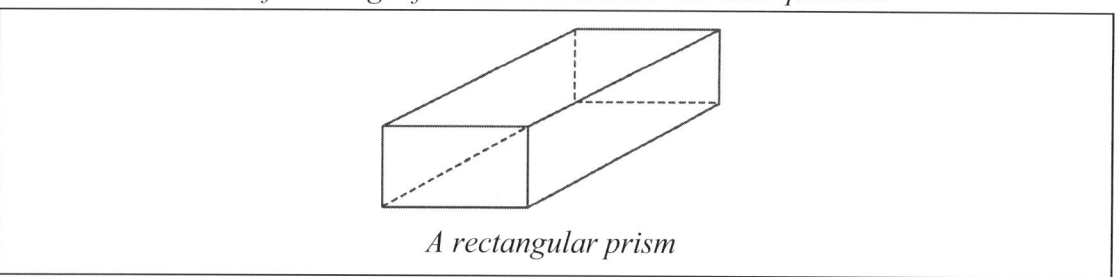

A rectangular prism

23. How many pairs of faces with the same area are found in a rectangular prism?

 A. 3   **B.** 6

 C. 7   **D.** 8

Use the following information to answer the next question.

The base of a prism is a rectangle with sides of 5 cm and 3 cm. The height of the prism is 9 cm.

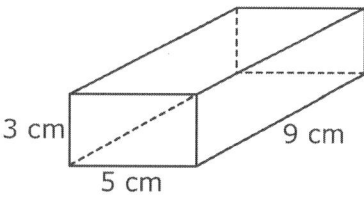

24. What is the surface area of the prism?

 A. 164 cm^2 **B.** 165 cm^2

 C. 170 cm^2 **D.** 174 cm^2

6m42 solve problems involving the estimation and calculation of the surface area and volume of triangular and rectangular prisms

SURFACE AREA AND VOLUME PROBLEMS

SURFACE AREA OF PRISMS

Example

How many square centimetres of wrapping paper are needed to wrap a box that is 30 cm long, 5 cm wide, and 45 cm high? Estimate first, and then calculate the surface area of the box.

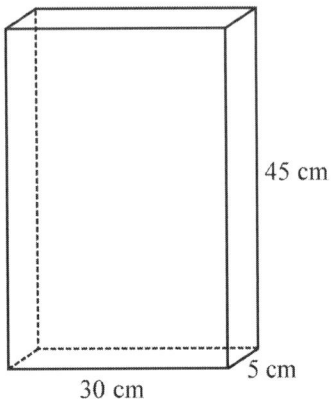

Solution

Transform the rectangular prism into its net.
Calculate the area of each rectangular face and find the sum of the areas of the rectangular faces.
Area of rectangle 1 is 45×30. There are 2 rectangles.
Area of rectangle 2 is 45×5. There are 2 rectangles.
Area of rectangle 3 is 30×5. There are 2 rectangles.

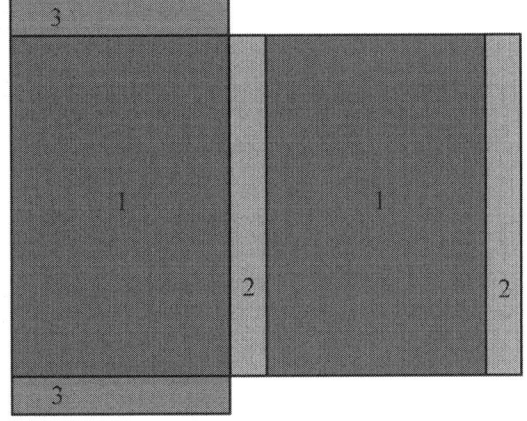

Surface Area $= (2 \times \text{Area}_1) + (2 \times \text{Area}_2) + (2 \times \text{Area}_3)$
Surface Area $= (2 \times 45 \text{ cm} \times 30 \text{ cm}) + (2 \times 45 \text{ cm} \times 5 \text{ cm}) + (2 \times 30 \text{ cm} \times 5 \text{ cm})$

Estimate using numbers that can be easily multiplied and added in your head.

$(2 \times 40 \times 30) + (2 \times 50 \times 5) + (2 \times 30 \times 5) \rightarrow 2\ 400 + 500 + 300 = 3\ 200$

About 3 200 cm² of wrapping paper will be needed to wrap the box.

Calculate using the actual numbers.

Surface Area = (2 × 45 cm × 30 cm) + (2 × 45 cm × 5 cm) + (2 × 30 cm × 5 cm)
Surface Area = 2 700 cm² + 450 cm² + 300 cm²
Surface Area = 3 450 cm²

This box will need 3 450 cm² of wrapping paper.

VOLUME OF PRISMS

Example
Find the volume of the triangular prism shown below. Estimate first, and then calculate the volume of the prism.

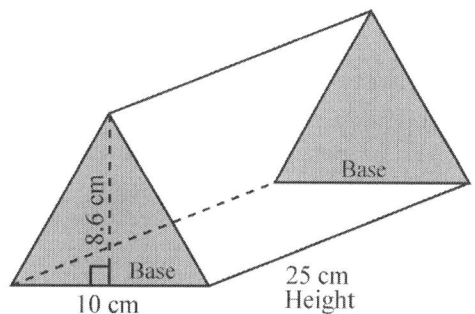

Solution
Use the formula for the volume of a triangular prism.

$$V = \frac{1}{2}(\text{area of the base}) \times \text{height}$$

$$V = \frac{1}{2}(10 \text{ cm} \times 8.6 \text{ cm}) \times 25 \text{ cm}$$

$$V = 43 \text{ cm}^2 \times 25 \text{ cm}$$

Estimate using numbers that can be easily multiplied in your head:

43 cm² × 25 cm → 40 cm² × 25 cm = 1 000 cm³

The volume of the triangular prism is about 1 000 cm³.

Calculate using the actual numbers.

$$V = 43 \text{ cm}^2 \times 25 \text{ cm}$$

$$V = 1\ 075 \text{ cm}^3$$

The volume of the triangular prism is 1 075 cm³.

Use the following information to answer the next question.

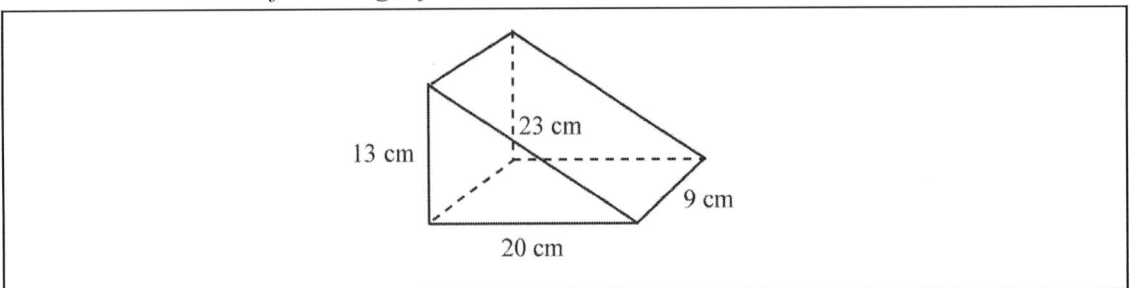

25. What is the surface area of the prism shown above?
    A. 560 cm^2 B. 634 cm^2
    C. 764 cm^2 D. 881 cm^2

26. The length of the base of a square-based prism is 8 cm, and the height is 10 cm. What is the volume of the prism?

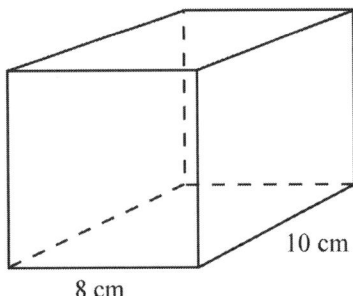

    A. 600 cm^3 B. 620 cm^3
    C. 640 cm^3 D. 700 cm^3

Use the following information to answer the next question.

A triangular prism is shown below.

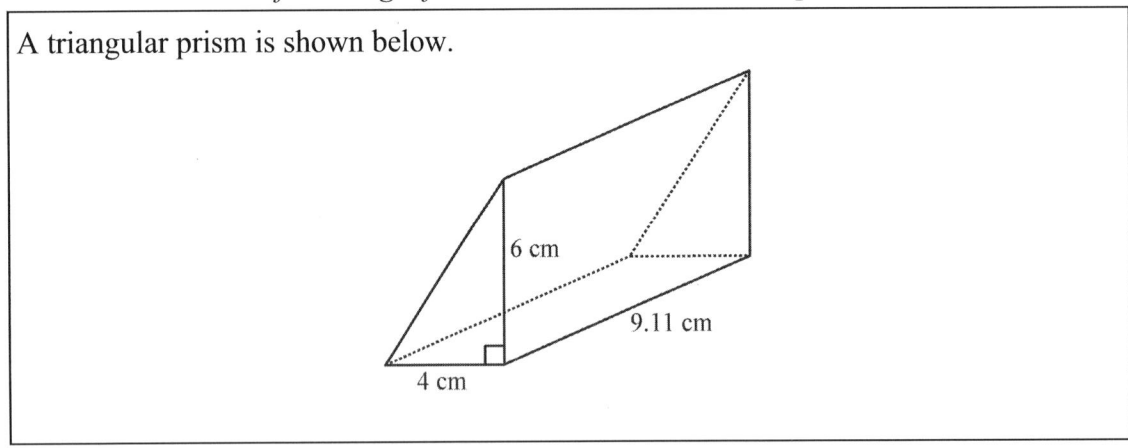

27. Which of the following volumes represents the **best** estimate of the volume of the triangular prism?
    A. 50 cm^3 B. 110 cm^3
    C. 200 cm^3 D. 280 cm^3

ANSWERS AND SOLUTIONS
MEASUREMENT

1. C	7. B	13. C	19. A	25. C
2. C	8. B	14. OR	20. C	26. C
3. B	9. D	15. A	21. OR	27. B
4. B	10. B	16. OR	22. A	
5. C	11. B	17. C	23. A	
6. D	12. D	18. C	24. D	

1. C

Ming is exactly 145 cm tall.

Because there are 100 centimetres in one metre, 145 cm can also be expressed as 1.45 m.

This can be rounded up to 1.5 m.

2. C

The ruler next to the pencil shows that the pencil measures precisely 9.5 cm.

3. B

When measuring the mass of an eraser, grams are the best units to use. Kilograms are too large of a unit. Millilitres are used to measure volumes. Centimetres are used to measure length.

Therefore, the best estimate of the mass of an eraser is 5 g.

4. B

If Jens puts all the train track pieces together, he will have a track that is 8 pieces long, each of which is 15 cm long.

The length of the track can be calculated by multiplying the number of tracks by the length of the tracks.

8×15 cm $= 120$ cm

Therefore, Jen's train track will be 120 cm long.

5. C

Step 1

Since $\begin{array}{l} 1\ 000\ mm = 1\ m \\ 100\ cm = 1\ m \end{array}$, millimetres and centimetres are much too small to measure the length of a car. You would be dealing with very large numbers, making the measurements impractical and ineffective.

Step 2

Since 10 m = 1 dam, decametres would be too large a unit. You would be dealing with a fractional amount, making the measurement less effective. As well, the decametre is not a commonly used unit, so it would also be impractical.

The most appropriate unit to use to measure the length of a car is the metre. It is a commonly used unit of measure, making it easily understood, and the numbers used for the length would not be very large, making it a practical unit.

6. D

Centimetres, decimetres, and metres are too small to measure the depth of an ocean. The most appropriate unit to measure the depth of the Pacific Ocean is kilometres (it is about 11km deep).

7. B

Millimetres are too small to measure the length of a book.

Metres and kilometres are too large to measure the length of a book.

It is most appropriate to measure the length of a book in centimetres.

8. B

To find the total number of kilometres Jean ran, find the total number of metres he ran during the practice.

1 500 m × 4 = 6 000 m

Convert to kilometres by dividing by 1 000, because 1 000 m is equal to 1 km.

6 000 m ÷ 1 000 = 6 km.

Jean ran a total of 6 km.

9. D

To compare the prices of the fruit, convert all of the weights to kilograms and find out the price of each fruit per kilogram.

Apples are $0.99 per kg.

Oranges are $3.95 per 5 kg or $0.79 per kg ($3.95 ÷ 5).

Bananas are $0.60 per 0.5 kg or $1.20 per kg ($0.60 × 2).

Kiwis are $1.89 per kg (1 000 g = 1 kg).

The prices per kilogram show that kiwis are the most expensive of the four fruits.

10. B

First, convert 1.7 kg into grams.
(1 kg = 1 000 g, so multiply 1.7 by 1 000)
1.7 kg = 1 700 g

Find the difference between the weight of the bag with the metal balls in it and the weight of the bag before the metal balls were put in it:
1 700 g – 800 g = 900 g

Find the weight of each metal ball.
900 g ÷ 18 = 50 g

Therefore, each metal ball weighs 50 g.

11. B

To find the area of the unfolded piece of paper, first find the length of each side. Because the figure is a square, each side is equal.

When folded, the perimeter of the piece of paper is 12 cm. The length of the longer side has to be twice the length of the shorter side because the unfolded figure is a square and all sides must add up to 12 cm.

Start with small numbers: 2 and 1.
(2 + 2 + 1 + 1 = 6 cm). These lengths are too small.

Try 4 and 2. (4 + 4 + 2 + 2 = 12 cm). Therefore, 4 and 2 are the lengths of the sides of the folded piece of paper.

Therefore, the sides of the unfolded square piece of paper are 4 cm.

To find the area of the unfolded piece of paper, multiply the length by the width.

$A = \text{length} \times \text{width}$

4 × 4 = 16

Therefore, the area of the unfolded piece of paper is 16 cm^2.

12. D

To find the dimensions of the soccer field, assume that the field is rectangular. Add each of the lengths to find the perimeter that matches 140 m.

The dimensions 5 m × 225 mA

The dimensions 9 m × 125 mABA

The dimensions 15 m × 75 mACA

The dimensions 25 m × 45 mADAD

13. C

The figure formed by joining the two triangles could be a rectangle. The area of the resulting figure is twice the area of the two triangles. To find the area of the two triangles, use the formula:

$$A = 2 \times \frac{b \times h}{2}$$
$$= b \times h$$
$$= 3 \text{ cm} \times 4 \text{ cm}$$
$$= 12 \text{ cm}^2$$

The figure could also be a quadrilateral with the same area and opposite sides of different lengths.

14. OR

Points	Sample Answer
4	Thorough understanding that a parallelogram can be made up of two congruent triangles. Is able to calculate the area of a triangle and parallelogram.

The area of the parallelogram would be equal to the area of the two triangles. To find the area of the parallelogram, find the area of one triangle and multiply by 2.

To find the area of the triangle, multiply the base (8) by the height (5) and divide by 2.

$$\frac{1}{2} \times 5 \times 8 = 20$$

The area of two triangles is twice the area, which is $20 \times 2 = 40$.

The area of the parallelogram made by combining 2 triangles is 40 square units.

3	Considerable understanding that a parallelogram can be made up of two congruent triangles. Is able to calculate the area of a triangle and parallelogram with minor errors.
2	Some understanding that a parallelogram can be made up of two congruent triangles. Is somewhat able to calculate the area of a triangle and/or parallelogram.
1	Limited understanding that a parallelogram can be made up of two congruent triangles. Is not able to calculate the area of a triangle and/or parallelogram.

15. A

A parallelogram can only be formed by triangles of the same shape and size.
Therefore, identical triangles used to form a parallelogram would have identical areas. So, the area of the parallelogram would be twice that of one of the triangles.

16. OR

Points	Sample Answer
4	Thorough understanding that a parallelogram can be composed of two identical triangles. Shows the ability to calculate the area of a triangle and parallelogram.

To determine if the parallelogram has more area than the two triangles, find out if the area of the two congruent triangles is equal to the area of the parallelogram.

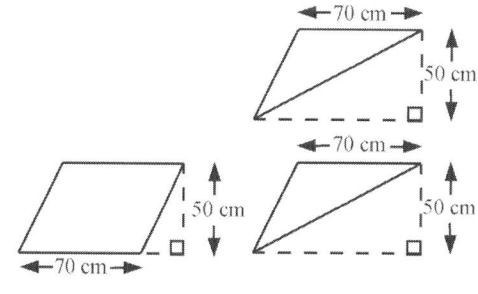

$$= \frac{1}{2} \times \text{base} \times \text{height}$$

$$\text{Area of one triangle} = \frac{1}{2} \times 70 \times 50$$

$$= 35 \times 50$$

$$= 1\ 750 \text{cm}^2$$

The area of the two congruent triangles is $1\ 750 \times 2 = 3\ 500$.

To find the area of the parallelogram, use the formula Area of a parallelogram
$= \text{base} \times \text{height}$.

$$= \text{base} \times \text{height}$$

$$\text{Area of a parallelogram} = 70 \times 50$$

$$= 3\ 500 \text{cm}^2$$

Therefore, the two congruent triangles have the same area as the parallelogram.

3	Demonstrates an understanding that a parallelogram can be composed of two identical triangles. Shows the ability to calculate the area of a triangle and parallelogram with minor errors.

Points	Sample Answer
2	Some understanding that a parallelogram can be composed of two identical triangles. Shows the ability to calculate the area of a triangle and parallelogram with minor errors.
1	Limited understanding that a parallelogram can be made up of two identical triangles. Is not able to calculate the area of a triangle and parallelogram.

17. C

Step 1

Determine the area of Martin's triangle.

Count the number of full squares. There are 6 full squares.

Count the number of half squares. There are 6 half squares. Since two half squares equals one full square, 6 half squares = 3 full squares.

Add the two amounts together.

$6 + 3 = 9$

The area of Martin's triangle is 9 cm^2.

Step 2

Use the area formula to determine the areas of the triangles in the given options.

$$A = \frac{b \times h}{2}$$

- Triangle A: $A = \dfrac{5 \times 3}{2} = 7.5$ cm^2

- Triangle B: $A = \dfrac{4 \times 5}{2} = 10$ cm^2

- Triangle C: $A = \dfrac{3 \times 6}{2} = 9$ cm^2

- Triangle D: $A = \dfrac{8 \times 3}{2} = 12$ cm^2

Triangle C has an area of 9 cm^2, which is the same area as the figure drawn by Martin.

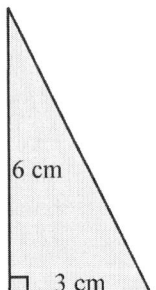

18. C

Base of the triangle = 4 m

Height of the triangle = 6 m

The area of a triangle $= \dfrac{1}{2} \times$ base $\times$ height

$A = \dfrac{1}{2} \times 4$ m $\times 6$ m

$A = \dfrac{1}{2} \times 24$ m^2

$A = 12$ m^2

19. A

Step 1

Determine the area of a tile (cm^2) and the area of the floor (m^2). Use the area formula $A = b \times h$.

Area of a tile: 60 cm $\times$ 50 cm = 3 000 cm^2

Area of the floor: 2.4 m $\times$ 2.0 m = 4.8 m^2

Step 2

Convert the m^2 to cm^2.

1 m^2 = 10 000 cm^2

4.8 m^2 = 4.8 $\times$ 10 000

4.8 m^2 = 48 000 cm^2

An easy way to multiply 4.8 by 10 000 is to move the decimal point 4 places to the right because there are four zeros in 10 000. Since there are not enough digits to the right of the decimal point, you will need to add three zeros after the 8. 4.8 → 48 000

The area of the floor is 48 000 cm^2.

Step 3

Determine the number of tiles that will fit on the floor.

To find how many tiles can fit on the floor, divide the area of the floor by the area of the tiles.

48 000 cm^2 ÷ 3 000 cm^2 = 16

An easy way to divide 48 000 by 3 000, is to divide both numbers by 1 000. When you do this, you will be removing the three zeros in each number and will be left with 48 ÷ 3 = 16

Therefore, 16 tiles will fit on the floor.

20. C

The length of the rectangle is 0.6 m.

There are 100 cm in 1 m, so to convert 0.6 m to centimetres, multiply by 100.

$0.6 \times 100 = 60$ cm

The width of the rectangle is 40 cm

Area of the rectangle $=$ length $\times$ width

60 cm $\times$ 40 cm = 2400 cm^2

Therefore, the area of the rectangle is 2 400 cm^2.

21. OR

Points	Sample Answer
4	Is able to calculate the area of a rectangle. Is able to convert square metres to square centimetres.

To determine how many boxes will fit onto the floor of the storage shed, find the area of the storage shed floor and the area of a box.

Area of the shed floor:
$= 2.5$ m $\times$ 1.5 m $= 3.75$ m^2

Area of a box: 50 cm $\times$ 50 cm $= 2$ 500 cm^2

Because the shed floor and the boxes are in different units, convert both to the same unit.

There are 10 000 cm^2 in 1 m^2.

Therefore, 3.75 m^2 $\times$ 10 000 = 37 500 cm^2

To find out how many boxes will fit onto the floor of the storage shed, divide the area of the shed floor by the area of 1 box.

37 500 cm^2 $\div$ 2 500 cm^2 = 15

Therefore, the greatest number of boxes that will fit onto the floor of the storage shed is 15.

Points	Sample Answer
3	Is able to calculate the area of a rectangle. Is able to convert square metres to square centimetres with minor errors.
2	Is able to calculate the area of a rectangle with minor errors. Is able to convert square metres to square centimetres with minor errors.

Points	Sample Answer
1	Is somewhat able to calculate the area of a rectangle and/or somewhat able to convert square metres to square centimetres.

22. A

Step 1
To find the volume of a triangular prism, use the formula: $V =$ area of the base $\times$ height

Step 2
Determine the area of the triangular base.
The formula for determining the area of a triangle is $A = \dfrac{b \times h}{2}$

Substitute the numbers for the length of the base (1.5 m) and the height of the base (2 m) into the formula.

$A = \dfrac{1.5 \times 2}{2} = 1.5$ m^2

Step 3
Determine the volume of the tent.
Substitute the area of the triangular base (1.5 m^2) and the height of the prism (3 m) into the volume formula.

$V = 1.5$ m^2 $\times$ 3 m $= 4.5$ m^3

The volume of space in the tent is 4.5 m^3.

23. A

The two bases of a rectangular prism are congruent. They have the same area.

The top and bottom of a rectangular prism are congruent. They have the same area.

The two side faces of a rectangular prism are congruent. They have the same area.

Therefore, there are 3 pairs of faces with the same area in a rectangular prism.

24. D

To find the surface area of the rectangular prism, find the area of each side:

Area of the 2 bases = 2 × 3 cm × 5 cm

$$= 2 \times 15 \text{ cm}^2$$

$$= 30 \text{ cm}^2$$

Area of the 2 sides = 2 × 3 cm × 9 cm

$$= 2 \times 27 \text{cm}^2$$

$$= 54 \text{ cm}^2$$

Area of the top and bottom = 2 × 5 cm × 9 cm

$$= 2 \times 45 \text{ cm}^2$$

$$= 90 \text{ cm}^2$$

Add up the areas of all the sides:

$30 \text{ cm}^2 + 54 \text{ cm}^2 + 90 \text{ cm}^2 = 174 \text{ cm}^2$.

The surface area of the rectangular prism is 174 cm^2.

25. C

To find the surface area of the triangular prism, find the area of each of the sides:

Area of the 2 bases = $2 \times \dfrac{1}{2} \times 20$ cm × 13 cm

$$= 1 \times 20 \text{ cm} \times 13 \text{ cm}$$

$$= 260 \text{ cm}^2$$

Area of 1 side = 20 cm × 9 cm

$$= 180 \text{ cm}^2$$

Area of 1 side = 23 cm × 9 cm

$$= 207 \text{ cm}^2$$

Area of 1 side = 13 cm × 9 cm

$$= 117 \text{ cm}^2$$

Add the areas of all the sides:

$260 \text{ cm}^2 + 180 \text{ cm}^2 + 207 \text{ cm}^2$
$+117 \text{ cm}^2 = 764 \text{ cm}^2$

Therefore, the surface area of the triangular prism is 764 cm^2.

26. C

To find the volume of the prism, use the formula:

$V = B \times H$, where B is the area of the base of the prism and H is the height

$B = 8$ cm × 8 cm

$B = 64 \text{ cm}^2$

H = 10

$V = B \times H$

$V = 64 \text{ cm}^2 \times 10$ cm

$V = 640 \text{ cm}^3$

The volume of the prism is 640 cm^3.

27. B

To calculate the volume of a prism, use the formula $V = B \times H$, where B is the area of the base of the prism and H is the height of the prism.

This prism has a triangular base. The length of the base of the triangle is 4 cm, and the height of the triangle is 6 cm.

$B = \dfrac{1}{2} \times 4$ cm × 6 cm

$B = 12 \text{ cm}^2$

The height of the prism is 9.11 cm, or about 9 cm.

$V = B \times H$

$V = 12 \text{ cm}^2 \times 9$ cm

$V = 108 \text{ cm}^3$

The best choice is 110 cm^3.

UNIT TEST — MEASUREMENT

Use the following information to answer the next question.

Three students finished a race. Their times are shown in the table.

Students	Time (min)
Caitlin	1.23
Mark	1.24
Nathan	1.28

1. Which of the following units of time gives the **most** precise results when recording the students' finish times?

   A. Hundredths of a minute

   B. Tenths of a minute

   C. Seconds

   D. Minutes

2. A school yard is 60 m long and 35 m wide. What is the distance covered by a boy if he runs around the outside of the playground once?

   A. 95 m

   B. 130 m

   C. 190 m

   D. 2 100 m

Use the following information to answer the next question.

Joey wants to measure the volume of a stone. To do so, he places it in a beaker containing water, as shown in the given figure.

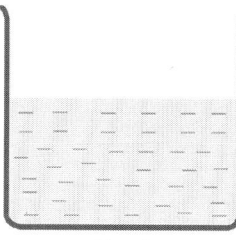 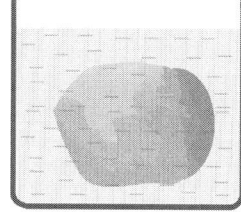

50 mL   70 mL

3. What is the volume of the stone?

   A. 20 mL

   B. 50 mL

   C. 70 mL

   D. 90 mL

4. Which of the following units would be most appropriate to use to measure the length of a pencil?

   A. Centimetre

   B. Decimetre

   C. Metre

   D. Decametre

5. Leela was asked by her father to measure the perimeter of their garage. What is the **best** unit of measurement for Leela to use?

   A. Centimetres   **B.** Metres

   C. Decametres   **D.** Kilometres

6. Mihn buys a bag of sugar that has a mass of 1.4 kg. What is the mass of the bag in grams?

   A. 104 g   **B.** 140 g

   C. 1 040 g   **D.** 1 400 g

Use the following information to answer the next question.

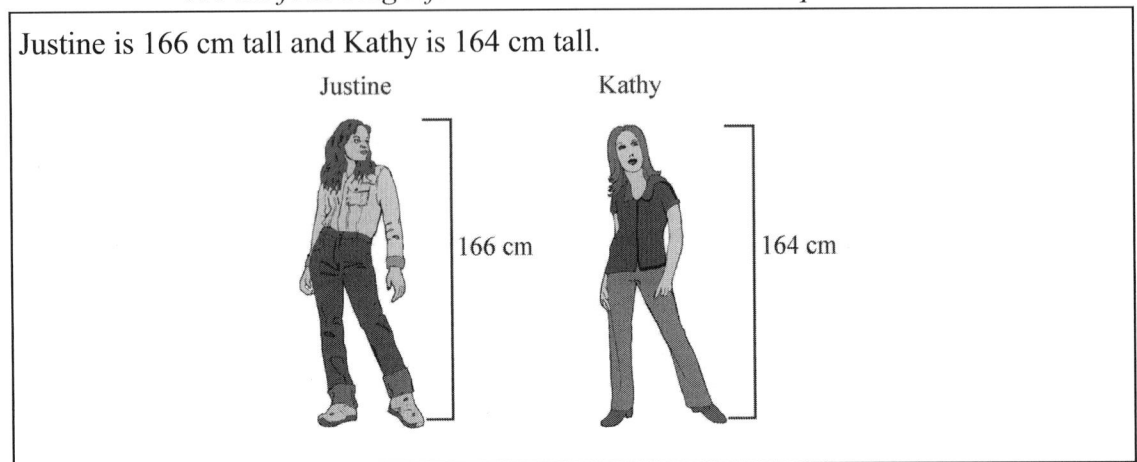

Justine is 166 cm tall and Kathy is 164 cm tall.

7. What is the combined height of Justine and Kathy in metres?

   A. 0.33 m   **B.** 3.30 m

   C. 33.0 m   **D.** 330.0 m

8. Which of the following rectangles has an area of 96 cm^2?

   A. 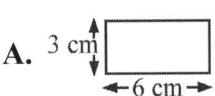   **B.**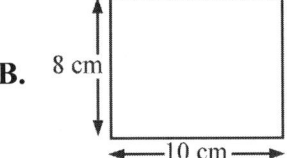

   C. 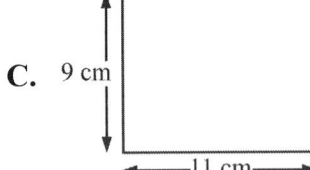   **D.**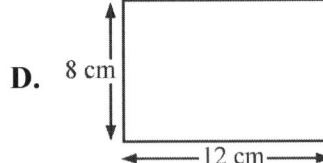

Use the following information to answer the next question.

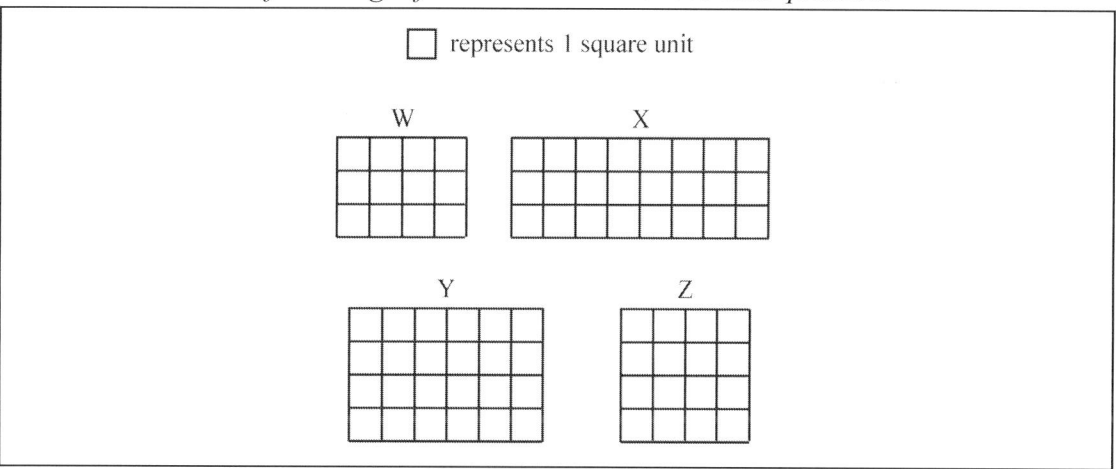

□ represents 1 square unit

W   X

Y   Z

9. Which two sets of figures have the same area?

    A. W and X   **B.** W and Z

    C. X and Y   **D.** Y and Z

Use the following information to answer the next question.

A parallelogram and a rectangle that have the same length of base and the same height are shown.

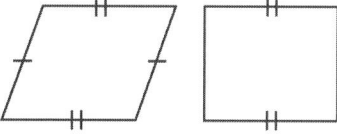

10. What is the relationship between a parallelogram and a rectangle if they have the same base length and the same height?

    A. Area of a rectangle= area of a parallelogram

    B. Area of the parallelogram = 2 × area of a rectangle

    C. Perimeter of a rectangle= perimeter of a parallelogram

    D. Perimeter of a rectangle = 2 × perimeter of a parallelogram

Use the following information to answer the next question.

A parallelogram has a base that is 4.5 cm long and a height that is 3 cm.

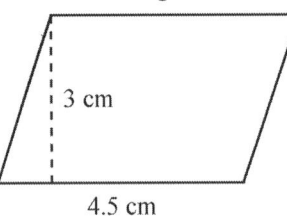

3 cm

4.5 cm

11. What is the area of the parallelogram?

    A. 7 cm^2 **B.** 12 cm^2

    C. 13.5 cm^2 **D.** 14.5 cm^2

12. What is the area of a right triangle that has a base measuring 12 cm and a height measuring 12 cm?

    A. 62.35 cm^2 **B.** 72 cm^2

    C. 124.7 cm^2 **D.** 144 cm^2

13. A living room floor has an area of 30 m^2. What is the area of the floor in square centimetres?

    A. 30 cm^2 **B.** 3 000 cm^2

    C. 30 000 cm^2 **D.** 300 000 cm^2

Use the following information to answer the next question.

This square has an area of 40 000 cm^2.

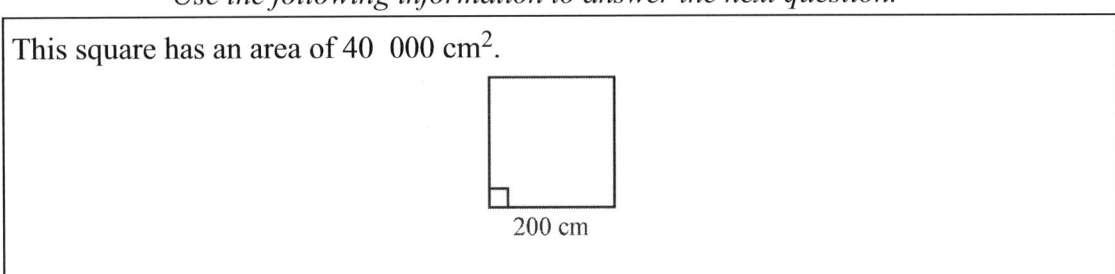

200 cm

14. What is the area of the square in square metres?

    A. 4 m^2 **B.** 40 m^2

    C. 400 m^2 **D.** 1 600 m^2

Use the following information to answer the next question.

A garden measures 3 m × 2 m. Each plant needs 20 cm × 20 cm of space in the garden.

Open Response

15. How many plants can be planted in the garden? Show your work.

16. Which of the following expressions is the formula for the volume of a triangular prism?

A. Length × width

B. $\frac{1}{2}$ × base × height

C. Area of base × height

D. Length × width × height

17. What is the surface area of a rectangular prism that is 4 m long by 6 m wide by 7 m high?

A. 160 m^2

B. 172 m^2

C. 188 m^2

D. 204 m^2

Use the following information to answer the next question.

A crystal box measures 11 cm in length, 5 cm in width, and 3 cm in height.

5 cm

3 cm

11 cm

18. What is the surface area of the crystal box?

A. 106 cm^2

B. 125 cm^2

C. 162 cm^2

D. 206 cm^2

19. A mattress measures 200 cm in length, 140 cm in width, and 50 cm in height. What is the surface area of the mattress?

A. 70 000 cm^2

B. 80 000 cm^2

C. 90 000 cm^2

D. 100 000 cm^2

20. A triangular prism has a height of 4 m. The height of the base is 3.11 m, and the length of the base is 1.9 m. Which of the following volumes is the **best** estimate of the volume of the prism?

A. 1 m^3

B. 12 m^3

C. 25 m^3

D. 38 m^3

ANSWERS AND SOLUTIONS — UNIT TEST

1. A	5. B	9. C	13. D	17. C
2. C	6. D	10. A	14. A	18. D
3. A	7. B	11. C	15. OR	19. C
4. A	8. D	12. B	16. C	20. B

1. A

In order to get the most precise results, it is important to record the students' finish times to the nearest hundredth of a minute. All three students finished the race in the same tenth of a minute (1.2 minutes). It is necessary to record the hundredths of a minute in order to determine who had the fastest time in this race.

2. C

The perimeter of the playground is a rectangle, so to find the perimeter of the playground, use the formula:

perimeter = length + width + length + width

= 2 × length + 2 × width

= (2 × 60) + (2 × 35)

= 120 m + 70 m

= 190 m

The boy covers a distance of 190 m.

3. A

The volume of the stone is equal to the change in the level of water in the beaker after the stone is placed in it: 70 mL – 50 mL = 20 mL. The water level in the beaker increases by 20 mL when the stone is placed in the beaker. Therefore, the volume of the stone is 20 mL.

4. A

Step 1

Since $\begin{array}{l} 1 \text{ m} = 100 \text{ cm} \\ 1 \text{ dam} = 1\ 000 \text{ cm} \end{array}$, metres and decametres are much too big to measure the length of a pencil.

Step 2

Since 1 dm = 10 cm, decimetres could be used to measure the length of a pencil, but the length would most likely be in fractions or decimals, so it would not be too effective. As well, decimetres are not commonly used, so it would not be too practical.

Since 1 cm = 10 mm, it would be most appropriate to use a smaller unit like centimetres to measure the length of a pencil. Most new pencils are about 17 or 18 cm long. Used pencils can be considerably shorter.

5. B

Perimeter is the distance around an object.

Centimetres are too small to measure the perimeter of a garage.

Metres are the best unit of measurement to use.

Decametres and kilometres are too large to measure the perimeter of a garage.

6. D

There are 1 000 g in 1 kg.

So, to convert 1.4 kg into grams, multiply 1.4 by 1 000.

1.4 × 1 000 = 1400 g

Therefore, the bag of sugar has a mass of 1 400 g.

7. B

To find the combined height of the girls, first add the two heights.

166 cm + 164 cm = 330 cm

There are 100 cm in 1 m.

So, to convert 330 cm to metres, divide 330 by 100.

330 ÷ 100 = 3.30 m

Therefore, the combined height of Justine and Kathy is 3.30 m.

8. D

To find the area of each rectangle, use the formula for the area of a rectangle:

Area of a rectangle = length × width

Rectangle A $A = 3$ cm × 6 cm. So, $A = 18$ cm^2

Rectangle B

$A = 8$ cm × 10 cm. So, $A = 80$ cm^2

Rectangle C

$A = 11$ cm × 9 cm. So, $A = 99$ cm^2

Rectangle D

$A = 12$ cm × 8 cm. So, $A = 96$ cm^2

Therefore, the rectangle with an area of 96 cm^2 is rectangle D.

9. C

To find the area of each figure, count the total number of units of each figure.

Figure W is 12 square units.

Figure X is 24 square units.

Figure Y is 24 square units.

Figure Z is 16 square units.

Therefore, the two figures with the same area are X and Y.

10. A

The perimeters of the rectangle and the parallelogram are different because the parallelogram's sides must be longer in order for the shape to be the same height as the rectangle. The areas of the two shapes, however, are the same.

11. C

The area of a parallelogram can be found by using the formula

$A = $ base × height.

The base of the parallelogram is 4.5 cm.

The height of the parallelogram is 3 cm.

$A = 4.5$ cm × 3 cm

$A = 13.5$ cm^2

Therefore, the area of the parallelogram is 13.5 cm^2.

12. B

To find the area of a triangle, use the formula:

$A = \dfrac{1}{2} \times$ base × height

$A = \dfrac{1}{2} \times 12$ cm × 12 cm

$A = \dfrac{1}{2} \times 144$ cm^2

$A = 72$ cm^2

Therefore, the area of the triangle is 72 cm^2.

13. D

To convert square metres to square centimetres, remember that 1 m^2 = 10 000 cm^2.

$30 \times 10\ 000 = 300\ 000$

Therefore, the area of the living room floor in square centimetres is 300 000 cm^2.

14. A

The area of the square = 40 000 cm^2

To convert square centimetres to square metres, remember that 1 m^2 = 10 000 cm^2.

$40\ 000 \div 10\ 000 = 4$

Therefore, the area of the square is 4 m^2.

15. OR

Points	Sample Answer
4	Thorough understanding of how to calculate the area of a rectangle. Is able to convert square metres to square centimetres.

To determine how many plants can be planted in the garden, you must find the area of the garden and the area of space each plant needs.

Points	Sample Answer

Area of the garden = 3 m × 2 m = 6 m^2

Area of space = 20 cm × 20 cm = 400 cm^2

Because each area is in different units, you must convert both to the same unit.

There are 10 000 cm^2 in 1 m^2.

6 × 10 000 = 60 000 cm^2.

To determine how many plants can be planted in the garden, you must divide the area of the garden by the area of space each plant needs in the garden.

60 000 cm^2 ÷ 400 cm^2 = 150

Therefore, 150 plants can be planted in the garden.

3	Considerable understanding of how to calculate the area of a rectangle with minor errors. Is able to convert square metres to square centimetres with minor errors.
2	Some understanding of how to calculate the area of a rectangle and is somewhat able to convert square metres to square centimetres.
1	Limited understanding of how to calculate the area of a rectangle and is not able to convert square metres to square centimetres.

16. C

The volume of a triangular prism can be found my multiplying the area of the base of the triangle by the height of the prism.

Volume = area of base × height

17. C

To find the surface area of the prism, use the formula:

$A = 2 × [(l × w) + (l × h) + (w × h)]$

Substitute the given values to find the solution.

$A = 2 × [(4 × 6) + (4 × 7) + (6 × 7)]$

$A = 2 × [24 + 28 + 42]$

$A = 2 × [94]$

$A = 188$ m^2

Therefore, the surface area of the prism is 188 m^2.

18. D

Calculate the area of each pair of faces and find the sum.

Area of top and bottom:

$A = 11 × 3 × 2$

$A = 66$ cm^2

Area of sides:

$A = 5 × 3 × 2$

$A = 30$ cm^2

Area of front and back

$A = 11 × 5 × 2$

$= 110$ cm^2

$SA = 66 + 30 + 110$

$SA = 206$ cm^2

Therefore, the surface area of the box is 206 cm^2.

19. C

To find the surface area of the mattress, use the formula $SA = 2B + pH$, where B is the area of the base, p is the perimeter of the base, and H is the height of the prism.

$B = \text{length} \times \text{width}$

$B = 200 \text{ cm} \times 140 \text{ cm}$

$B = 280 \text{ cm}^2$

$p = \text{side} + \text{side} + \text{side} + \text{side}$

$p = (200 + 200 + 140 + 140) \text{ cm}$

$p = 680 \text{ cm}$

$H = 50$

$SA = 2B + pH$

$SA = (2 \times 280 \text{ cm}^2) + (680 \text{ cm} \times 50 \text{ cm})$

$SA = 560 \text{ cm}^2 + 340 \text{ cm}^2$

$SA = 900 \text{ cm}^2$

Therefore, the surface area of the mattress is 90 0 cm^2.

20. B

First, round the dimensions to the nearest metre.

3.11 is rounded down to 3.
1.9 is rounded up to 2.

The volume V of a prism $= B \times h$, where B is the area of the base and h is the height.

This prism has a triangular base. The base of the triangle is 2 m, and the height of the triangle is 3 m.

$B = \dfrac{1}{2} \times 2 \text{ cm} \times 3 \text{ cm}$

$B = 3 \text{ cm}^2$

The height of the prism is 4 m.

$V = B \times H$

$V = 3 \text{ cm}^2 \times 4 \text{ cm}$

$V = 12 \text{ cm}^3$

The best estimate is 12 m^3.

Geometry and Spatial Sense

GEOMETRY AND SPATIAL SENSE

Table of Correlations

Specific Expectation		Practice Questions	Unit Test Questions	Practice Test 1	Practice Test 2
6m43	Geometric Properties				
6m46	*sort and classify quadrilaterals by geometric properties related to symmetry, angles, and sides, through investigation using a variety of tools and strategies*	1, 2, 3	9	35	
6m47	*sort polygons according to the number of lines of symmetry and the order of rotational symmetry, through investigation using a variety of tools*	4, 5, 6	10, 11, 12	36	34
6m48	*measure and construct angles up to 180° using a protractor, and classify them as acute, right, obtuse, or straight angles*	7	13		35
6m49	*construct polygons using a variety of tools, given angle and side measurements*	8, 9, 10	14, 15		36
6m44	Geometric Relationships				
6m50	*build three-dimensional models using connecting cubes, given isometric sketches or different views (i.e., top, side, front) of the structure*	11, 12			
6m51	*sketch, using a variety of tools, isometric perspectives and different views (i.e., top, side, front) of three-dimensional figures built with interlocking cubes*	13, 14, 15	1	1	
6m45	Location and Movement				
6m52	*explain how a coordinate system represents location, and plot points in the first quadrant of a Cartesian coordinate plane*	16, 17, 18	2	10	9
6m53	*identify, perform, and describe, through investigation using a variety of tools, rotations of 180° and clockwise and counter clockwise rotations of 90°, with the centre of rotation inside or outside the shape*	19, 20, 21	3, 4		10
6m54	*create and analyse designs made by reflecting, translating, and/or rotating a shape, or shapes, by 90° or 180°*	22, 23, 24, 25	5, 6, 7, 8	11, 12	11

6m46 sort and classify quadrilaterals by geometric properties related to symmetry, angles, and sides, through investigation using a variety of tools and strategies

PROPERTIES OF QUADRILATERALS

SORTING AND CLASSIFYING QUADRILATERALS

A quadrilateral is any two-dimensional (2-D) figure or polygon that has four straight sides. Quadrilaterals can be classified or sorted by their different properties or characteristics. For example, they may be sorted by the number of congruent sides or parallel sides. Two sides of a quadrilateral are congruent if they are the same length.

They may be sorted by the number of lines of symmetry. A quadrilateral may have no lines of symmetry, one line of symmetry, or more than one line of symmetry.

Quadrilaterals can also be sorted or classified according to the types and measurement of their angles.

TYPES OF QUADRILATERALS

Kites, trapezoids, parallelograms, rectangles, rhombus, and squares are different types of quadrilaterals that are defined by the characteristics below.

A parallelogram is a quadrilateral with two pairs of parallel sides. They can have either no right angles (Parallelogram 1) or four right angles (parallelograms 2 and 3). They may have either two pairs of congruent sides (parallelograms 1 and 2) or four congruent sides (Parallelogram 3). They can have no lines of symmetry (Parallelogram 1), two (Parallelogram 2), or four (Parallelogram 3) lines of symmetry.

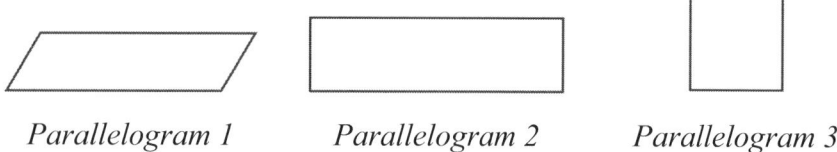

Parallelogram 1   *Parallelogram 2*   *Parallelogram 3*

A rectangle is a parallelogram with two pairs of parallel sides and four right angles. Rectangles may have two lines of symmetry (Rectangle 1) or four lines of symmetry (Rectangle 2).

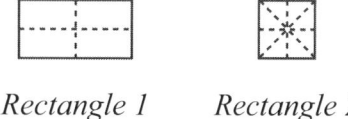

Rectangle 1   *Rectangle 2*

A rhombus is a parallelogram with two pairs of parallel sides and four congruent sides. Rhombi, more than one rhombus, may have two lines of symmetry (Rhombus 1) or four lines of symmetry (Rhombus 2).

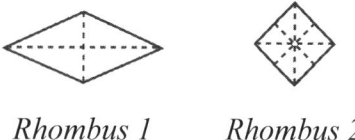

Rhombus 1   *Rhombus 2*

A square is a parallelogram with two pairs of parallel sides, all sides congruent, and four right angles. Squares have four lines of symmetry.

Square

A kite is a quadrilateral that has only one line of symmetry. Kites never contain right angles or parallel sides.

Kite

A trapezoid is a quadrilateral with two parallel sides and two non-parallel sides. Trapezoids may have one line of symmetry and no right angles (Trapezoid 1) or no lines of symmetry and two right angles (Trapezoid 2). They may have only two congruent sides (Trapezoid 1) or no congruent sides (Trapezoid 2).

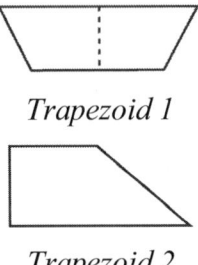

Trapezoid 1

Trapezoid 2

The tree diagram below shows the relationships between the different types of quadrilaterals.

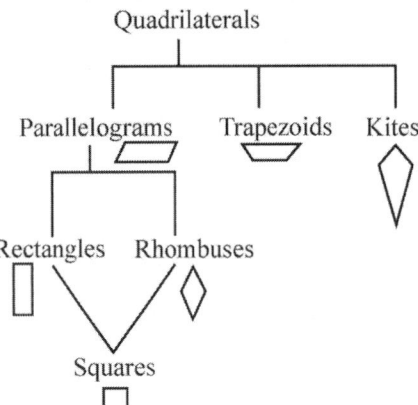

These diagrams show that a square is a rectangle, a rhombus, a parallelogram, and a quadrilateral.

Use the following information to answer the next question.

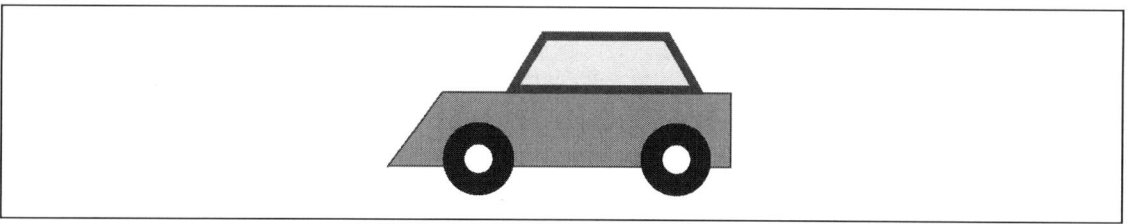

1. Jamie drew a picture of a car using three shapes. The top of the car that is outlined in thick lines is in the shape of a

   A. rhombus   **B.** rectangle

   C. trapezoid   **D.** parallelogram

2. Which of the following statements about squares and rectangles is **false**?

   A. Squares and rectangles are both rhombuses.

   B. Squares and rectangles are both parallelograms.

   C. Both squares and rectangles have the same number of right angles.

   D. Both squares and rectangles have the same number of parallel edges.

3. Which of the following polygons is **not** a quadrilateral?

   A.   **B.**

   C.   **D.**

6m47 sort polygons according to the number of lines of symmetry and the order of rotational symmetry, through investigation using a variety of tools

SORTING POLYGONS ACCORDING TO SYMMETRY

A **polygon** is a closed, two-dimensional figure with straight sides.

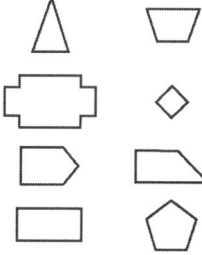

A **regular polygon** is a polygon in which all angles are congruent and all sides are congruent.

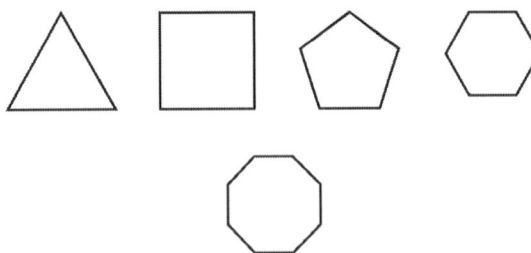

An **irregular polygon** is a polygon in which all sides and angles are *not* congruent.

SYMMETRY

Reflection Symmetry

You can find **lines of symmetry** on regular and irregular polygons.

The following regular and irregular polygons are sorted according to the number of lines of symmetry.

No lines of symmetry:

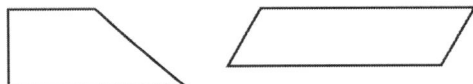

One line of symmetry:

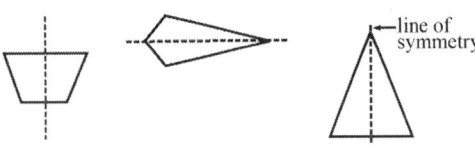

Two lines of symmetry:

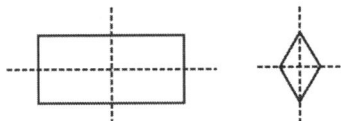

More than two lines of symmetry:

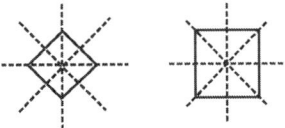

A general rule for symmetry in regular polygons is that the number of sides of the regular polygon is the same as the number of lines of symmetry.

ROTATIONAL SYMMETRY

Rotational symmetry is seen in shapes that can be turned about a point of rotation so that the rotated shape exactly coincides with its original position at least once in a complete rotation (360°).

If a shape that is rotated about its centre comes to rest in a position and looks exactly like the original, then it has rotational symmetry. The number of times that the rotated shape looks exactly like the original is called the **order of rotational symmetry** for that shape.

A rectangle has rotational symmetry. If the rectangle is rotated about its centre, then in two successive rotations of 180°, the rectangle coincides with its original position twice.

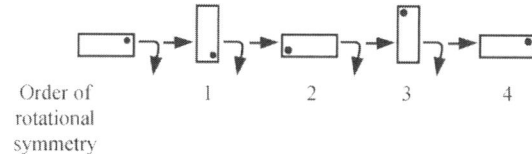

Notice that the rectangle in positions 2 and 4 look exactly like the rectangle in the original position. Therefore, the rectangle has an order of rotational symmetry of 2.

An **equilateral triangle** has rotational symmetry. If the triangle is rotated about its centre, then in three successive rotations of 120° clockwise the triangle coincides with its original position three times.

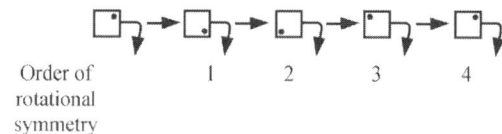

Notice that the triangles in position 1, 2, and 3 look exactly like the rectangle in the first or original position.
Therefore, the equilateral triangle has an order of rotational symmetry of 3.

A square has rotational symmetry. If the square is rotated about its centre, then in four successive rotations of 90° clockwise the square coincides with its original position 4 times. Therefore, the square has an order of rotational symmetry of 4.

4. Which of the following quadrilaterals has only 1 line of symmetry?

A.

B.

C.

D.

Use the following information to answer the next question.

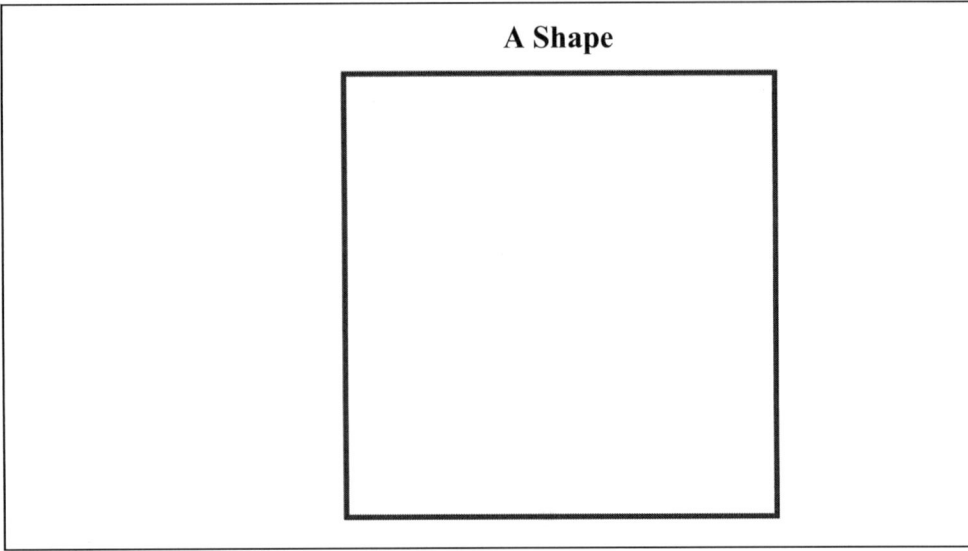

A Shape

5. How many lines of symmetry does this shape have?

   A. 1   **B.** 2

   C. 3   **D.** 4

Use the following information to answer the next question.

Elva plans to draw a line of symmetry through as many of these numbers as she can.

1 2 3 4 5

6 7 8 9 0

6. How many numbers **cannot** have a line of symmetry drawn through them?

   A. 4   **B.** 5

   C. 6   **D.** 7

6m48 measure and construct angles up to 180° using a protractor, and classify them as acute, right, obtuse, or straight angles

CLASSIFYING, MEASURING, AND CONSTRUCTING ANGLES

CLASSIFYING ANGLES

Angles are classified into different types based on their measures.

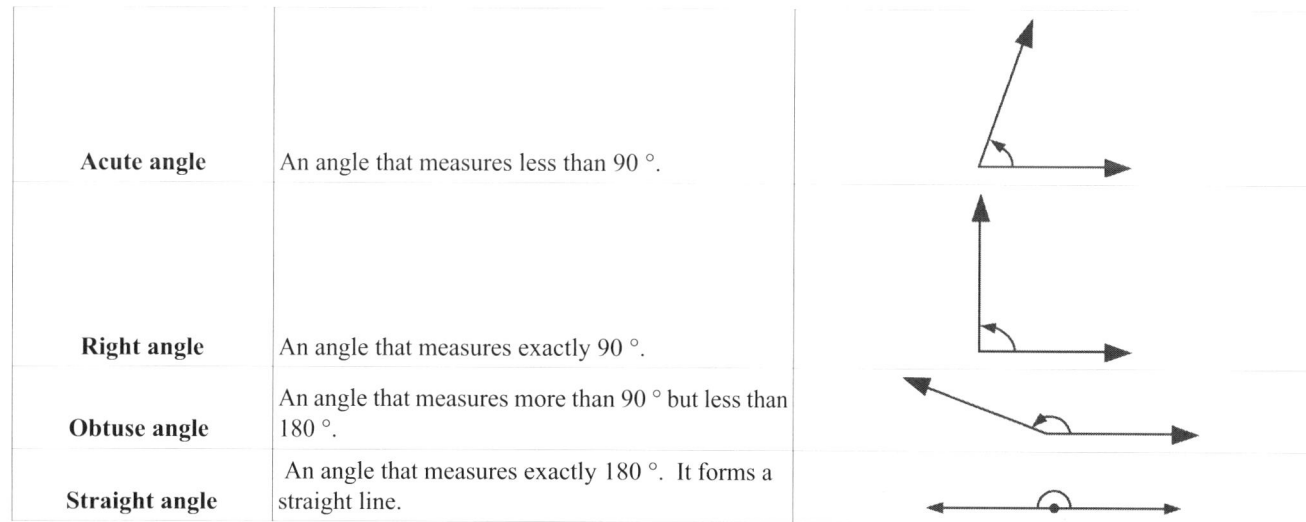

Acute angle	An angle that measures less than 90 °.	
Right angle	An angle that measures exactly 90 °.	
Obtuse angle	An angle that measures more than 90 ° but less than 180 °.	
Straight angle	An angle that measures exactly 180 °. It forms a straight line.	

MEASURING ANGLES

A **protractor** is an instrument for measuring angles. It is usually in the shape of a semicircle or circle and is marked around the edge in **degrees**.

Semicircle Protractor   **Circular Protractor**

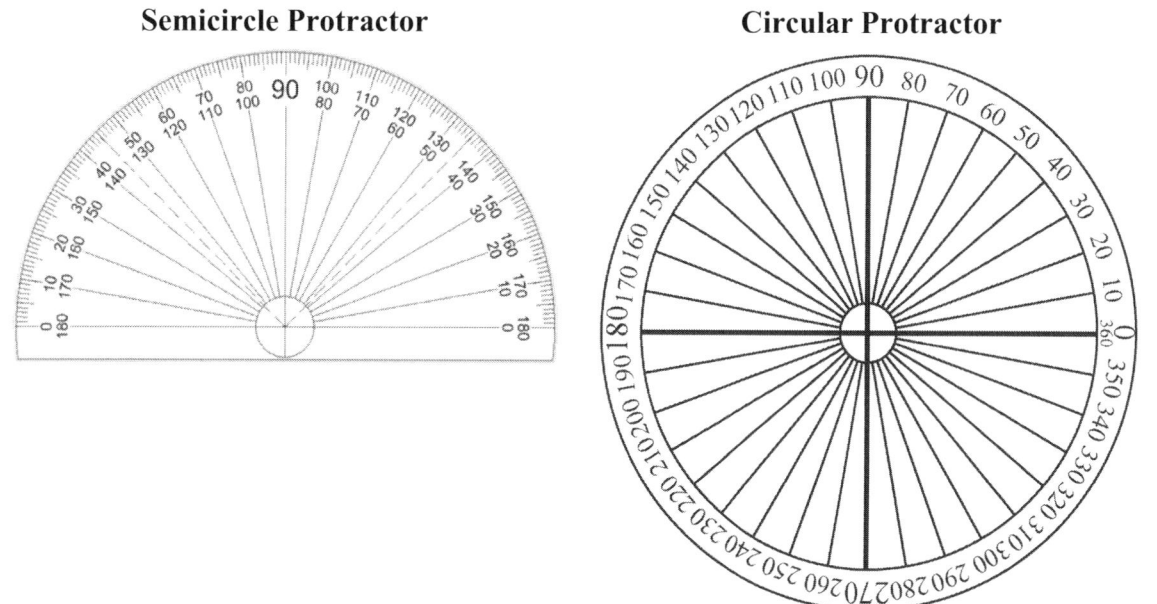

To find the measure of the following angle, you can use a semicircle protractor.

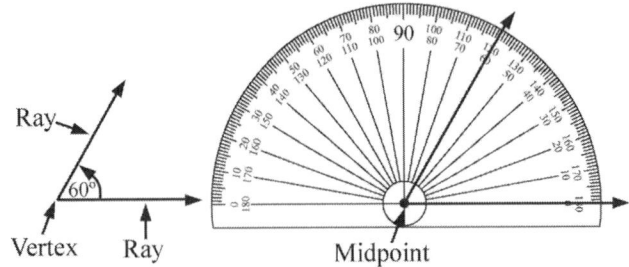

Ray

Vertex   Ray

Midpoint

By counting the degrees between the two rays, you see that the measure of the angle is 60°.

Example

Use a protractor to measure the size of the given angle.

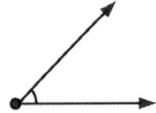

Solution

Step 1

Place the midpoint of the protractor on the vertex of the angle. The 0° line on the right side of the protractor's inner scale should line up with the end of the bottom ray of the angle.

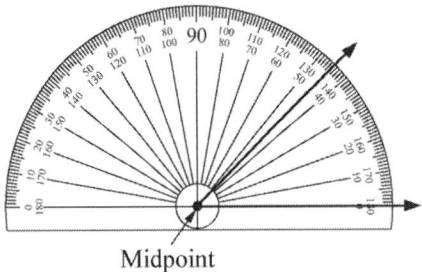

Midpoint

Start at the right side of the protractor's inner scale, at the 0° line, and count by tens until you reach the number of degrees closest to the upper ray without passing it.

10°, 20°, 30°, 40°

Step 2

Count the individual ticks after 40° by ones until you reach the upper ray of the angle.

...41°, 42°, 43°, 44°, 45°

The measure of the given angle is 45°.

Geometry and Spatial Sense   114   Castle Rock Research

CONSTRUCTING ANGLES

You can use either a semicircular or a circular protractor to construct angles.

To draw an angle using a protractor, follow these steps:

1. Draw a ray.
2. Place the protractor on the ray so that the midpoint of the protractor lines up with the end of the ray.
3. Starting at 0°, count the number of degrees needed to construct the angle.
4. Remove the protractor, and join the point that you marked and the endpoint of the ray that was drawn.

Example

Use a semicircular protractor to construct an angle of 145°.

Solution

Step 1

Draw a ray.

Step 2

Place the protractor on the ray so that the midpoint of the protractor lines up with the end of the ray.

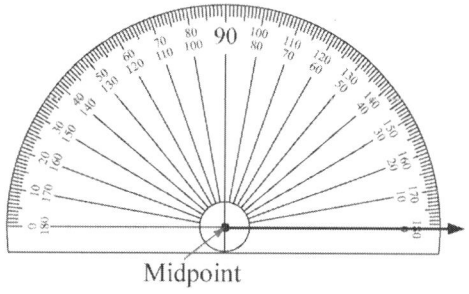

Midpoint

Step 3

Starting at 0°, count the number of degrees needed to construct the angle.

If the ray is pointing to the right, use the inside of the scale. If the ray is pointing to the left, use the outside scale. Always start measuring at 0°.

The angle needs to be 145°, so stop at 145. Using your pencil, mark the point that shows 145°.

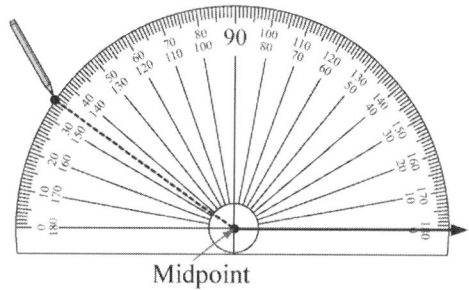

Midpoint

Step 4

Remove the protractor, and join the point that you marked and the endpoint of the ray that was drawn.

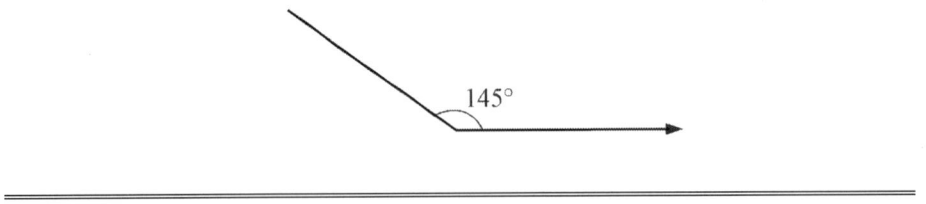

145°

Use the following information to answer the next question.

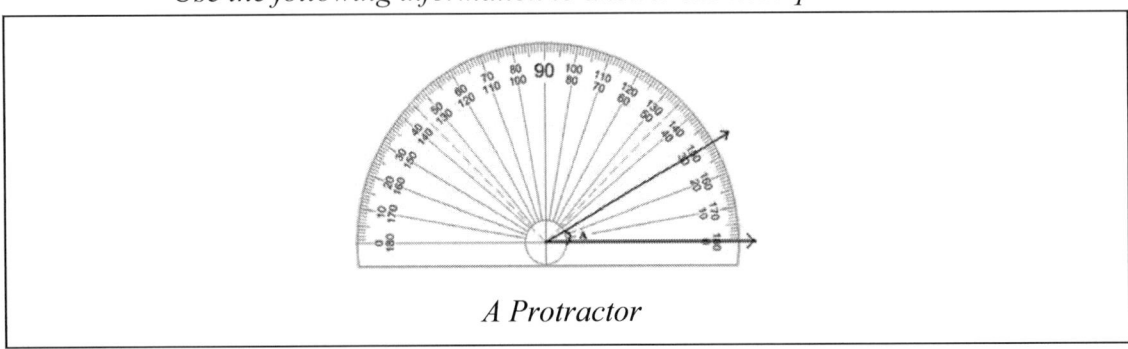

A Protractor

7. What is the measure of the angle to the nearest degree?

    A. 20°   **B.** 30°

    C. 50°   **D.** 150°

6m49 construct polygons using a variety of tools, given angle and side measurements

Constructing Polygons

In geometry, you will need to draw a variety of shapes. One method for constructing polygons is to use a protractor and ruler. You can use a protractor to measure out the exact angle that you want. For example, if you want to make a square or a rectangle, all the angles must be exactly 90°. You can draw each corner using the same procedure for making an angle.

To construct an **isosceles triangle** with a base measuring 4 cm and two congruent angles of 45°, use the following steps.

Step1– Using a centimetre ruler, draw a line segment that is 4 cm long.

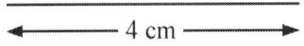

◀———— 4 cm ————▶

Step2– At one endpoint of the line segment, construct a 45° angle using a protractor. At the other endpoint of the line segment, construct another 45° angle using a protractor.

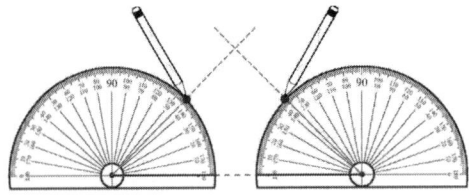

Step3– The two rays of the constructed angles will intersect to form the third angle of the triangle. Since the total number of degrees in any triangle is 180°, the measure of the third angle is 90°.

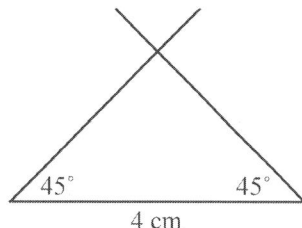

Your completed isosceles triangle should look like the triangle below.

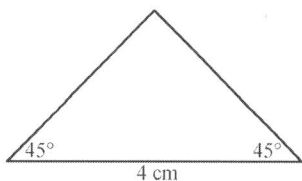

Use the following information to answer the next question.

Tina has a copper wire that is 42 cm long. She bends the wire and makes an equilateral triangle.

8. What is the length of each side of the equilateral triangle?
   A. 7 cm   **B.** 14 cm
   C. 21 cm   **D.** 126 cm

9. Ram wants to draw a regular pentagon with a perimeter of 40 cm. What length should he make each side?
   A. 5 cm   **B.** 6 cm
   C. 8 cm   **D.** 10 cm

| Open Response |

10. Using a ruler and a protractor, draw an equilateral triangle, *ABC*, with sides measuring 6 cm. What are the measures of each angle?

Show your work. Explain your answer

6m50 *build three-dimensional models using connecting cubes, given isometric sketches or different views (i.e., top, side, front) of the structure*

BUILDING 3-D MODELS

In order to build a 3-D model, you must look at the different views that make up the model. Given different views, you can build a 3-D model using connecting cubes. You can generally make a 3-D model if you have the front, side, and top views of the object. The following diagrams show sketches of different views of a 3-D model.

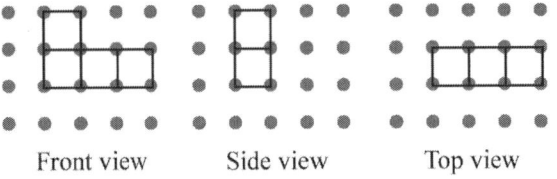

Front view   Side view   Top view

By looking at the different views, you can build the stack of cubes.

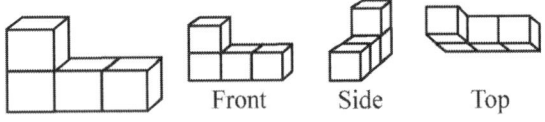

Front   Side   Top

Example
Raquel built a tower of blocks. The different views of her tower are shown below.

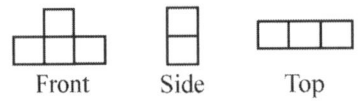

Front   Side   Top

Using the views above, you can see what Raquel's 3-D tower looked like.

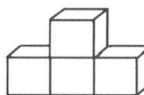

Looking at the front view of Raquel's tower, you can see that there are two blocks stacked high in the middle of the tower and one block on each side of these.

Looking at the side view of Raquel's tower, you can see that the tower is two blocks high.

Looking at the top view of Raquel's tower, you can see that there are three blocks side by side.

Use the following information to answer the next question.

The given diagrams represent the top, front, and side views of a group of geometric blocks.

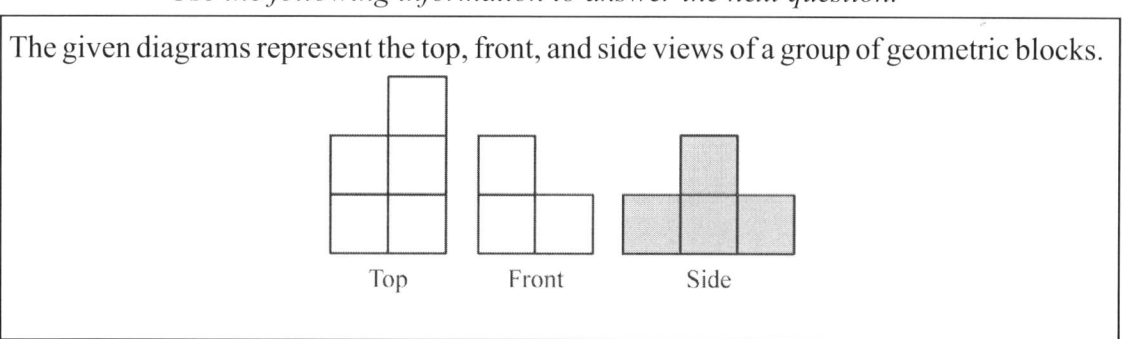

Top   Front   Side

11. Which of the following groups of blocks is **best** represented by the given diagrams?

A.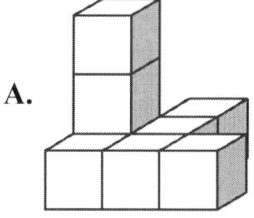

B.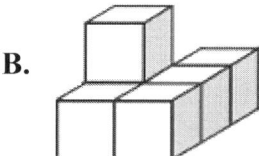

C.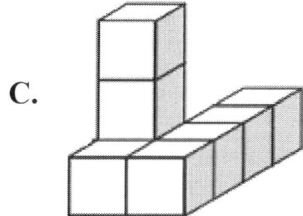

D.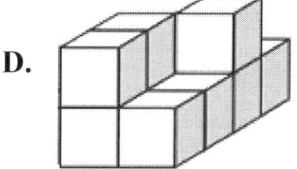

Use the following information to answer the next question.

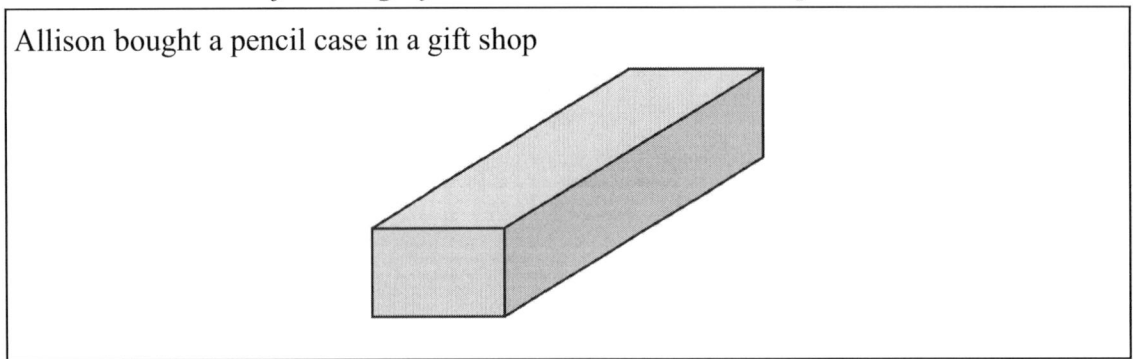

Allison bought a pencil case in a gift shop

12. Which of the following nets could be folded to make the shape of Allison's pencil case?

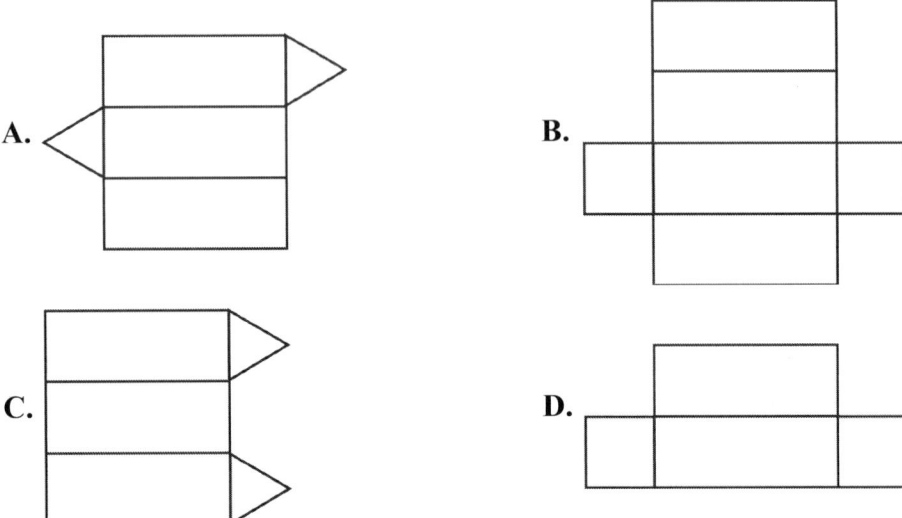

A.

B.

C.

D.

6m51 sketch, using a variety of tools, isometric perspectives and different views (i.e., top, side, front) of three-dimensional figures built with interlocking cubes

SKETCHING DIFFERENT VIEWS OF 3-D OBJECTS

In the last lesson, you learned how to build a 3-D model given the 2-D sketches of the different views. You can also draw 2-D views of an object on isometric dot paper. For example, following is a three-dimensional object built with connecting cubes.

By labelling each perspective or view, you can examine the individual sides of the object to see what they look like.

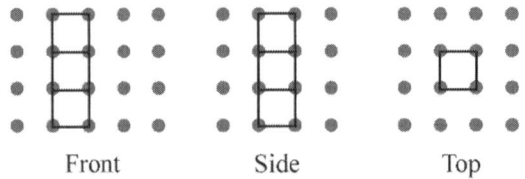

Front   Side   Top

Example

Abdi stacked three identical boxes in his storage shed.

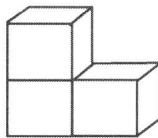

The following sketches show the different views of the boxes.

If you look at the front view of Abdi's boxes, you can see that the boxes are stacked two high on the left side and two boxes side by side on the bottom.

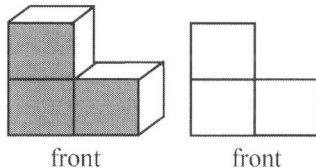

If you look at the side view of Abdi's boxes, you can see that the boxes are stacked two high.

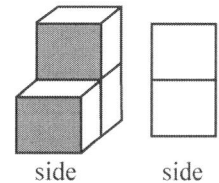

If you look at the top view of Abdi's boxes, you can see that the two boxes are side by side.

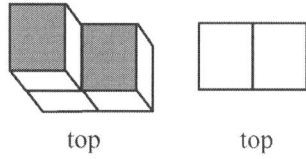

Use the following information to answer the next question.

The given diagrams represent the top, front, and side views of a group of geometric blocks.

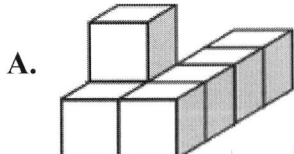 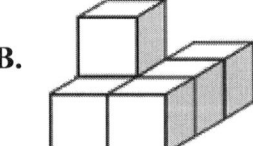

Top Front Side

13. Which of the following groups of blocks is **best** represented by the given diagrams?

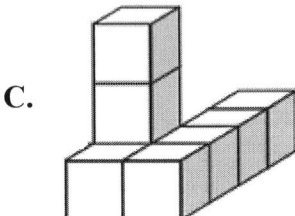

A.

B.

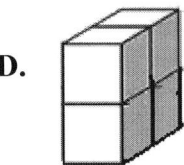

C.

D.

Use the following information to answer the next question.

Zara made this house out of cardboard.

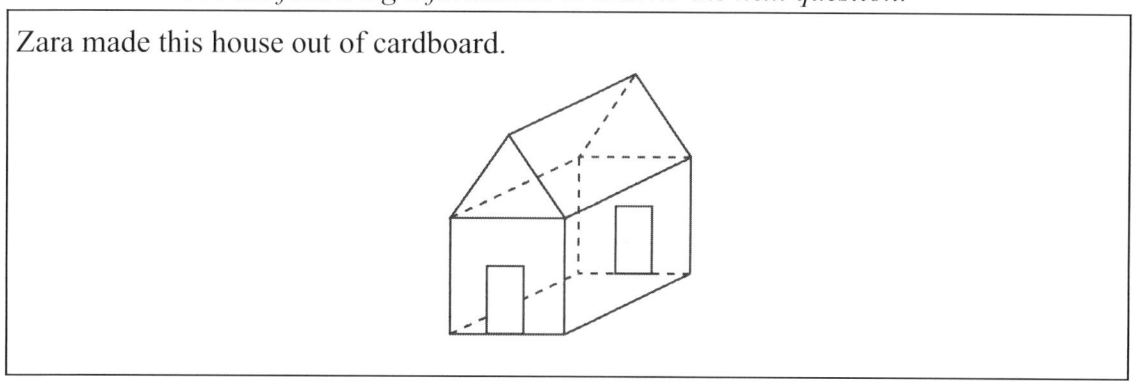

14. Which of the following views of the house is **not** correct?

A.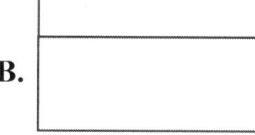

Front view

B.

Side view

C.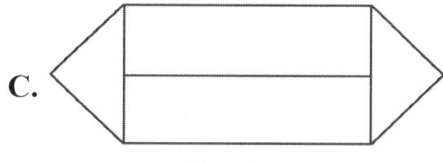

Top view

D.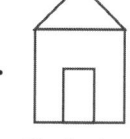

Back view

Use the following information to answer the next question.

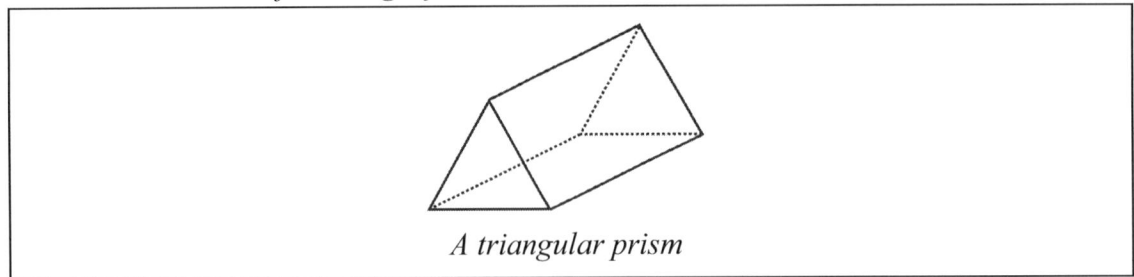

A triangular prism

Open Response

15. Sketch the faces of the given triangular prism.

   Show your work. Explain your answer

6m52 explain how a coordinate system represents location, and plot points in the first quadrant of a Cartesian coordinate plane

PLOTTING POINTS AND LOCATING POINTS ON A GRID

The following grid is called a coordinate plane or a Cartesian plane. It is a grid made up of a horizontal *x*-axis and a vertical *y*-axis. The *x*-axis and *y*-axis are numbered, starting with 0 in the bottom corner, which is called the origin. As you move right on the *x*-axis, the numbers get larger. As you move up on the *y*-axis, the numbers get larger. Grids can be used to represent location.

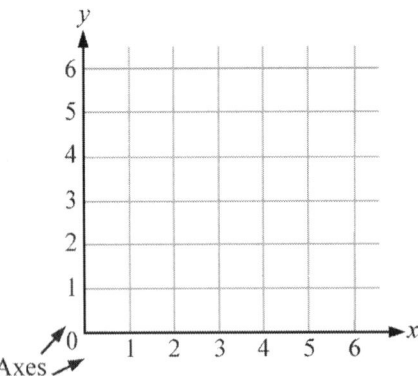

LOCATING A POINT ON A GRID

Coordinates are ordered pairs of numbers used to show a location on a grid. Together, the x-coordinate and y-coordinate make up an ordered pair (x, y).
Coordinates are located at the intersecting point of imaginary lines that extend from each axis.

To read the location of the point on the grid and write its coordinates, first look along the x-axis to see how far over the point is. This point is sitting on the x-axis at 4. Then, look along the y-axis to see how far up the point is sitting. This point is sitting on the y-axis at 3.

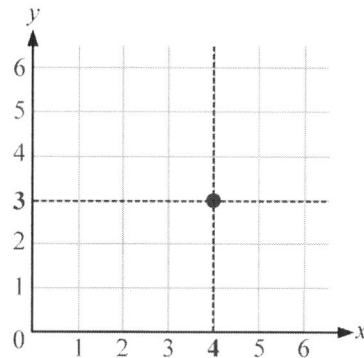

Therefore, the location of the point on the grid is $(4, 3)$. When writing coordinates, the order is important.
Be sure to write the number of the x-coordinate first and then the number of the y-coordinate (x, y).
You can also locate more than one point on the coordinate grid.

Example

To find the coordinates of point A, look along the x-axis to the 2 and then the y-axis up to the 4. The coordinates for point A are $(2, 4)$ and can be written as $A(2, 4)$. To find the coordinates of point B, look along the x-axis to the 5 and then the y-axis up to the 3. The coordinates for point B are $(5, 3)$ and can be written as $B(5, 3)$.

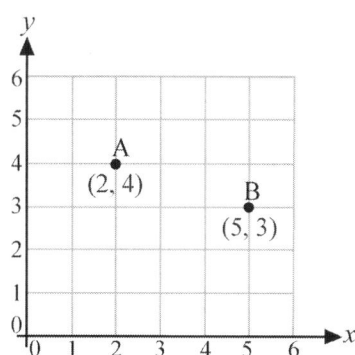

PLOTTING A POINT ON A GRID

You can also plot points on a grid if you are given the point's coordinates.

Example

Given the coordinates (2, 2), (3, 4), and (4, 2), plot the points on the grid to see what shape they make.

To plot the ordered pair (2, 2) on the grid, look along the *x*-axis until you get to 2, then look up the *y*-axis until you get to 2. Plot the point where these two lines meet.

To plot the ordered pair (3, 4) on the grid, look along the *x*-axis until you get to 3, then look up the *y*-axis until you get to 4. Plot the point where these two lines meet.

To plot the ordered pair (4, 2) on the grid, look along the *x*-axis until you get to 4, then look up the *y*-axis until you get to 2. Plot the point where these two lines meet. Join the points with a line to see what shape they make.

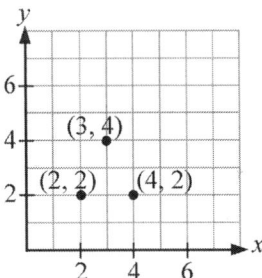

Use the following information to answer the next question.

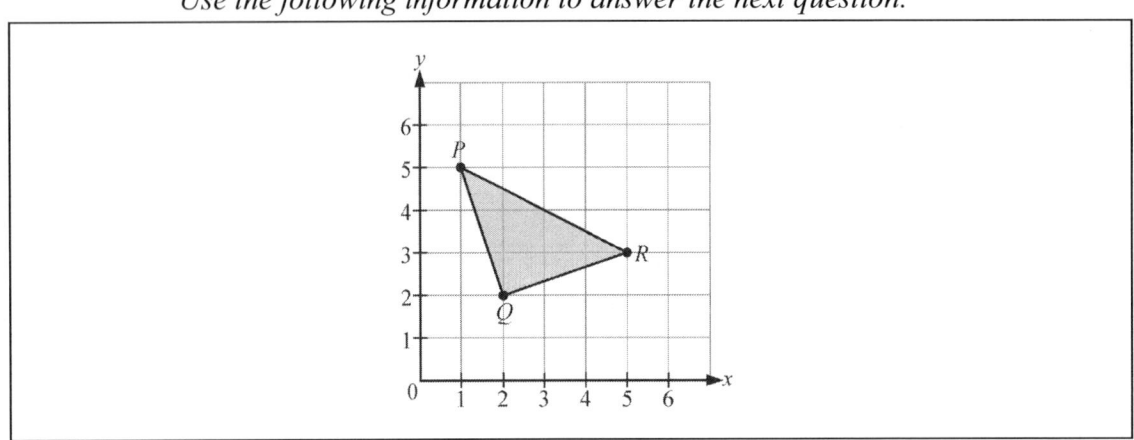

16. What are the coordinates of points P, Q, and R?

    A. P (5, 1), Q(2, 2), R(5, 3)   **B.** P(2, 2), Q(5, 3), R(1, 5)

    C. P(1, 5), Q(2, 2), R(3, 5)   **D.** P(1, 5), Q(2, 2), R(5, 3)

Use the following information to answer the next question.

Josie plotted the following points on a coordinate grid.

A (2, 2)

B (3, 3)

C (2, 5)

D (0, 3)

She then joined point *A* to point *B*, point *B* to point *C*, point *C* to point *D*, and point *D* to point *A*.

17. Which design did Josie make?

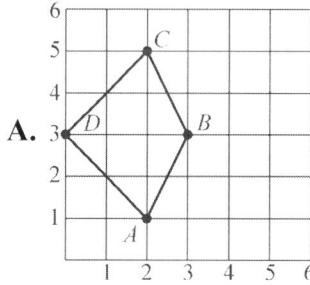

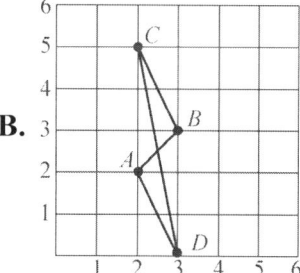

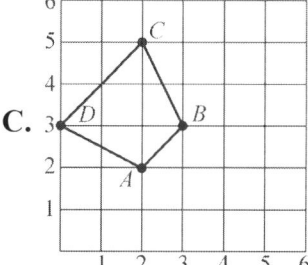

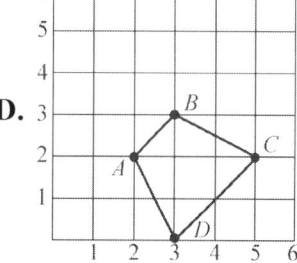

Open Response

18. Plot the coordinates $A(5, 8)$, $B(7, 5)$, $C(5, 2)$, and $D(3, 5)$ on the grid. Connect the points to form a polygon shape, and identify the type of polygon formed.

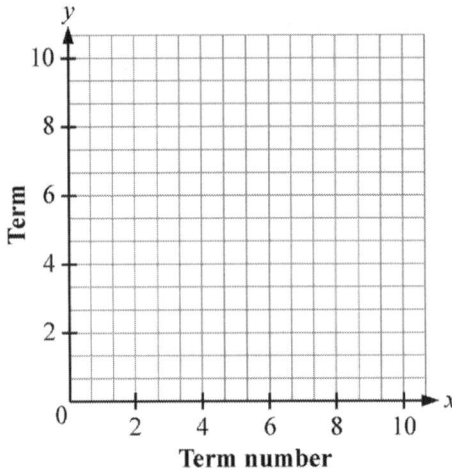

6m53 identify, perform, and describe, through investigation using a variety of tools, rotations of 180° and clockwise and counter clockwise rotations of 90°, with the centre of rotation inside or outside the shape

ROTATIONS

A rotation is a transformation in which a shape is turned about a point to create a congruent image of the original shape.

Remember:

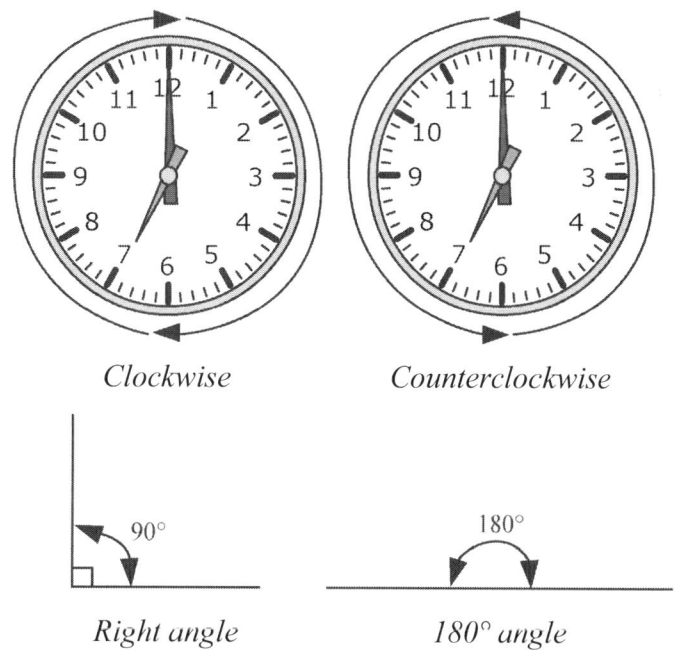

ROTATING A SHAPE

Shapes can be rotated in either a clockwise (cw) or counterclockwise (ccw) direction. A 90° rotation is a $\frac{1}{4}$ turn, and a 180° rotation is a $\frac{1}{2}$ turn.

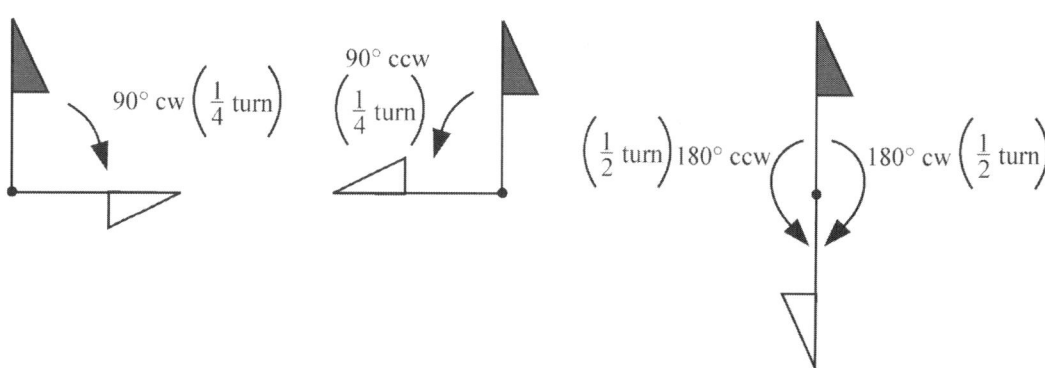

Example

Rotate the foot clockwise 90°, counterclockwise 90°, and clockwise 180°.

Solution

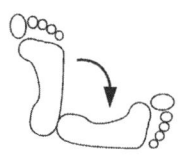

clockwise 90°

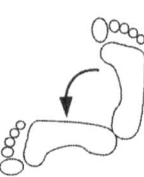

counterclockwise 90°

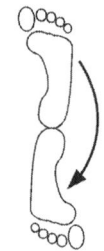

clockwise 180°

Use the following information to answer the next question.

The given picture shows a transformation.

19. Which of the following transformations is seen in the given picture?

   A. Rotation   **B.** Reflection

   C. Translation   **D.** Rotation and Reflection

20. Which of the following transformations turns the letter **N** into a **Z**?

   A. A diagonal translation   **B.** A reflection across a flip line

   C. A 90° rotation around the centre   **D.** A 180° rotation around the centre

21. Which of the following pairs of figures shows a rotation?

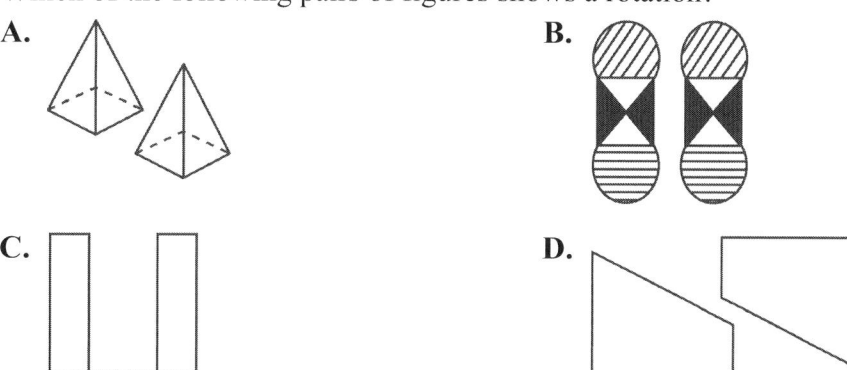

A.

B.

C.

D.

6m54 create and analyse designs made by reflecting, translating, and/or rotating a shape, or shapes, by 90° or 180°

TRANSFORMATIONS

A **transformation** is a change in a figure that results in a different position, direction, or size. Transformations include translations, reflections, and rotations.

A **translation**, or slide, is the movement of a figure in which each point of the figure is moved the same distance and direction.

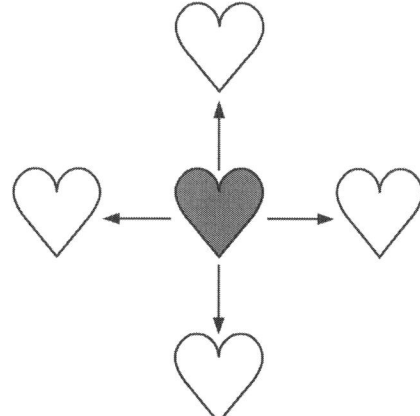

A **reflection**, or flip, is when a figure is flipped along a line of reflection to create a mirror image of the original figure.

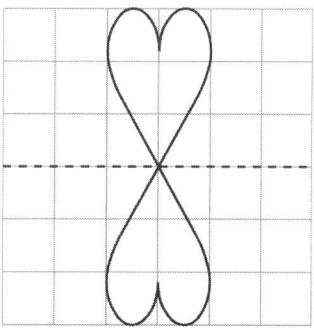

A **rotation**, or **turn**, is when a figure is rotated around a fixed point.

Example

Translate Figure I to the right 5 (R5) and up 2 (U2), then reflect (flip) the new figure (Figure II) along the line of reflection given.

Solution

To translate Figure I, start at point *A* and count right 5 units and up 2 units.

At point *B*, count right 5 units and up 2 units.

At point *C*, count right 5 units and up 2 units.

At point *D*, count right 5 units and up 2 units.

At point *E*, count right 5 units and up 2 units.

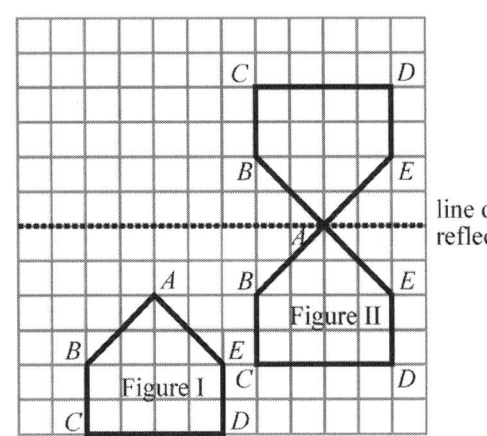

To reflect the new figure (Figure II), flip the figure along the line of reflection.

Example

Translate or slide the flag (Figure I) to the right 6 and up 5, and then rotate the flag 180°.

Solution

To translate the flag (Figure I), move the flag to the right 6 units and up 5 units.

Rotate the new flag (Figure II) 180°.

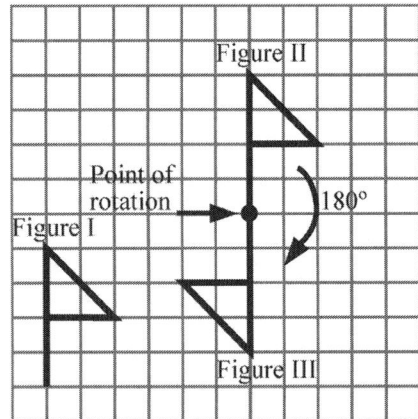

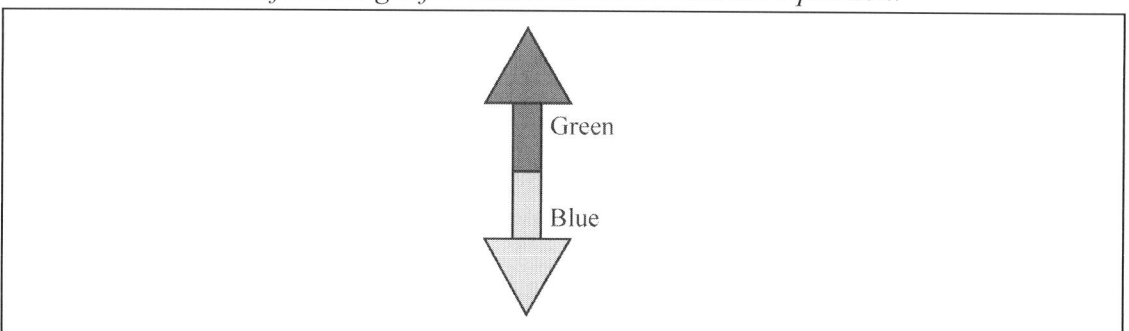 *Use the following information to answer the next question.*

22. Which of the following figures shows the given figure rotated clockwise 180° and then reflected across a horizontal line?

A.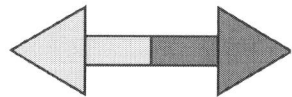

B.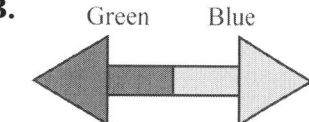

C.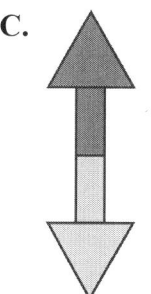

D.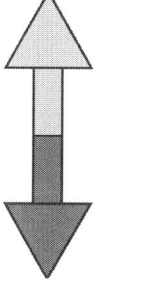

Use the following information to answer the next question.

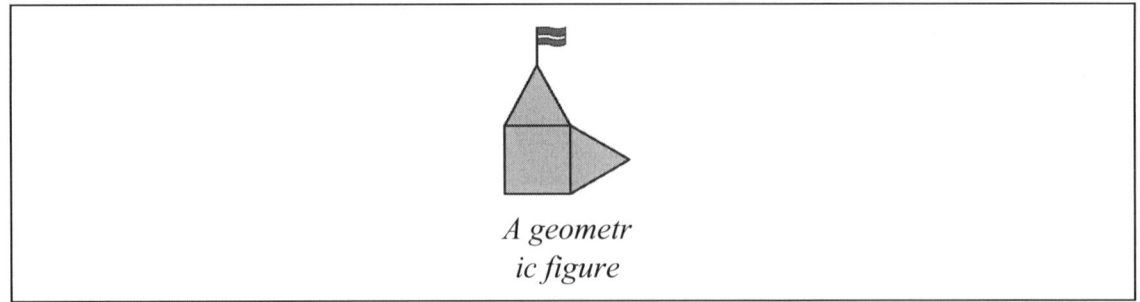

A geometr
ic figure

23. Which of the following figures shows the given figure after it has been rotated in a clockwise direction by 180°?

A.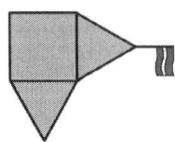

B.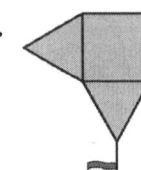

C.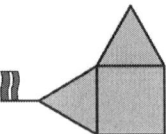

D.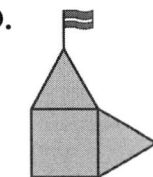

24. Which of the following diagrams shows an example of a reflection?

A.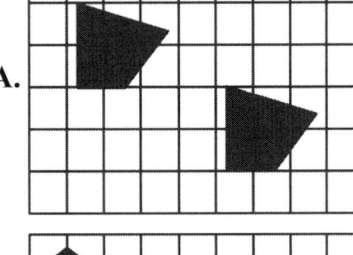

B.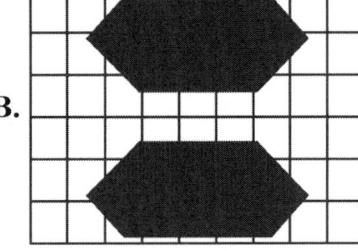

C.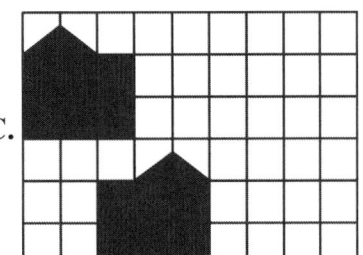

D.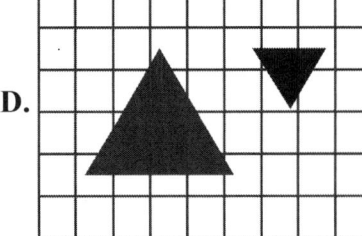

Use the following information to answer the next question.

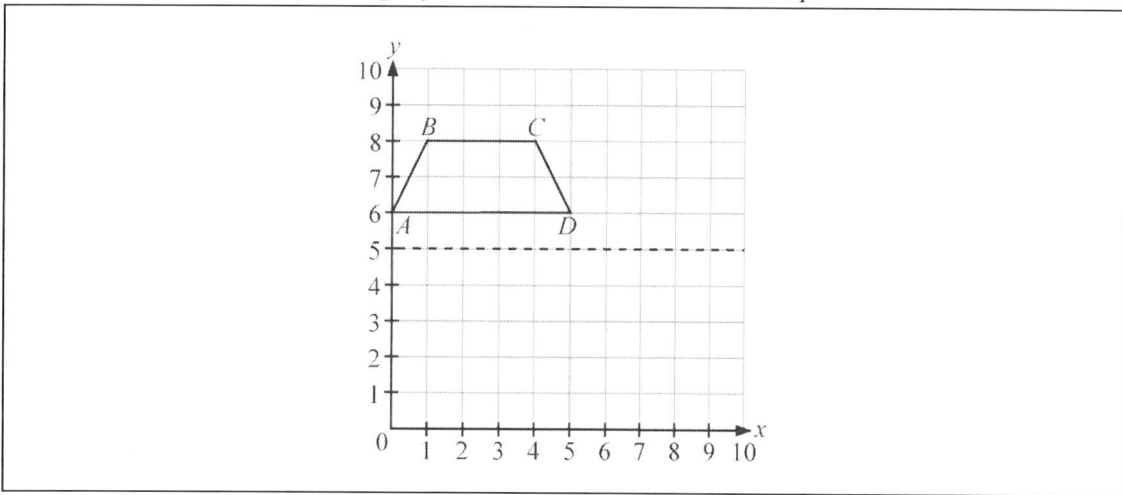

Open Response

25. Translate Figure *ABCD* to the right 6 units and reflect the new figure across Line 1.

ANSWERS AND SOLUTIONS
GEOMETRY AND SPATIAL SENSE

1. C	6. C	11. B	16. D	21. D
2. A	7. B	12. B	17. C	22. C
3. C	8. B	13. D	18. OR	23. B
4. D	9. C	14. C	19. A	24. B
5. D	10. OR	15. OR	20. C	25. OR

1. C

Step 1

Consider the characteristics of each given quadrilateral.

- A rhombus has two pairs of parallel sides and congruent sides.
- A rectangle has two pairs of parallel sides and four right angles.
- A trapezoid has one pair of parallel sides. It may or may not have right angles.
- A parallelogram has two pairs of parallel and congruent sides.

Step 2

Identify the description that matches the given shape.

The given shape has one set of parallel lines. It does not have any right angles.

The given shape is a trapezoid.

2. A

Step 1

Consider the statement in each given option. This diagram may help you consider the statements.

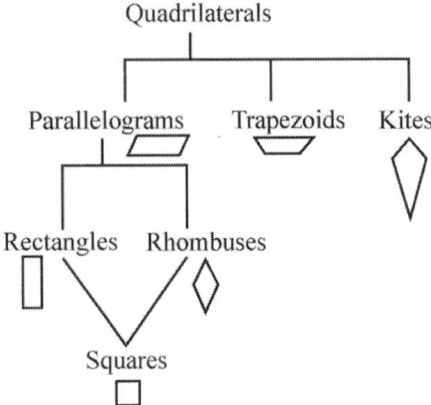

- Option *A*: All rhombuses have four congruent sides. Squares have four congruent sides and rectangles have two sets of congruent sides.
- Option *B*: All parallelograms have two sets of congruent and parallel sides. Squares and rectangles both have two sets of congruent and parallel sides.
- Option *C*: Both squares and parallelograms have four right angles.
- Option *D*: Both squares and parallelograms have two sets of parallel edges.

Step 2

Identify the stated characteristic that is not true of squares and rectangles.

Although squares are rhombuses, rectangles are not rhombuses. A rhombus has four congruent sides, while rectangles have two pairs of congruent sides. Therefore, the statement that is false is that squares and rectangles are both rhombuses.

3. C

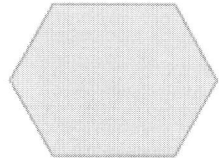

A quadrilateral is a four-sided enclosed figure.

The figure in C is a six-sided figure. Therefore, it is not a quadrilateral.

4. D

A The figure has 2 lines of symmetry: two diagonal lines from corner to corner.

B The figure has 2 lines of symmetry: a vertical line down the middle and a horizontal line across the middle.

C The figure has no line of symmetry.

D The figure has only 1 line of symmetry: a vertical line down the middle of the figure. So, this is the correct answer.

The correct answer is D.

5. D

A square has four lines of symmetry: two diagonal lines from corner to corner, a vertical line down the middle, and a horizontal line across the middle.

6. C

A line of symmetry divides a shape (in this case the number) into two halves that are exactly the same in size and shape.

The number 3 has one line of symmetry, and the numbers 0, 1, and 8 each have two lines of symmetry.

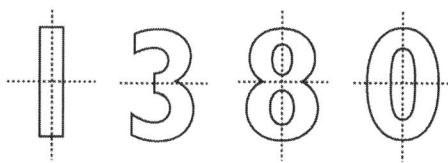

This means that Elva cannot draw lines of symmetry through the other six numbers. 2, 4, 5, 6, 7, and 9.

7. B

The centre of the protractor is on the vertex on the angle. One ray is lined up with the 0 degree mark on the inner scale. The other ray crosses the protractor at 30° on the inner scale. Thus, angle measures 30°.

The correct answer is B.

8. B

An equilateral triangle has 3 sides of equal length. To find the length of each side, divide 42 by 3.

$42 \div 3 = 14$ cm

Therefore, the length of each side of the triangle is 14 cm.

9. C

A regular pentagon has 5 sides of equal length. To find the length of each side, divide 40 by 5.

$40 \div 5 = 8$

Therefore, the length of each side of the pentagon is 8 cm.

10. OR

Points	Sample Answer
4	Thorough ability in drawing an equilateral triangle using a protractor.

In an equilateral triangle, all sides are equal and all angles are equal. The inside angles of all triangles add up to 180°. Therefore, in an equilateral triangle where all the sides are equal, each angle must equal 60° (180 ÷ 3).

Points	Sample Answer
	Using a ruler, draw a line that is 6 cm.
	At one end of the line, use your protractor to draw an angle of 60°.
	Make this line 6 cm also. Draw a connecting line that is also 6 cm.
	The equilateral triangle should have three 60° angles and three sides that each measure 6 cm.
3	Considerable ability in drawing an equilateral triangle using a protractor.
2	Some ability in drawing an equilateral triangle using a protractor.
1	Limited ability in drawing an equilateral triangle using a protractor.

11. B

In the given diagrams, the front view has two columns. However, the group of blocks in A has three columns as its front view. Therefore, A is incorrect.

The group of blocks in B has three columns on the side and two columns in the front. Therefore, B is correct.

In the given diagrams, the side view has three columns. However, the group of blocks in C and D would have four columns as their side views. Therefore, C and D are incorrect.

12. B

The pencil case is a rectangular prism. Therefore, the net would have four long rectangular sides with two smaller rectangles at each end of the middle rectangle (like the net shown in B.)

13. D

Compare all of the given views with the given groups of blocks. Only the group of blocks in D corresponds to a diagram with a side view, top view, and front view with 2 columns, 1 column, and 1 column respectively. Therefore, D is the correct answer.

14. C

Alternative A is the correct front view.

Alternative B is the correct side view.

Alternative C is not a correct sketch of the top view.

When viewed from the top, the sketch should look like this:

Top view

Alternative D is the correct back view.

15. OR

Points	Sample Answer
4	Thorough ability in sketching the faces of a triangular prism.
	A triangular prism has two faces that are triangles and three faces that are rectangles. The faces would look like this: 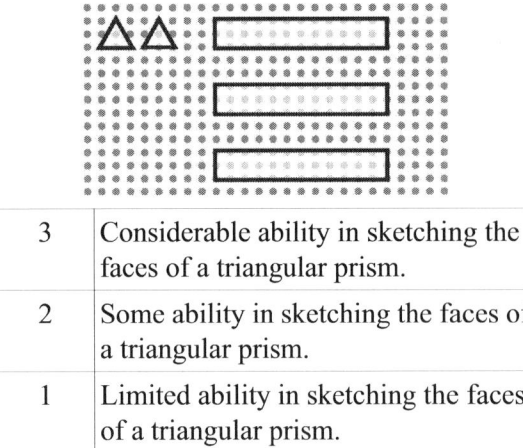
3	Considerable ability in sketching the faces of a triangular prism.
2	Some ability in sketching the faces of a triangular prism.
1	Limited ability in sketching the faces of a triangular prism.

16. D

When finding coordinates, remember to always read the x-coordinate first and then the y-coordinate.

Point P is 1 unit to the right and 5 units up. The coordinates for point P are (1, 5).

Point Q is 2 units to the right and 2 units up. The coordinates for point Q are (2, 2).

Point R is 5 units to the right and 3 units up. The coordinates for point R are (5, 3).

Therefore, the coordinates for the design are P (1, 5), Q (2, 2), and R (5, 3), which correspond to **D**.

17. C

Begin with the horizontal bottom line (*x*-axis) and then go up the vertical line (*y*-axis).

To plot point *A*(2, 2), go right 2 and then up 2

To plot point *B*(3, 3), go right 3 and then up 3

To plot point *C*(2, 5), go right 2 and then up 5

To plot point *D*(0, 3), go up 3.

Connect the points *A*, *B*, *C*, *D*. The design in **C** is correct.

18. OR

Points	Sample Answer
4	Thorough ability in plotting points on a coordinate plane.

To plot the points on the coordinate plane, remember to always plot the *x*-coordinate first and then the *y*-coordinate.

To plot *A*(5,8), look along the *x*-axis to the 5 and then look up the *y*-axis to the 8.

To plot *B*(7,5), look along the *x*-axis to the 7 and then look up the *y*-axis to the 5.

To plot *C*(5,2), look along the *x*-axis to the 5 and then look up the *y*-axis to the 2.

To plot *D*(3,5), look along the *x*-axis to the 3 and then look up the *y*-axis to the 5.

Connect the points and you should see a rhombus.

3	Considerable ability in plotting points on a coordinate plane.
2	Some ability in plotting points on a coordinate plane.
1	Limited ability in plotting points on a coordinate plane.

19. A

The gorilla has been rotated 180°. It has not been reflected or translated.

Choice A is the correct answer.

20. C

To change the letter **N** into the letter **Z**, it must be rotated 90°. The rotation can be either clockwise or counterclockwise. Both rotations will turn the N into a Z.

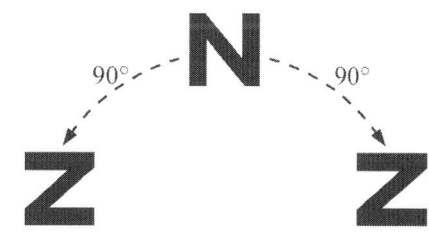

21. D

Analyze each set of figures to determine what transformations have taken place.

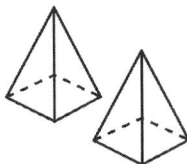

The figure has been translated diagonally.

The figure has been translated to the right.

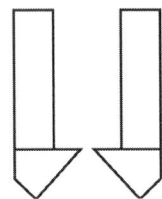

The figure has been flipped over a vertical flip line, making a mirror image.

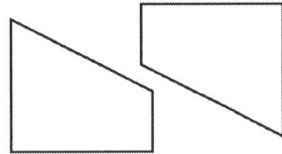

The figure has been turned or rotated 180°.

22. C

A reflection, or flip, is a transformation in geometry in which an object is reflected in a straight line to form a mirror image. If you took the image and rotated it 180°, then the dark arrow, which was initially on the top, would be at the bottom, like the figure in D. However, the image would still need to be reflected across a horizontal line. Once this occurred, the image reflected would look like the original image. Therefore, A and B do not show a 180° rotation or a reflection.

C is the correct answer.

D only shows a 180° rotation.

23. B

This figure shows a rotation of 180°.

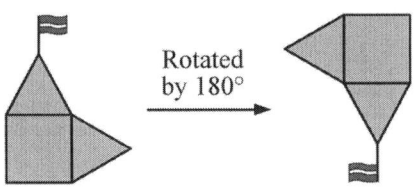

24. B

A reflection is a transformation in geometry in which an object is reflected in a straight line to form a mirror image.

Choice A is incorrect. It is a translation 3 units to the right and 2 units down.

Choice B is correct. It is a reflection across a horizontal line.

Choice C is incorrect. It is an example of a reflection and a translation.

Choice D is incorrect. It does not represent a true transformation because the sizes of the images are not consistent.

25. OR

Points	Sample Answer
4	Thorough ability in translating and reflecting a figure on a coordinate plane.

The figure, when translated to the right 6 units, should sit at $A(6, 6)$, $B(7, 8)$, $C(9, 8)$, $D(10, 6)$.

The figure, when reflected across line 1 from its translated position, should sit at $A(6, 4)$, $B(7, 2)$, $C(9, 2)$, $D(10, 4)$.

Points	Sample Answer
	The new figure, when translated to the right 6 units and reflected across line 1, should look like this: 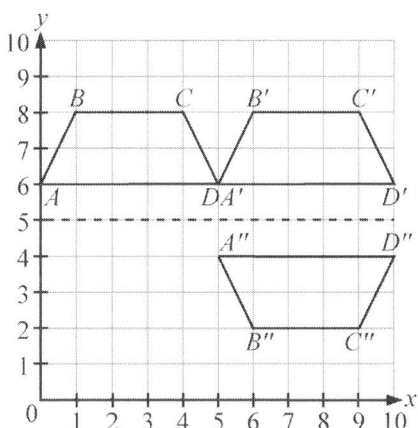
3	Considerable ability in translating and reflecting a figure on a coordinate plane.
2	Some ability in translating and reflecting a figure on a coordinate plane.
1	Limited ability in translating and reflecting a figure on a coordinate plane.

UNIT TEST — GEOMETRY AND SPATIAL SENSE

Use the following information to answer the next question.

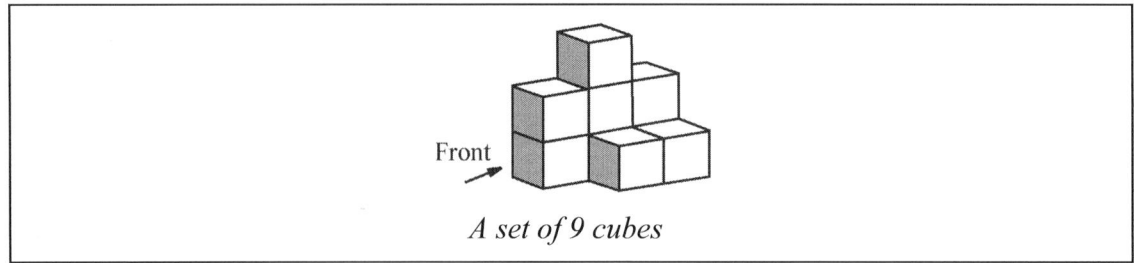

Front

A set of 9 cubes

1. Which of the following sets of perspectives represents the layout for the given set of 9 cubes?

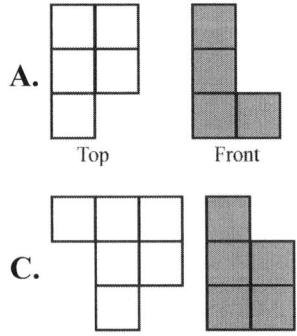

A.

Top   Front

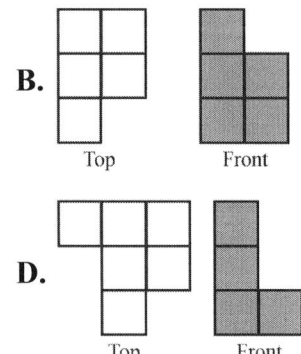

B.

Top   Front

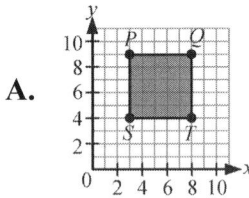

C.

Top   Front

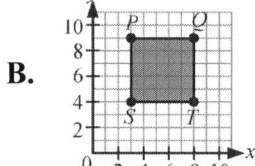

D.

Top   Front

2. Which of the following figures correctly places the points $P(3, 9)$, $Q(8, 9)$, $T(8, 4)$, and $S(3,4)$ on the coordinate plane?

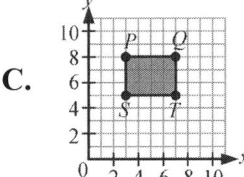

A.

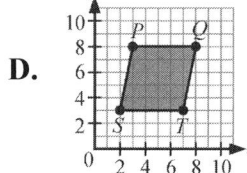

B.

C.

D.

Use the following information to answer the next question.

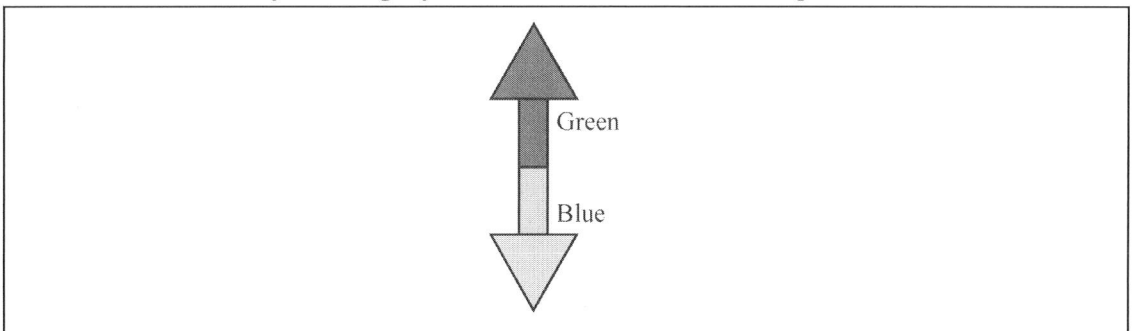

3. Which of the following figures shows the given figure after it has been rotated counterclockwise 90°?

A.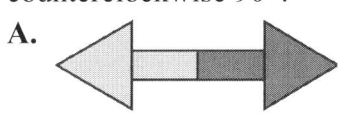

B.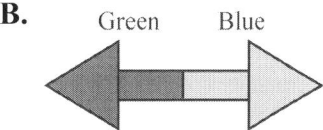

C.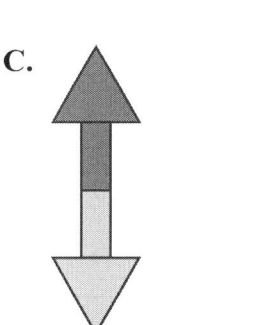

D.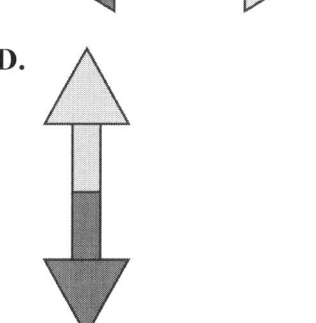

Use the following information to answer the next question.

Triangle 1 was rotated clockwise about point *A* to form Triangle 2, as shown in the diagram.

4. How many degrees was the triangle rotated?

    A. 0°   **B.** 90°

    C. 180°   **D.** 270°

Use the following information to answer the next question.

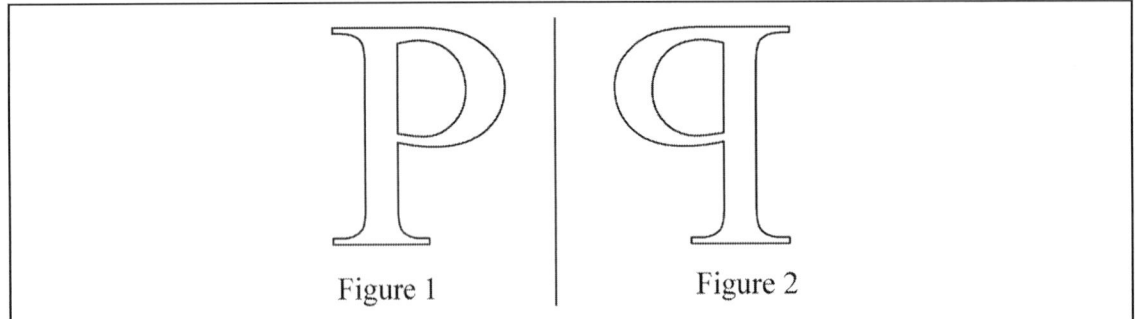

Figure 1   Figure 2

5. Which of the following transformations could produce Figure 2 from Figure 1?

A. A rotation   **B.** A reflection

C. A translation   **D.** A translation and a rotation

6. Which of the following diagrams shows a horizontal translation?

A. 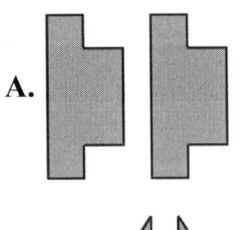   **B.**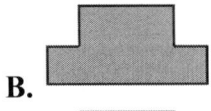

C. 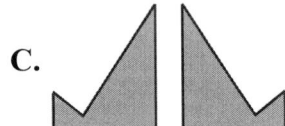   **D.**

Use the following information to answer the next question.

Horizontal line

7. What is the resulting image when the given figure is reflected over the horizontal line and then rotated clockwise 90°?

A. 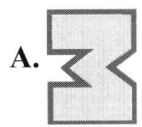   **B.**

C.    **D.**

Use the following information to answer the next question.

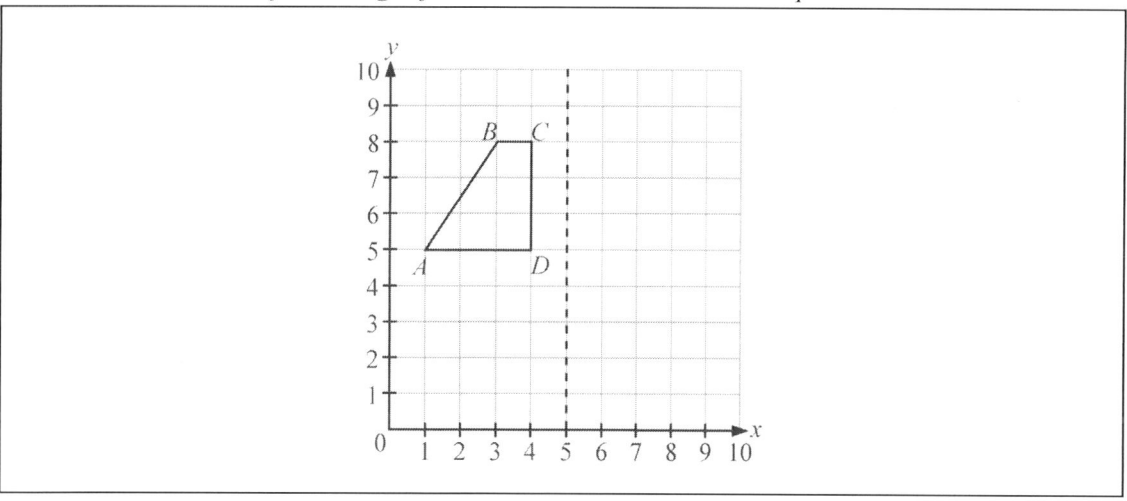

Open Response

8.   Reflect figure *ABCD* across line 2, and slide the new figure down 3 units.

Use the following information to answer the next question.

Marty uses characteristics of quadrilaterals to sort the following shapes into two groups.
Group 1 will have right angles and parallel lines.

Shape L   Shape M   Shape N   Shape O

9.   Which two shapes should Marty place in Group 1?
   A. L and M   **B.** L and N
   C. M and O   **D.** N and M

10. Which of the following sets of pattern blocks has 6 lines of symmetry?

A.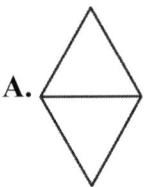

B.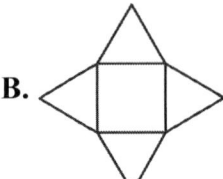

C.

D.

Use the following information to answer the next question.

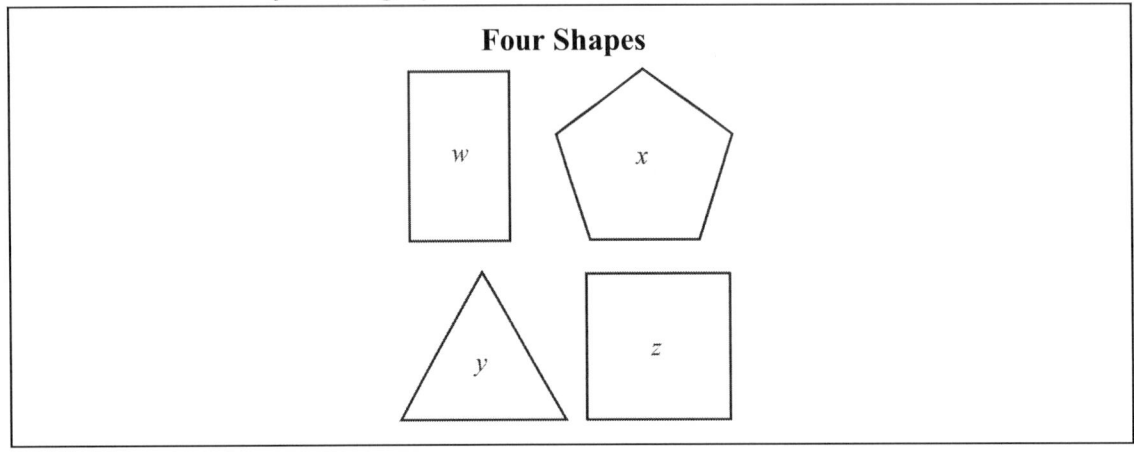

Four Shapes

11. Which of the following sets lists the four shapes in order, from the shape with the fewest lines of symmetry to the shape with the most lines of symmetry?

   A. w, y, z, and x   **B.** w, z, y, and x

   C. x, z, y, and w   **D.** y, w, z, and x

12. Which of the following shapes does **not** have a line of symmetry?

A.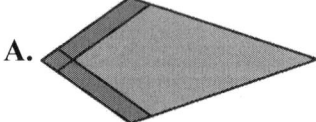

B.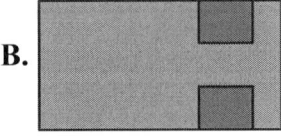

C.

D.

13. Which of the following triangles has at least one obtuse angle and one acute angle?

A.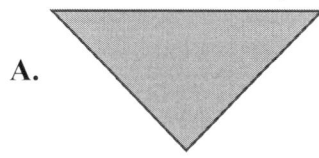

B.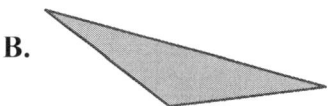

C.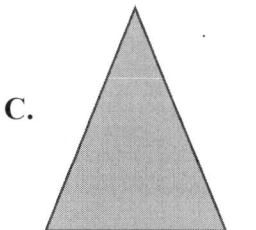

D.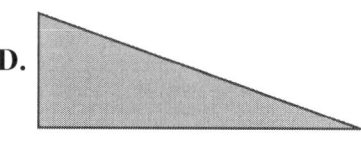

Use the following information to answer the next question.

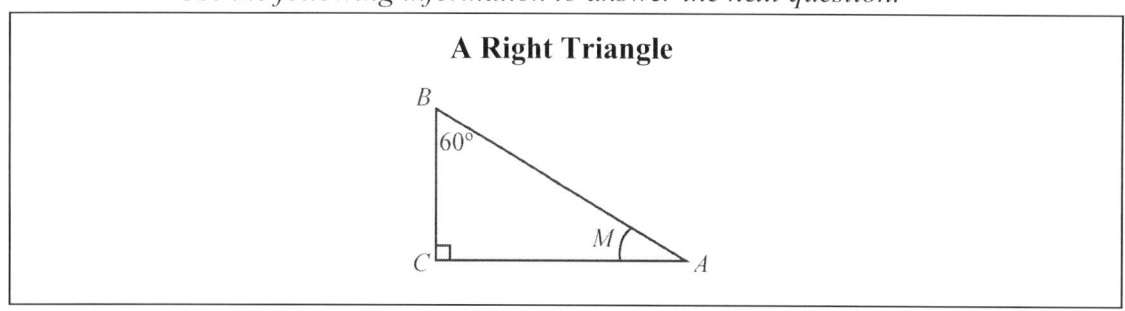

14. What is the measurement of ∠*A*?

  A. 20°   B. 30°

  C. 60°   D. 120°

Use the following information to answer the next question.

A triangle has angles measuring 42° and 53°.

15. What is the value of the triangle's third angle?

  A. 28°   B. 35°

  C. 48°   D. 85°

ANSWERS AND SOLUTIONS — UNIT TEST

1. A	5. B	9. B	13. B
2. A	6. A	10. D	14. B
3. B	7. D	11. A	15. D
4. B	8. OR	12. D	

1. A

When viewed from the top, a total of 5 blocks should be visible. When viewed from the front, 4 blocks should be visible. Perspective A correctly represents the layout of the 9 cubes.

When viewed from the front, a total of 4 blocks should be visible. Perspective B shows 5. This choice is incorrect.

A total of 5 blocks should be visible from the top and 4 blocks should be visible from the front. Perspective C shows 6 blocks from the top view and 5 from the front. This choice is incorrect.

When viewed from the top, a total of 5 blocks should be visible. Perspective D shows 6. This choice is incorrect.

2. A

The plotted points are identical to the coordinate plane given in A:

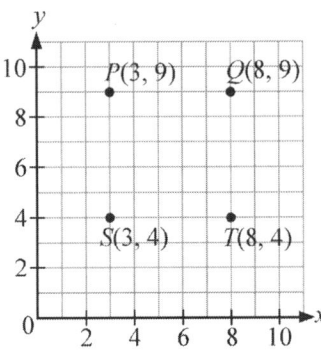

3. B

In the given figure, the darker arrow is pointing up and the lighter arrow is pointing down. If the whole arrow is rotated counterclockwise 90°, the lighter arrow will point right and the darker arrow will point left.

4. B

The triangle was rotated clockwise 90°.

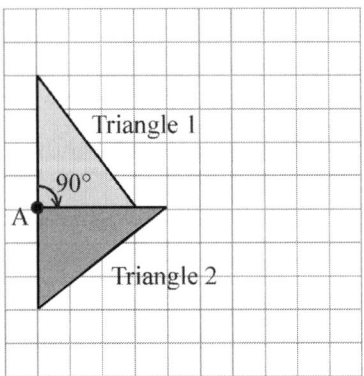

5. B

In a reflection, every point on the object moves to a point that is the same distance on the opposite side of a fixed line. The figure and its image are directly opposite each other. Therefore, this diagram shows a reflection.

6. A

A This shows a horizontal slide. This choice is correct.

B This is a vertical slide.

C This is a reflection.

D This is a reflection.

7. D

If the image is reflected across the horizontal line it will look like an upside-down M. Then, if that figure is rotated clockwise 90°, it will look like the figure in D.

8. OR

Points	Sample Answer
4	Thorough ability in reflecting and translating a figure on a coordinate plane.

Points	Sample Answer
	The new figure, when reflected across Line 2, should sit at A(9, 5), B(7, 8), C(6, 8), D(6, 5). 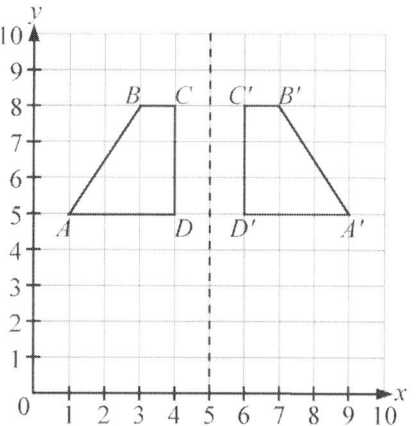 The new figure, when translated down 3 units, should sit at $A(9, 2)$, $B(7, 5)$, $C(6, 5)$, $D(6, 2)$. The new figure, when reflected across Line 2 and translated down 3 units would look like this: 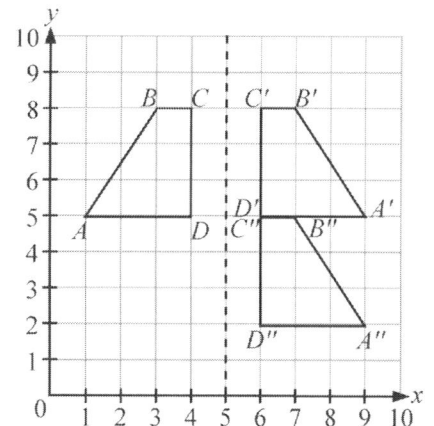
3	Considerable ability in reflecting and translating a figure on a coordinate plane.
2	Some ability in reflecting and translating a figure on a coordinate plane.
1	Limited ability in reflecting and translating a figure on a coordinate plane.

9. B

Step 1

Analyze each shape according to right angles and parallel lines.

- Shape L (the square) has four right angles and two sets of parallel lines.
- Shape M (the kite) has no right angles and no parallel lines.
- Shape N (the trapezoid) has two right angles and one set of parallel lines.
- Shape O (the rhombus) has no right angles and two sets of parallel lines.

Step 2

Identify the shapes with both right angles and parallel lines.

Shape L (the square) and Shape N (the trapezoid) both have right angles and parallel lines.

10. D

A line of symmetry is a line that divides a figure into two congruent parts that are mirror images of one another.

Figure A has 2 lines of symmetry.

Figure B has 4 lines of symmetry.

Figure C has 3 lines of symmetry.

Figure D has 6 lines of symmetry.

11. A

Shape w is a rectangle with 2 lines of symmetry.

Shape x is a pentagon with 5 lines of symmetry.

Shape y is an equilateral triangle with 3 lines of symmetry.

Shape z is a square with 4 lines of symmetry.

The correct order is w, y, z, and x.

12. D

A The kite has a horizontal line of symmetry across the middle.

B The rectangle has a horizontal line of symmetry across the middle.

C The rectangle has a horizontal line of symmetry across the middle.

D The triangle has no line of symmetry.

The correct answer is D.

13. B

A This triangle has 1 right angle and 2 acute angles.

B This triangle has 1 obtuse angle and 2 acute angles. This is the correct answer.

C This triangle has 3 acute angles

D This triangle has 1 right angle and 2 acute angles.

The correct answer is B.

14. B

The sum of the angles of a triangle is 180°.
It is given that $\angle B = 60°$.
In a right triangle, one angle $= 90°$.

$\angle A + \angle B + \angle C = 180°$
$\angle A + 60° + 90° = 180°$
$\angle A + 150° = 180°$
$\angle A = 180° - 150°$
$\angle A = 30°$

15. D

The sum of the angles of a triangle is 180°.
Label the first two angles A and B, and label the unknown angle C.

$\angle A + \angle B + \angle C = 180°$
$42° + 53° + \angle C = 180°$
$95° + \angle C = 180°$
$\angle C = 180° - 95°$
$\angle C = 85°$

Patterning and Algebra

PATTERNING AND ALGEBRA

	Specific Expectation	Practice Questions	Unit Test Questions	Practice Test 1	Practice Test 2
6m55	Patterns and Relationships				
6m57	*identify geometric patterns, through investigation using concrete materials or drawings, and represent them numerically*	1	1		14
6m58	*make tables of values, for growing patterns given pattern rules, in words, then list the ordered pairs (with the first coordinate representing the term number and the second coordinate representing the term) and plot the points in the first quadrant, using a variety of tools*	2, 3	2, 3		15
6m59	*determine the term number of a given term in a growing pattern that is represented by a pattern rule in words, a table of values, or a graph*	4, 5, 6	4, 5, 6	15, 16, 17	16
6m60	*describe pattern rules (in words) that generate patterns by adding or subtracting a constant, or multiplying or dividing by a constant, to get the next term, then distinguish such pattern rules from pattern rules, given in words, that describe the general term by referring to the term number*	7, 8	7, 8	18	
6m61	*determine a term, given its term number, by extending growing and shrinking patterns that are generated by adding or subtracting a constant, or multiplying or dividing by a constant, to get the next term*	9, 10, 11	9, 10, 11	19, 20	
6m62	*extend and create repeating patterns that result from rotations, through investigation using a variety of tools*	12, 13	12		17
6m56	Variables, Expressions, and Equations				
6m63	*demonstrate an understanding of different ways in which variables are used*	14	13		18
6m64	*identify, through investigation, the quantities in an equation that vary and those that remain constant*	15, 16	14		19
6m65	*solve problems that use two or three symbols or letters as variables to represent different unknown quantities*	17, 18, 19	15, 16		20
6m66	*determine the solution to a simple equation with one variable, through investigation using a variety of tools and strategies*	20, 21	17, 18	21	

Table of Correlations

6m57 identify geometric patterns, through investigation using concrete materials or drawings, and represent them numerically

REPRESENT GEOMETRIC PATTERNS NUMERICALLY

Patterns are repeated sequences of numbers, shapes, colours, or behaviours. Patterns can be represented visually with shapes, diagrams, or charts. Patterns can be **repeating patterns** where a **pattern core** repeats to make the pattern. The following example shows a pattern core.

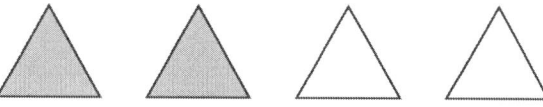

The pattern core repeats to become an increasing pattern or growing pattern.

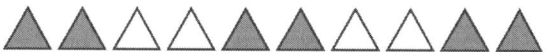

By looking at the pattern, you are able to predict what comes next and you can extend the pattern.

To describe the relationship between shaded triangles and non-shaded triangles, you would say that for every two shaded triangles, two non-shaded triangles follow. Unlike increasing patterns, shrinking patterns or decreasing patterns decrease by the same amount with each term.

Example

The pattern 3, 4, 5, 6, 7, can be represented as follows:

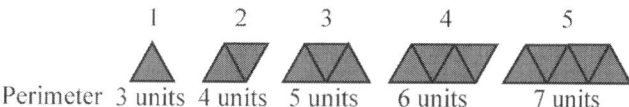

The first term of the pattern shows one triangle with a perimeter of 3 units, the second term shows two triangles with a perimeter of 4 units, the third term shows three triangles with a perimeter of 5 units, and so on. The perimeter of each geometric figure increases by 1 unit as the number of triangles increases by 1.

Example

Robin creates a pattern by placing building blocks in the following order:

△ △ ■ △ △ △ △ ■ △ △ △ △ ■ △ △

Which set of blocks is repeated to create this pattern?

Solution

The set of blocks that form the repeating part of the pattern are 2 triangles, 1 square, and 2 triangles.

2△ +1■ +2△

Use the following information to answer the next question.

Robin creates a pattern by placing building blocks in the following order:

1. Which set of blocks is repeated to create this pattern?

    A. $2\triangle + 1\blacksquare + 1\triangle$

    B. $2\triangle + 1\blacksquare + 2\triangle$

    C. $2\triangle + 1\blacksquare + 3\triangle$

    D. $2\triangle + 1\blacksquare + 4\triangle$

6m58   *make tables of values, for growing patterns given pattern rules, in words, then list the ordered pairs (with the first coordinate representing the term number and the second coordinate representing the term) and plot the points in the first quadrant, using a variety of tools*

6m59   *determine the term number of a given term in a growing pattern that is represented by a pattern rule in words, a table of values, or a graph*

GRAPHING PATTERNS

A **pattern rule** is a statement that describes how to find the next term in a pattern.

A pattern rule must state the first number or first term in the pattern. The pattern rule explains what should be done with this first term in the pattern to get the second term in the pattern. Similarly, this pattern rule explains what should be done with the second term in the pattern to get the third term in the pattern, and so on.

Example
The pattern rule for the terms in the second row of the table of values below is: *start with 1 and add 2 to each term to get the next term.*
Use the pattern rule to find the other terms in the pattern and place these numbers in the second row of a table of values.

Term Number	1	2	3	4	5	6	7
Term	1						

Solution
To find the second term, use the pattern rule. Add 2 to each term to get the next term. Since the first term is 1, add 2 to 1 to get 3. Place 3 in the second row directly under term number 2. To find the third term, use the pattern rule again but this time, add 2 to 3 to get 5. For the fourth term, add 2 to 5 to get 7. Continue using the pattern rule to complete the table of values.

Term Number	1	2	3	4	5	6	7
Term	1	3	5	7	9		

To list the ordered pairs from the table of values, write the term number first and then the term.
Term Number → (1, 1) ← Term

The ordered pairs that appear in the table of values are: (1, 1), (2, 3), (3, 5), (4, 7), (5, 9), … To graph the ordered pairs, remember that the first member of each ordered pair is the coordinate on the horizontal axis of the graph and the second member is the coordinate on the vertical axis of the graph.

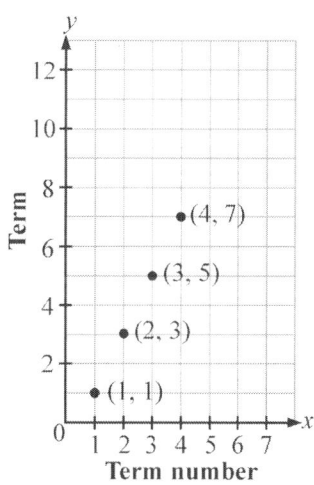

DETERMINING THE TERM NUMBER USING A GRAPH

A pattern rule is used to find each successive term in a pattern. By studying the pattern, you can find the term number if you are given the pattern rule and the value for a specific term.

If the term numbers and their corresponding terms are written as coordinates, you can find the term number by looking at the first number of the coordinate.

If the coordinates are plotted on a graph, you can find the term number by identifying where the x-axis and given value on the y-axis intersect. Most graphs record the term numbers on the x-axis and the terms on the y-axis.

Example

In this graph, you can see five sets of coordinates plotted on the graph. The coordinates are joined together by a dotted line. The coordinates are written beside each intersection to help you clearly see where the number on the x-axis (the term number) and the number on the y-axis (the term value) intersect.

Remember, the first number of a coordinate is the term number and the second number of the coordinate is the term value.

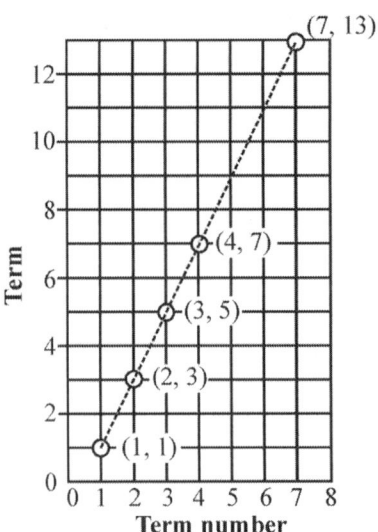

Using this graph, you can determine the term number for a given term by following these directions.

- To determine which term number has a value of 7, start at the zero and move vertically up the y-axis (↑)until you reach the term value of 7 (halfway between 6 and 8).
- Then move horizontally to the right (→) until you reach the dotted line.
- Move vertically downward (↓) until you reach the number on the x-axis, which is 4.

The 4th term number has a value of 7. Its coordinates are (4, 7)

2. Which of the following ordered pairs corresponds to the pattern rule, **start with 12, subtract 2, and double the result**?
   A. (12, 20), (20, 18), (18, 34)   **B.** (12, 10), (10, 8), (8, 6)
   C. (12, 20), (20, 36), (36, 68)   **D.** (12, 24), (24, 48), (48, 96)

   Open Response

3. Start a pattern rule with 100, and then subtract 20 from each term. List the values as ordered pairs. Explain your thinking.

4. There are four numbers in a series. The first three numbers are 12, 9, and 6. If the series continues in the same pattern, what will the fourth number be?
   A. 1   **B.** 2
   C. 3   **D.** 4

Use the following information to answer the next question.

In divided by 2 = **Out**

5. Which of the following tables follows the given rule?

A.

In	10	24	76	92
Out	5	12	39	47

B.

In	18	28	52	98
Out	9	14	26	48

C.

In	16	32	54	68
Out	8	16	27	35

D.

In	22	38	74	96
Out	11	19	37	48

Use the following information to answer the next question.

A Number Pattern

6. Which of the following numbers completes the pattern?

A. 20   B. 21

C. 22   D. 23

6m60 describe pattern rules (in words) that generate patterns by adding or subtracting a constant, or multiplying or dividing by a constant, to get the next term, then distinguish such pattern rules from pattern rules, given in words, that describe the general term by referring to the term number

6m61 determine a term, given its term number, by extending growing and shrinking patterns that are generated by adding or subtracting a constant, or multiplying or dividing by a constant, to get the next term

PATTERN RULES

A pattern rule is a general statement that describes how a pattern increases or decreases.

A **constant** is a value that does not change. An example of a pattern growing by addition is 2, 4, 6, 8, …, where the constant, 2, is added to each term to get the next term. An example of a pattern growing by multiplication is 2, 4, 8, 16, …, where the constant, 2, is multiplied by each term to get the next term.

There are two types of pattern rules. The first type of pattern rule is one that describes the growth of a pattern from one term to the next. It describes the relationship among the numbers in one row in a table of values.

The second type of pattern rule is one that describes the growth of a pattern by relating the term number to the value of the term. It describes the relationship between two rows in a table of values. Using this second type of pattern rule, you could find the value of the 100 th term without having to write out all 100 terms.

These two types of pattern rules are represented in the example below.

Example

In the diagram below, you can see a pattern. The first figure has 4 parts the second figure has 7 parts, the third figure has 10 parts and the fourth figure has 13 parts.

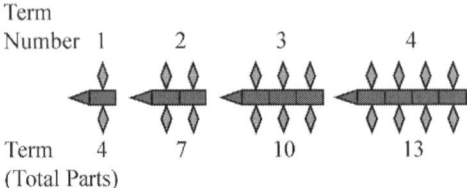

The information from the diagram can be summarized in a table of values or a chart as shown below:

Term Number	1	2	3	4	5	6	7
Term	4	7	10	13	16	19	22

Now, look at the two types of pattern rules that describe the growth of the pattern shown in the table of values.

a) The first type of pattern rule describes the growth of a pattern from one term to the next.

Term Number	1	2	3	4	5	6	7	8
Term	4	7	10	13	16	19	22	

To describe the pattern 4, 7, 10, 13, 16, …, you can use the following pattern rule: Start with 4 and add 3 to each term to get the next term.

Using this pattern rule, you can find the 8th term by adding 3 to 22. The 8th term is 25. However, it would be inefficient to find the value of the 100th term using this pattern rule.

b) The second type of pattern rule describes the growth of a pattern by relating the term number to the value of the term. This type of pattern rule describes the relationship between two rows in a table of values.

Study the diagram below to determine the pattern rule that tells you what to do with each term number to get the term value or the total parts.

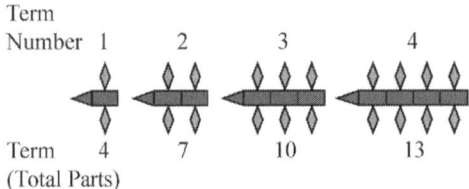

The pattern rule that relates the term number to the total parts or the value of that term is multiply the term number by 3 and add 1.

The table of values shows the relationship between the term number and the term.

Term Number	1	2	3	4	5	6	7	8
Term number × 3 + 1 = Term								
Term (Total Parts)	4	7	10	13	16	19	22	

EXTENDING PATTERNS

You can use the pattern rule from the previous example to extend the pattern. For example, the value of the 8th term is $8 \times 3 + 1 = 25$.

You can also find the value of the 100th term using the same pattern rule: $100 \times 3 + 1 = 301$. The value of the 100th term is 301.

SHRINKING PATTERNS

Shrinking patterns can be made by either subtracting a constant or dividing by a constant. An example of a pattern shrinking by subtraction is 96, 94, 92, 90, …, where the constant, 2, is subtracted from each term to get the next term. An example of a pattern shrinking by division is 96, 48, 24, 12, …, where each term is divided by the constant, 2, to get the next term.

Use the following information to answer the next question.

Frances wrote the following number pattern. 9 045, 8 035, 7 025, 6 015

7. What pattern rule did Frances use to write the pattern?
   A. Subtract 1 010 each time
   B. Subtract 1 000 each time
   C. Add 1 010 each time
   D. Add 1 000 each time

Use the following information to answer the next question.

Each term number has the same relation to its corresponding term.

Term Number	Term
2	5
5	11
8	17
9	?
12	25

8. Which of the following pattern rules can be used to find the missing term in the given table?

   A. Add 1 to the term number and double the result.

   B. Double the term number and add 1 to the result.

   C. Subtract 1 from the term number and double the result.

   D. Double the term number and subtract 1 from the result.

Use the following information to answer the next question.

Mia uses this chart to help her determine how many grams of beef and beans she needs to make chili.

Number of servings	Grams of beef	Grams of beans
4	500	175
6	750	350
8	1 000	525
10	1 250	700
12	1 500	875

9. For every 2 servings, how many more grams of beef and beans does Mia need?

   A. 500 g more of beef and 175 g more of beans

   B. 250 g more of beef and 150 g more of beans

   C. 250 g more of beef and 175 g more of beans

   D. 150 g more of beef and 175 g more of beans

10. What is the next term in the number pattern 94, 84, 75, 67, 60, 54, __?

   A. 42   **B.** 45

   C. 47   **D.** 49

Open Response

11. The xth term of a pattern is $\dfrac{x}{4}$. What are the 8th and 16th terms of this pattern? Show your work.

6m62 extend and create repeating patterns that result from rotations, through investigation using a variety of tools

ROTATING PATTERNS

A rotation is a change in a figure or shape resulting from a turn of that figure about a fixed point. The fixed point is called a point of rotation. The shape or the size of the shape does not change. An example of a rotation of a shape is shown below.

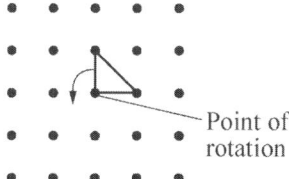

The triangle shown above is the core unit. The core unit is then rotated counterclockwise.

Original triangle (core unit)

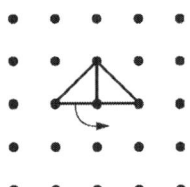

Original triangle and 1 image after a
90 ° counterclockwise rotation

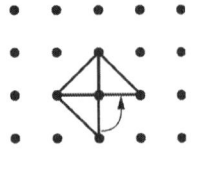

Original triangle and 2 images after
a second 90 ° counterclockwise
rotation

Original triangle and 3 images after
a third 90 ° counterclockwise
rotation

Use the following information to answer the next question.

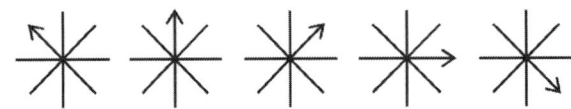

12. If the given pattern continues, which diagram will be next?

A.

B.

C.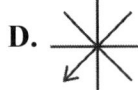

D.

Use the following information to answer the next question.

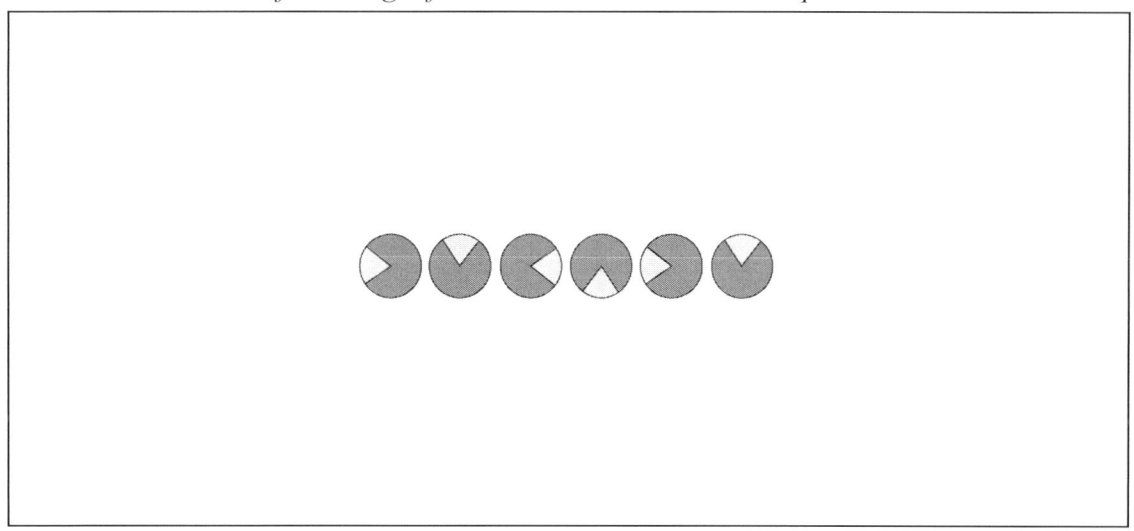

13. What will be the next figure in the given pattern?

A.    B.

C. 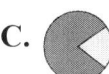   D.

6m63 demonstrate an understanding of different ways in which variables are used

VARIABLES

A **variable** is a symbol or letter that can be used to represent an unknown quantity or value in an equation. A variable can also represent a changing quantity. A constant is a value that does not change.

VARIABLE AS AN UNKNOWN QUANTITY

In the equation $2n + 1 = 9$, the numbers 1 and 9 are the constants. They do not change. The letter n is the variable. It represents an unknown value or quantity. The value of the unknown quantity must make the equation true.

The equation is only true if $n = 4$.
You can check this by replacing n with 4 in the equation: $2 \times 4 + 1 = 9$.
If n has any other value, the equation is false. Therefore, n is a variable that has only one quantity that will make the equation a true statement.

Any symbol or letter can be used to represent the unknown quantity in an equation. For example, all the following equations have the same quantity for the variable:
$n + 1 = 18$
$p + 1 = 18$
$\Delta + 1 = 18$

When one variable is used in an equation but appears more than once, the variable still has only one value.

For example, in the equation $n + n = 4$, the variable n has only one unknown quantity that will make the equation a true statement: $n = 2$.

You can check this by replacing n with 2 in the equation: $2 + 2 = 4$
The value of n is the same in all parts of the equation.
Therefore, the variable has only one value. In this case, $n = 2$.

VARIABLE AS A CHANGING QUANTITY

The formula for the area of a rectangle is Area = base × height or $A = b \times h$. There are three variables in the formula: A, b, and h. One of the variables could be held constant and the other two variables could each have a changing quantity. For example, if $A = 12$, the formula becomes $12 = b \times h$, where 12 is the constant and b and h are variables. The number 12 is the constant because it does not change. If $b = 2$, then h must equal 6 in order to make the formula a true statement: $12 = 2 \times 6$. If $b = 3$, then $h = 4$.

When there are two different variables in an equation, the values for those variables may be equal or unequal.

For example, in the equation $a + n = 4$, when $a = 1$, $n = 3$, and after replacing a with 1 and n with 3, the equation becomes $1 + 3 = 4$. If $a = 2$, then $n = 2$ and the equation becomes $2 + 2 = 4$. If $a = 3$, then $n = 1$ and the equation becomes $3 + 1 = 4$.

There are many possible solutions, and one solution could include a being the same number as n. Therefore, the variables have changing quantities.

Equations that have a variable as a changing quantity must have at least two different variables in the same equation.

Use the following information to answer the next question.

A square is represented by the variable y, as shown in the diagram.

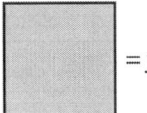

$= y$

14. If y represents one square, then $4y$ represents

A. 1 square   **B.** 2 squares

C. 3 squares   **D.** 4 squares

6m64 identify, through investigation, the quantities in an equation that vary and those that remain constant

QUANTITIES IN EQUATIONS THAT CAN CHANGE OR REMAIN CONSTANT

An **expression** is a collection of symbols representing numbers and operations that represent a quantity. Examples of expressions are $3 + 2$, $7 + n$, and $4 \times a$. The last two expressions are general terms because they can represent many different quantities, depending on the values of their variables.

An **equation** is a statement that says that two mathematical expressions have the same value. It uses an equal sign (=) to tell you that the two expressions have the same value. An example of an equation is $4 \times a = 12$. It states that $4 \times a$ and 12 have the same value. This is true only if $a = 3$.

$4 \times a = 12$

$4 \times 3 = 12$

$12 = 12$

Quantities in an equation that vary or change are represented by variables in the equation. The quantities in an equation that remain constant are represented by numbers. An equation that has two different variables has many possible quantities for these two variables to make the equation a true statement.

Example

The area of a rectangle is calculated using the formula $A = b \times h$. If you are told that the area of the rectangle is 48 cm², then the equation becomes $48 = b \times h$. The area is a constant value of 48 cm². The quantities in this equation that change are represented by b for the base length and h for the height or width. As the base length increases, the height decreases, since the product or area is constant.

The following table shows the value that is constant and the values that change.

Area (constant)	Base (changes)	Height (changes)
48 cm²	48 cm	1 cm
48 cm²	24 cm	2 cm
48 cm²	16 cm	3 cm
48 cm²	12 cm	4 cm
48 cm²	8 cm	6 cm

Example

The formula for the area of a triangle is $A = \dfrac{b \times h}{2}$.

The variables in the formula $A = \dfrac{b \times h}{2}$ are A, b, and h. Therefore, the quantities represented by these variables vary. As the length of the base and the height of the triangle change, the area may change. Similarly, as the area of the triangle and the length of the base change, the height may change. Also, as the area of the triangle and the height of the triangle change, the base may change. To find the area of a triangle, the product of the base and the height is always divided by 2. Therefore, the number 2 remains constant in the formula.

---

15. Which of the following values changes at a constant rate?

    A. Age   **B.** Weight

    C. Rainfall   **D.** Temperature

16. How many variables and constants are in the equation $y = 3x + z + 6$?

    A. Two constants and one variable   **B.** Two variables and one constant

    C. Three constants and one variable   **D.** Three variables and one constant

6m65 solve problems that use two or three symbols or letters as variables to represent different unknown quantities

SOLVING MULTIPLE RELATED EQUATIONS

When solving problems involving variables in which two equations are provided, one equation can be used to solve the other equation.

Example

Given the two equations: $n + 2 = 16$, $n + 2 + s = 17$, you can find the value of s.

By examining the two equations, you can see that $n + 2$ appears in both equations.
Since $n + 2 = 16$, you can replace $n + 2$ in the second equation with 16.

     $n + 2 + s = 17$ becomes $16 + s = 17$

To solve the equation, $16 + s = 17$, ask yourself, "What number is added to 16 to equal 17?"
Since $16 + 1 = 17$, $s = 1$.

Example

Given the two equations $x - 8 = 2$ and $y + x - 8 = 15$, what value does the y represent?

Equation 1: $x - 8 = 2$
Equation 2: $y + x - 8 = 15$

There are two methods you can use to solve this problem.

Solution 1

Examining the two equations, you can see that $x - 8$ appears in both equations.
Since $x - 8 = 2$, you can replace $x - 8$ in the second equation with 2.

$y + x - 8 = 15$	Replace $x - 8$ with 2
$y + 2 = 15$	Ask yourself, "What number plus 2 equals 15?"
$y = 13$	$13 + 2 = 15$

Solution 2

By examining the two equations, you can see that the first equation has only one variable and the second equation has two variables.

First, solve the first equation: $x - 8 = 2$
Ask yourself, "What number minus 8 equals 2?"
$10 - 8 = 2$
Therefore, $x = 10$.

Now, solve the equation.

$y + x - 8 = 15$	Replace the x with 10
$y + 10 - 8 = 15$	Solve the part of the equation $10 - 8$
$y + 2 = 15$	Now, ask yourself, "What number plus 2 is the same as 15?"
$y = 13$	$13 + 2 = 15$

---

17. If $(m + 10) \times 6 = [(n \times 2) + 10] \times 6$, then the variable m is equal to
    A. n **B.** $2n$

    C. $3n$ **D.** $4n$

18. If $x - 6 = 14$ and $2x - 30 + 5y = 35$, what is the value of y?
    A. 3   **B.** 5

    C. 10   **D.** 12

Use the following information to answer the next question.

Yoshi and Masa are two brothers whose birthday falls on the same day. In the year 2006, the relation between Yoshi's age (x) and Masa's age (y) is $y = x + 5$.

19. Which of the following statements is **best** supported by the equation?

   A. Yoshi is five years younger than Masa.

   B. Yoshi is five years older than Masa.

   C. Yoshi is five times as old as Masa.

   D. Yoshi and Masa are twins.

6m66 determine the solution to a simple equation with one variable, through investigation using a variety of tools and strategies

SOLVING EQUATIONS

An equation with one variable is a number sentence that includes an equals sign with one letter or symbol for the variable. An example of an equation that includes one variable is

   $2 \times n + 3 = 7$.

There are a variety of methods to use to find the value of a variable in a simple equation.

SOLVING AN EQUATION USING BALANCE SCALE RULES

The equals sign in an equation means "the same quantity as". To show that each side of the equals sign represents the same quantity, you can use the idea of a balance scale.
When the scale is balanced, you know that both sides of the scale contain the same quantity in terms of mass.

To keep the scale balanced, you must remember that any operation that is performed on one side of the equation or balance must be performed on the other side of the equation or balance in order to keep the equation or scale balanced.

The following are four rules to follow when solving an equation:

- Any quantity that is added to one side must be added to the other side.
- Any quantity that is subtracted from one side must be subtracted from the other side.
- Any quantity that is multiplied on one side must be multiplied on the other side.
- Any quantity that is divided on one side must be divided on the other side.

Example
To balance the second balance scale, how many blocks would have to be placed on the right side? Assume that each cylinder weighs the same and that each block weighs the same. Explain your thinking.

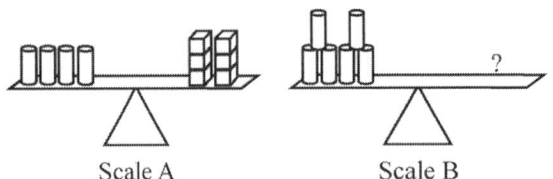

Scale A   Scale B

Solution

On scale *A*, you can divide the number of cylinders in half on the left side and also divide the number of blocks in half on the right side. Therefore, 2 cylinders will balance 3 blocks as shown below. For every 2 cylinders, you need 3 blocks.

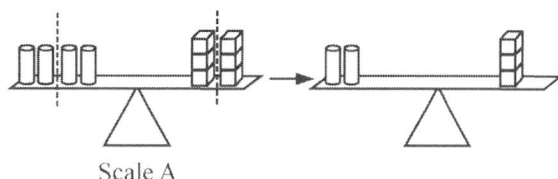

Scale A

Since there are three groups of 2 cylinders on the left of scale *B*, three groups of 3 blocks are needed on the right of scale *B* to show equality.

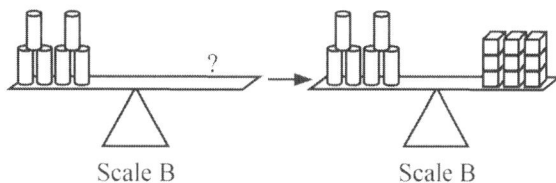

Scale B   Scale B

Nine blocks must be placed on the right side to balance the 6 cylinders on the balance scale.

Example

Use the balance scale below to illustrate and solve the equation $7 = \square + 5$.

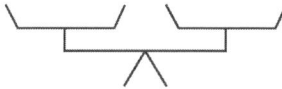

Solution

Use blocks to represent the constants on the balance scale. The constants are 7 and 5.

Use a bag to represent the variable. The variable in the equation is $\square$.

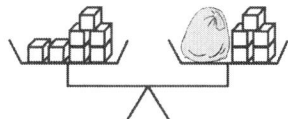

Following the second rule, remove 5 blocks from each side of the scale.

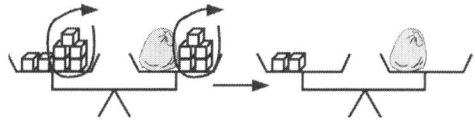

The balances 2 cubes, and therefore has the same number quantity as 2.

The solution to the equation is $\square = 2$.

Then you have

$$7 = 2 + 5$$
$$7 = 7$$

Both sides of the equation have the same quantity.
There is only one solution because there is only one variable in the equation. Therefore, there is only one number that will make the equation a true statement.

SOLVING AN EQUATION USING AN ALGORITHM

When solving equations, the same rules that apply to the balance scale apply to the equation. What you do to one side, you must do to the other side.
To solve for a variable, you must get the variable alone on one side of the equation.

Example
Solve the equation $2 + a = 6$.

Solution

According to the second rule, if a constant is added to the variable, you must subtract that constant from both sides. To find the value of a, subtract 2 from both sides:

$$\begin{array}{rcl} 2+\ a= & & 6 \\ \underline{-2\ \ \ \ = -2} & & \\ 0+\ a= & & 4 \\ a= & & 4 \end{array}$$

20. Ali has $2 more than twice the amount of money that Roy has. If Roy has $2, how much money does Ali have?

    A. $4   B. $6

    C. $10   D. $12

21. What is the value of y in the equation $3y + 1 = 28$?

    A. 1   B. 3

    C. 5   D. 9

ANSWERS AND SOLUTIONS
PATTERNING AND ALGEBRA

1. B	6. C	11. OR	16. D	21. D
2. C	7. A	12. B	17. B	
3. OR	8. B	13. C	18. B	
4. C	9. C	14. D	19. A	
5. D	10. D	15. A	20. B	

1. B

The set of blocks that form the repeating part of the pattern are 2 triangles, 1 square, and 2 triangles.

$$2 \triangle + 1 \blacksquare + 2 \triangle$$

2. C

Start with 12 and follow the given rule: subtract 2, and double the result.

$12 - 2 = 10 \times 2 = 20$

$20 - 2 = 18 \times 2 = 36$

$36 - 2 = 34 \times 2 = 68$

To make it easier to see the ordered pairs, put them in a table.

12	20
20	36
36	68

These values are the same as the pairs in C.

(12, 20), (20, 36), (36, 68)

3. OR

Points	Sample Answer
4	Is able to extend a pattern given the pattern rule and list the ordered pairs.

For the pattern rule,
start with 100, then subtract 20 from each term, the table of values would look like this:

Term Number	100	80	60	40	20
Term Value	80	60	40	20	0

In ordered pairs, the term number comes first, then the term value. For the given rule, the ordered pairs are as follows:

(100, 80), (80, 60), (60, 40), (40, 20), (20,0)

Points	Sample Answer
3	Is able to extend a pattern, given the pattern rule, and list the ordered pairs with minor errors.
2	Is somewhat able to extend a pattern, given the pattern rule, and list the ordered pairs, but with errors.
1	Is somewhat able to extend a pattern, given the pattern rule, and somewhat able to list the ordered pairs, but with errors.

4. C

The pattern shows that each number decreases by 3. To find the next number in the pattern, subtract 3 from 6.

$6 - 3 = 3$

The next number in the pattern is 3.

5. D

To find the correct table, look at each **In** term and divide it by 2 to see if the **Out** terms match the pattern rule.

- In table, $76 \div 2$ does not equal 39, so the table does not follow the pattern rule.
- In table , $98 \div 2$ does not equal 48, so the table does not follow the pattern rule.
- In table , $68 \div 2$ does not equal 35, so the table does not follow the pattern rule.
- In table , all of the In numbers divided by 2 equal the corresponding Out numbers, so the table follows the pattern rule.

6. C

The pattern shows that each number increases by 5. To find the next number in the pattern, add 5 to 17.

$17 + 5 = 22$

The pattern is

7. A

The numbers in the pattern decrease. To find the pattern rule, find the difference between each number.

$9\ 045 - 8\ 035 = 1\ 010$

$8\ 035 - 7\ 025 = 1\ 010$

$7\ 025 - 6\ 015 = 1\ 010$

Therefore, the pattern rule is to subtract 1 010 each time.

8. B

Identify the pattern by applying each pattern rule to the first term number and term.

For alternative A: $2 + 1 = 3 \times 2 = 6$. This term does not correspond to the one in the given table.

For alternative B: $2 \times 2 = 4 + 1 = 5$. This term does correspond to the one in the given table.

For alternative C: $2 - 1 = 1 \times 2 = 2$. This term does not correspond to the one in the given table.

For alternative D: $2 \times 2 = 4 - 1 = 3$. This term does not correspond to the one in the given table.

The following table represents the pattern when the correct pattern rule is applied.

Term Number	Term
2	$2 \times 2 + 1$
5	$5 \times 2 + 1$
8	$8 \times 2 + 1$
9	$9 \times 2 + 1$
12	$12 \times 2 + 1$

The expression that can be used to find the missing term in the given table is: double the term number and add 1.

9. C

Step 1

The pattern shows that the amount of beef increases. Find the difference between each amount:

$1\ 500 - 1\ 250 = 250$
$1\ 250 - 1\ 000 = 250$
$1\ 000 - 750 = 250$
$750 - 500 = 250$

Therefore, the amount of beef increases by 250 g for every two servings.

Step 2

The pattern shows that the amount of beans increases. Find the difference between each amount:

$875 - 700 = 175$
$700 - 525 = 175$
$525 - 350 = 175$
$350 - 175 = 175$

Therefore, each amount of beans increases by 175 g for every two servings.

Mia needs 250 g more of beef and 175 g more of beans for every two servings.

10. D

The pattern shows that each term decreases. Find the difference between each term:

$94 - 84 = 10$

$84 - 75 = 9$

$75 - 67 = 8$

$67 - 60 = 7$

$60 - 54 = 6$

Therefore, between each term there is one less taken away each time. By following the pattern, the next amount to subtract from the previous term would be 5.
So, $54 - 5 = 49$.

The next term would be 49.

11. OR

Points	Sample Answer
4	Understands how to find the value of a term in a sequence, given the general term.

Points	Sample Answer
	The general term $= \dfrac{x}{4}$ 8th term $= \dfrac{8}{4} = 2$ 16th term $= \dfrac{16}{4} = 4$ Therefore, the required terms are 2 and 4.
3	Understands how to find the value of a term in a sequence given the general term, with minor errors.
2	Understands somewhat how to find the value of a term in a sequence given the general term, with errors.
1	Does not understand how to find the value of a term in a sequence given the general term.

12. B

If the rotating pattern continues, the arrow will continue to move clockwise and will be facing straight down. Diagram B shows the arrow facing straight down.

13. C

If the pattern continues, the triangle in the circle will move clockwise and will be facing to the right.

14. D

$4y$ is the same as $4 \times y$

$y + y + y + y = 4y$

Therefore, if 1 square $= y$, then $4y = 4$ squares.

15. A

The age of a person increases at a constant rate over time.

16. D

In the equation $y = 3x + z + 6$, when the value of x or z changes, the value of y also changes.

Therefore, x, y, and z are variables, and 6 is a constant.

There are three variables and one constant in the given equation.

17. B

$(m + 10) \times 6 = [(n \times 2) + 10] \times 6$

Divide each side by 6:

$m + 10 = n \times 2 + 10$

Subtract 10 from each side:

$m = n \times 2$

$n \times 2$ is the same as $2n$. Therefore, $m = 2n$.

18. B

$x - 6 = 14$

Add 6 to each side to get $x = 20$.

If $x = 20$, substitute 20 into $2x - 30 + 5y = 35$.

$2 \times 20 - 30 + 5y = 35$

$40 - 30 + 5y = 35$

$10 + 5y = 35$

$5y = 35 - 10$ (subtract 10 from each side)

$5y = 25$

$y = 25 \div 5$ (divide each side by 5)

$y = 5$

Therefore, the value of y is 5.

19. A

The variable x represents Yoshi's age, and the variable y represents Masa's age.

The relation $y = x + 5$ indicates that y is 5 more than x. So, $y = x + 5$ indicates that Masa's age is 5 more than Yoshi's age. In other words, Yoshi is 5 years younger than Masa.

Therefore, Yoshi is five years younger than Masa.

20. B

It is given that Ali has $2 more than twice the amount Roy has.

This can be expressed as $2R + \$2 = A$, where R is Roy's money and A is Ali's money.

Roy has $2. This can be expressed as $R = \$2$.

Substitute $2 for R and solve for A.

$A = (\$2 \times 2) + \$2$ $A = \$4 + \$2$ $A = \$6$

Ali has $6.

21. D

The only variable in the given equation is y.

$3y + 1 = 28$

Subtract 1 from both sides:

$3y = 27$

Divide both sides by 3:

$y = 9$

The correct answer is D.

UNIT TEST — PATTERNING AND ALGEBRA

1. Akeel uses shapes to make the given pattern.

    Which of the following pattern rules **best** describes Akeel's pattern?

    A. 1 + 1 + 1   **B.** 1 + 1 + 1 + 1

    C. 1 + 1 + 2 + 1   **D.** 1 + 1 + 2 + 1 + 1

2. Which of the following tables represents the pattern rule: double the term and add 2?

A.	Term	Result
	3	10
	10	24
	24	52
	52	108

B.	Term	Result
	3	6
	6	12
	12	24
	24	48

C.	Term	Result
	2	6
	6	14
	14	30
	30	62

D.	Term	Result
	2	5
	5	11
	11	23
	23	47

Use the following information to answer the next question.

A Pattern Rule

Start with 1, then double each term and add 1 to the result.

Open Response

3. Complete the table of values for the given pattern rule. Then, plot the ordered pairs on the grid.

Term Number				
Term Value				

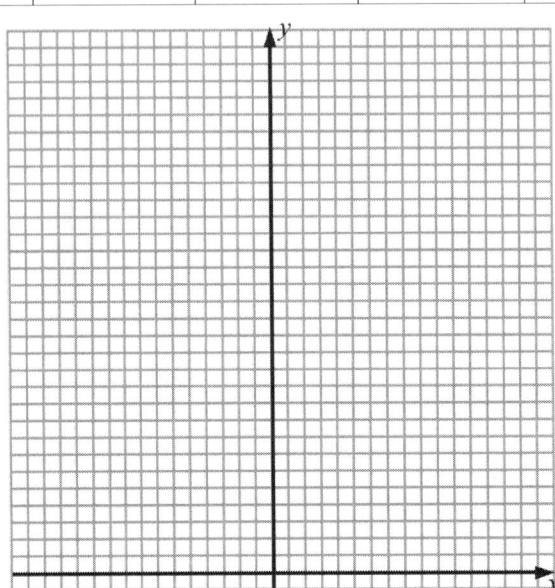

Mrs. Miller asked her students to bring pictures of their pets to school.
The following graph shows how many pictures of each animal the students brought to school. The number of fish pictures has not been filled in.

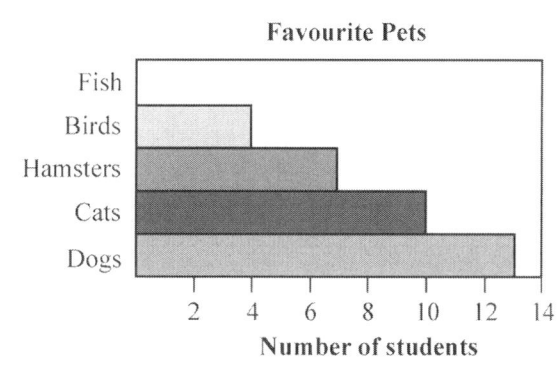

Favourite Pets

4. If the pattern on the graph continues, then how many students brought pictures of fish?
   A. 0   B. 1
   C. 2   D. 3

Use the following information to answer the next question.

A Number Pattern

(80) (73) (66) (59) (52) ( )

5. Which of the following numbers completes the pattern?
   A. 43   B. 44
   C. 45   D. 46

Use the following information to answer the next question.

The temperatures of a town over a few days in January are recorded in the following table.

Day	Temperature
January 16	8°C
January 17	6°C
January 18	4°C
January 19	2°C

6. If the temperature continues to drop at the same rate, what will the temperature on January 20 be?
   A. –4°C   B. 0°C
   C. 2°C   D. 4°C

Use the following information to answer the next question.

A Number Pattern
109, 104, 99, 94, 89

---

7. Which of the following pattern rules matches the given number pattern?
   A. Start with 109 and add 5   **B.** Start with 109 and add 10
   C. Start with 109 and subtract 5   **D.** Start with 109 and subtract 10

Use the following information to answer the next question.

A Number Pattern
5, 9, 17, 33, 65, 129

---

8. Which of the following statements describes the pattern for determining a term in the given number pattern?
   A. Double the previous term and add 1 to the result.

   B. Add 1 to the previous term and double the result.

   C. Subtract 1 from the previous term and double the result.

   D. Double the previous term and subtract 1 from the result.

9. What is the next number in the pattern 3, 7, 15, 31?
   A. 54   **B.** 56
   C. 58   **D.** 63

10. What is the missing term in the number pattern 30, 26, 22, __, 14, 10?
    A. 6   **B.** 16
    C. 18   **D.** 20

Use the following information to answer the next question.

A snowflake is a geometric pattern that is made up of smaller shapes that are copies of the original shape. The number of points created during the construction of a snowflake forms the geometric sequence 6, 18, 54, …

Open Response

11. What is the fifth term of this sequence? Explain your thinking.

Use the following information to answer the next question.

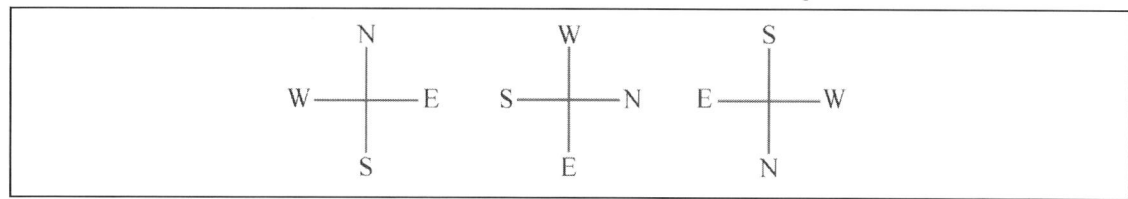

12. Which of the following figures comes next in the pattern?

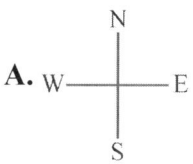 **A.**

B.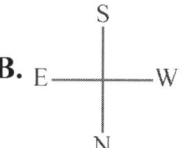

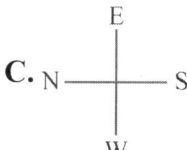 **C.**

D.

13. How many unknown variables are in the expression $n + n + 2n + n = 15$?

    A. 1   **B.** 2

    C. 3   **D.** 4

14. Which of the following situations is an example of a varying rate of change?

    A. Amount of snowfall in a year

    B. Distance covered by a car at a constant speed

    C. Time taken by Earth to complete one rotation about its axis

    D. Time taken by Earth to complete one revolution around the sun

15. If $x + 6 = 20$, and $x + 2y = 24$, what is the value of y?

    A. 3   **B.** 5

    C. 12   **D.** 14

16. If the symbol Δ represents 15, what is the value of the expression $\Delta \div \Delta$?

    A. 0   **B.** 1

    C. 15   **D.** 225

Use the following information to answer the next question.

Maria has 50 fewer marbles than Todd, who has n marbles.

17. What is the number of marbles that Maria has?

    A. $n - 50$ **B.** $n + 50$

    C. $n - 25$ **D.** $n + 25$

18. If $14.2 - x = 7.98$, what is the value of x?

    A. 0.18   **B.** 2.22

    C. 6.22   **D.** 22.18

ANSWERS AND SOLUTIONS — UNIT TEST

1.	D	6.	B	11.	OR	16.	B
2.	C	7.	C	12.	C	17.	A
3.	OR	8.	D	13.	A	18.	C
4.	B	9.	D	14.	A		
5.	C	10.	C	15.	B		

1. D

The core of the pattern must be known in order to identify this pattern. The pattern core of a repeating pattern is the smallest part that repeats. The pattern core in Akeel's pattern is small circle, large circle, small circle, small circle, large circle, and triangle.

Written in numbers, the pattern rule would be $1 + 1 + 2 + 1 + 1$.

Therefore, the pattern rule that Akeel uses is D.

2. C

Step 1

Apply the pattern rule to the first number of each table in the alternatives.

For alternative A: $3 \times 2 + 2 = 8$. This result does not correspond to the pattern rule.

For alternative B: $3 \times 2 + 2 = 8$. This result does not correspond to the pattern rule.

For alternative C: $2 \times 2 + 2 = 6$. This result follows the pattern rule

For alternative D: $2 \times 2 + 2 = 6$. This result does not correspond to the pattern rule.

Step 2

Identify the alternative that follows the given pattern rule.

C $2 \times 2 + 2 = 6$. This result follows the pattern rule of double the term and add 2C.

C To verify, apply the pattern rule to the next terms in the same table.
$6 \times 2 + 2 = 14$, $14 \times 2 + 2 = 30$,
$30 \times 2 + 2 = 62$.

3. OR

Points	Sample Answer
4	Is able to extend a pattern given the pattern rule and plot the ordered pairs.

For the pattern rule, *start with 1, then double each term and add 1*, a table of values would look like this:

Points	Sample Answer
	Term Number	1	3	7	15
	Term Value	3	7	15	31

The ordered pairs would be (1, 3), (3,7), (7, 15), (15, 31).

To plot the ordered pairs on the grid, the term number is plotted along the *x*-axis and the term is plotted along the *y*-axis.

3	Is able to extend a pattern given the pattern rule and plot the ordered pairs with minor errors.
2	Is somewhat able to extend a pattern given the pattern rule, and plot the ordered pairs with errors.
1	Is somewhat able to extend a pattern given the pattern rule, and somewhat able to plot the ordered pairs with errors.

4. B

To find the pattern on the graph, read each bar and then compare the numbers.

It would be best to start with the longest bar and work toward the shortest bar.

There are 13 dogs, 10 cats, 7 hamsters, and 4 birds.

The pattern rule is to subtract 3 each time, in decreasing order, or to add 3 each time in increasing order.

$4 - 3 = 1$

If the pattern continues, 1 student will bring a picture of a fish.

B is the correct answer.

5. C

The pattern shows that each number decreases by 7. To find the next number in the pattern, subtract 7 from 52. $52 - 7 = 45$

The pattern is:

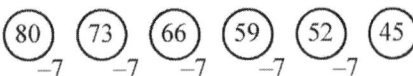

6. B

According to the table, the temperature decreases by 2°C each day.

The temperature on January 19 is 2°C.
2 − 2 = 0

Therefore, the temperature on January 20 should be 0°C.

7. C

The pattern shows that the numbers decrease, so the difference is found by subtracting five from the previous number.

109 − 104 = 5

104 − 99 = 5

99 − 94 = 5

94 − 89 = 5

Therefore, the pattern rule is to *start at 109 and subtract 5 each time*.

8. D

In A, starting with 5, the pattern would look like: 5(× 2 + 1), 11(× 2 + 1), 23, etc. This is incorrect.

In B, starting with 5, the pattern would look like: 5(+ 1 × 2), 12(+ 1 × 2), 26, etc. This is incorrect.

In C, starting with 5, the pattern would look like: 5(−1 × 2), 8(−1 × 2), 14, etc. This is incorrect.

In D, starting with 5, the pattern would look like: 5(× 2−1), 9(× 2−1), 17(× 2−1), 33(× 2−1), 65. This is correct.

9. D

The pattern shows that the numbers increase. The pattern rule is to multiply by 2 and add 1 each time.

3 × 2 + 1 = 7
7 × 2 + 1 = 15
15 × 2 + 1 = 31
31 × 2 + 1 = 63

Therefore, the next number in the pattern is 63.

10. C

The pattern shows to subtract 4 from each term to get the next term.

The number before the missing number is 22, so the missing number is 22 − 4.

22 − 4 = 18

The correct answer is C.

11. OR

Points	Sample Answer
4	Understands how to determine a pattern rule and extend a pattern.

The geometric sequence 6, 18, 54 is given.

The pattern rule can be found by calculating the number by which each term is multiplied to get the next term.

$\dfrac{18}{6} = 3$, $\dfrac{54}{18} = 3$.

The next number after 54 is equal to 54 × 3 = 162. Hence, 162 is the fourth term. To calculate the fifth term, multiply once more by 3.

Therefore, the fifth term is 162 × 3 = 486.

3	Understands how to determine a pattern rule and extend a pattern with minor errors.
2	Understands somewhat how to determine a pattern rule and extend a pattern with some errors.
1	Understands somewhat how to determine a pattern rule and extend a pattern with errors.

12. C

The first figure in the pattern is rotated clockwise 90° to become the second figure. The second figure is then rotated clockwise 90° to become the third figure. Thus, the third pattern can be rotated clockwise 90° to become the fourth pattern:

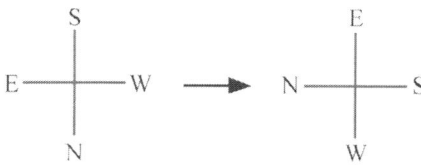

13. A

Unknown variables are variables with only one correct value. In the equation $n + n + 2n + n = 15$, there is only 1 unknown variable, n. Each variable, n, has the same value.

14. A

For a varying rate of change, the change does not occur at a constant rate. Since the amount of snowfall in a year is not constant, it has a varying rate of change.

15. B

If $x + 6 = 20$, then $x = 20 - 6$

Subtract 6 from each side to get $x = 14$.

Since $x = 14$, substitute 14 for x in $x + 2y = 24$.

$14 + 2y = 24$

Subtract 14 from each side.

$2y = 24 - 14$

$2y = 10$

Divide each side by 2.

$y = 5$

Therefore, the value of y is 5.

16. B

Since the value of the symbol Δ is 15,

$$\Delta \div \Delta = \frac{\Delta}{\Delta} = \frac{15}{15} = 1.$$

Thus, the value of $\Delta \div \Delta$ is 1.

17. A

The number of marbles Todd has $= n$.
Since Maria has 50 fewer marbles than Todd, the number of marbles Maria has $= n - 50$.

18. C

$14.2 - x = 7.98$

You know that if $14.2 - x = 7.98$, then $7.98 + x = 14.2$, and $14.2 - 7.98 = x$.

You can now find the value of x.

$14.2 - 7.98 = x$

$6.22 = x$

The value of x is 6.22.

NOTES

Data Management and Probability

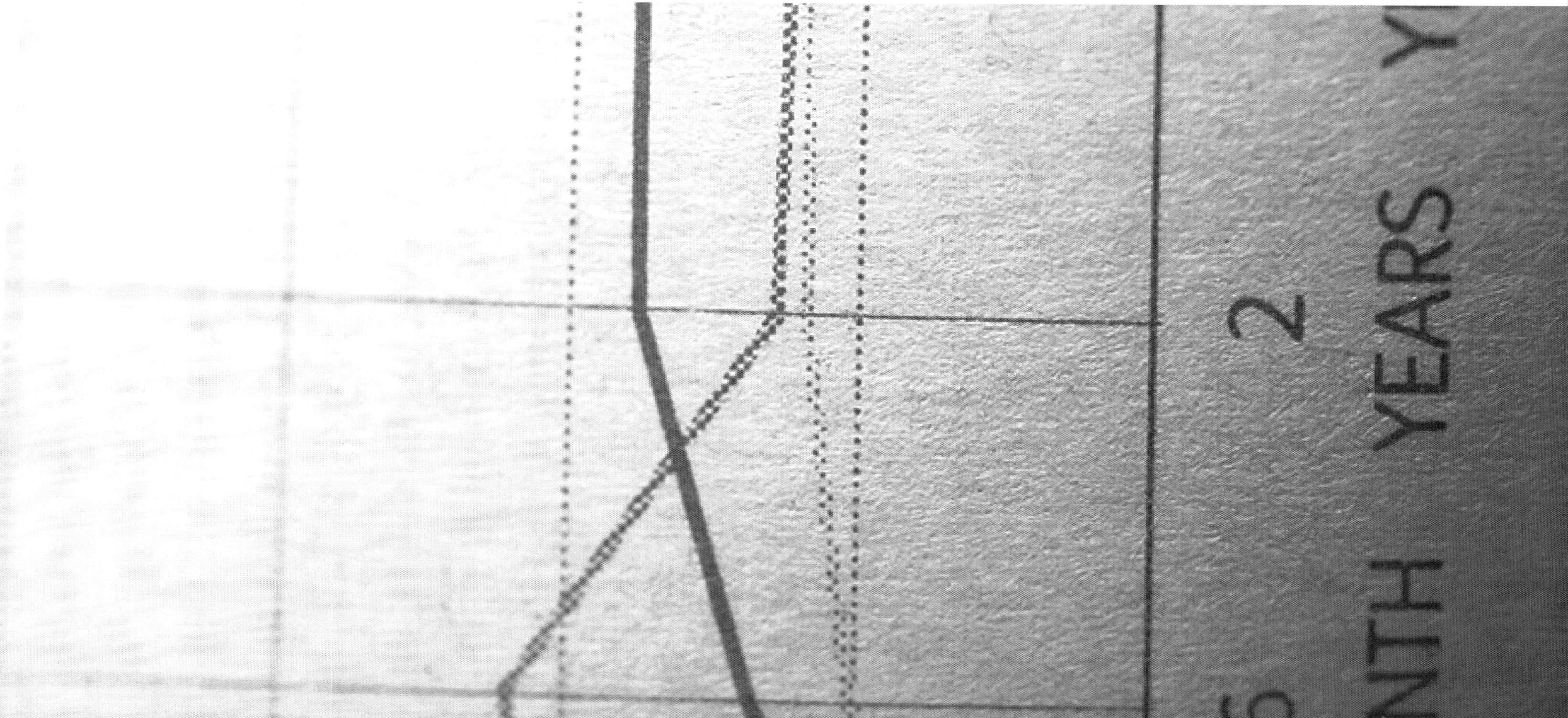

DATA MANAGEMENT AND PROBABILITY

Table of Correlations

Specific Expectation		Practice Questions	Unit Test Questions	Practice Test 1	Practice Test 2
6m67	Collection and Organization of Data				
6m70	*collect data by conducting a survey or an experiment to do with themselves, their environment, issues in their school or community, or content from another subject, and record observations or measurements*	1, 2	1	22	
6m71	*collect and organize discrete or continuous primary data and secondary data and display the data in charts, tables, and graphs (including continuous line graphs) that have appropriate titles, labels, and scales that suit the range and distribution of the data, using a variety of tools*	3, 4	2, 3		21
6m72	*select an appropriate type of graph to represent a set of data, graph the data using technology, and justify the choice of graph (i.e., from types of graphs already studied, such as pictographs, horizontal or vertical bar graphs, stem-and-leaf plots, double bar graphs, broken-line graphs, and continuous line graphs)*	5, 6	4	23	22
6m73	*determine, through investigation, how well a set of data represents a population, on the basis of the method that was used to collect the data*	7, 8	5, 6		23
6m68	Data Relationships				
6m74	*read, interpret, and draw conclusions from primary data and from secondary data, presented in charts, tables, and graphs (including continuous line graphs)*	9, 10	7	24	
6m75	*compare, through investigation, different graphical representations of the same data*	11, 12	8, 9		24
6m76	*explain how different scales used on graphs can influence conclusions drawn from the data*	13			
6m77	*demonstrate an understanding of mean, and use the mean to compare two sets of related data, with and without the use of technology*	14, 15	10	25	
6m78	*demonstrate, through investigation, an understanding of how data from charts, tables, and graphs can be used to make inferences and convincing arguments*	16	11		
6m69	Probability				
6m79	*express theoretical probability as a ratio of the number of favourable outcomes to the total number of possible outcomes, where all outcomes are equally likely*	17, 18, 19, 20	12, 13	32	31
6m80	*represent the probability of an event (i.e., the likelihood that the event will occur), using a value from the range of 0 (never happens or impossible) to 1 (always happens or certain)*	21, 22	14, 15		32
6m81	*predict the frequency of an outcome of a simple probability experiment or game, by calculating and using the theoretical probability of that outcome.*	23, 24, 25, 26	16, 17	33, 34	33

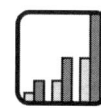

6m70 collect data by conducting a survey or an experiment to do with themselves, their environment, issues in their school or community, or content from another subject, and record observations or measurements

COLLECTING DATA

Data is information collected from observations, surveys, or an experiment. This information has been properly organized so that it may be understood by the person conducting the survey or experiment. Being able to organize and show the information collected is called data management.

EXPERIMENTS

In probability, an **experiment** is an activity completed in order to predict the chances of an event occurring in the future. For example, tossing a coin 4 times to see how many heads and tails occur. The results of the experiment are recorded.

SURVEYS

A **survey** is one method for gathering information. A survey is a list of questions that is asked to a group of people in order to discover their opinions. There are four steps to conducting a survey.

Step 1: Decide on the purpose of your survey
To help direct your purpose, you should ask yourself the following questions:
What do I want to find out about?
Why do I want to find this information?

Step 2: Create the survey by writing the questions to be asked
The survey will consist of questions you will ask a group of people to gather information about their opinions related to your objective. It is very important to ask questions that will get the best and most relevant data. You must also make sure that your questions do not mislead or influence the answer that may be given.

Examples of survey questions:

• How many students in Grade 6 like animated movies?
• What are the most popular weekend activities for students?
• What is the most favourite recess snack among Grade 6 students?

Step 3: Conduct the survey and record the results
Choose the method of recording your observations and organizing the data. To record your results, you can use a tally chart or a table.

Step 4: Read, describe, and interpret data
The final step is to read and interpret the data. These observations are what you see and what you learn from the results of your survey. These are the facts, or information, that you have discovered about your question.

Example

Survey question: What is your favourite weekend activity?

A specific question is being asked. You may choose to have options within your question where people can indicate which is their favourite activity.

Survey options: playing sports, reading books, spending time with friends, playing video games, or watching television.

You now need to organize your survey options to make it easier to record and interpret your results. Look at the sample chart below.

What is your favourite weekend activity?	Number of Students
Playing sports	50
Reading books	25
Watching television	12
Playing video games	19
Spending time with friends	45

Some sample observations that could be discovered from this kind of data are:

- The most favourite weekend activity is playing sports.
- The least favourite weekend activity is watching television.
- Six more people chose reading books than playing video games as their favourite weekend activity.
- More people chose spending time with friends as their favourite weekend activity than watching television.

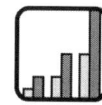

Use the following information to answer the next question.

Trisha surveys students in her class by asking them each a question. She makes this graph to show the results of the survey.

Trisha's Survey

Activities: Drawing, Painting, Clay work, Bead work

Number of students: 2 4 6 8 10 12

1. To get the results shown on the graph, which of the following survey questions could Trisha have asked the students?

   A. Is your favourite subject art?

   B. Do you prefer to paint or draw?

   C. Do you want to be a part of my survey?

   D. Which art class activity do you like the most?

2. Mrs. Smith's Grade 6 class wants to find out the average family size in Canada. Which of the following methods of data collection would be the **best** to obtain this information?

   A. Send out a questionnaire to all households.

   B. Go to public places and observe the size of all the families.

   C. Go to Statistics Canada's website and look at the recent Canadian census.

   D. Survey the school and use the information to estimate the average family size in Canada.

6m71 collect and organize discrete or continuous primary data and secondary data and display the data in charts, tables, and graphs (including continuous line graphs) that have appropriate titles, labels, and scales that suit the range and distribution of the data, using a variety of tools

DISPLAYING DATA

While collecting data, you can collect either discrete or continuous data. **Discrete data** is data that has a limited number of possible values, and all data is a whole number. For example, months of the year, days of the week, or students in a class. These are limited values to which you cannot add. **Continuous data** is data that has an unlimited number of possible values or is data that changes. For example, weather patterns, temperatures, or a tree's height over a long period of time.

All types of data can be displayed in charts, tables, and graphs. This helps to clearly communicate the data you have collected.

When you are displaying data in graphs, you need to be sure to label the *x*-axis and *y*-axis and give the graph a title. Here is an example of the location of these labels on a graph.

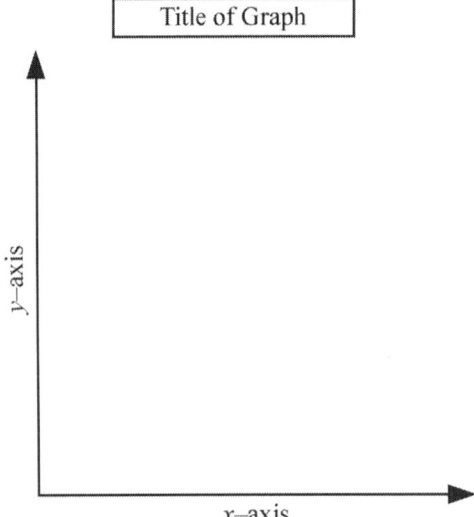

The *x*- and *y*-axis should be labelled with a proper name to indicate what they represent. In addition, the *x*- and *y*-axis should be labelled with appropriate number increments depending on what they represent. For example, if the *x*-axis represents cost, the increments should be shown as increments of a dollar value.

Having these labels will ensure that anyone trying to interpret your observations and data will be able to read the graph. People need to know what the numbers on the graph represent, so you must ensure that appropriate and equal increments, or intervals, are used and labelled properly.

Example

Here is a sample survey question that shows how to collect and record the data and display the results.

Step 1: Formulate your question
Which type of drink do students in Grade 6 drink the most in a one-week period?

Step 2: Choose a method of gathering data
In a survey: Ask students to keep track of which of the following types of drinks they consume in a one-week period: soft drinks, milk, water, and juice.

Step 3: Collect and record data
Use a table to gather data and enter the results on the table.

Type of Drink	Number of Drinks per Week
Soft drinks	15
Milk	30
Water	35
Juice	10

Step 4 Final presentation of results

Here you must show the results on a graph or chart with all the areas properly labelled.

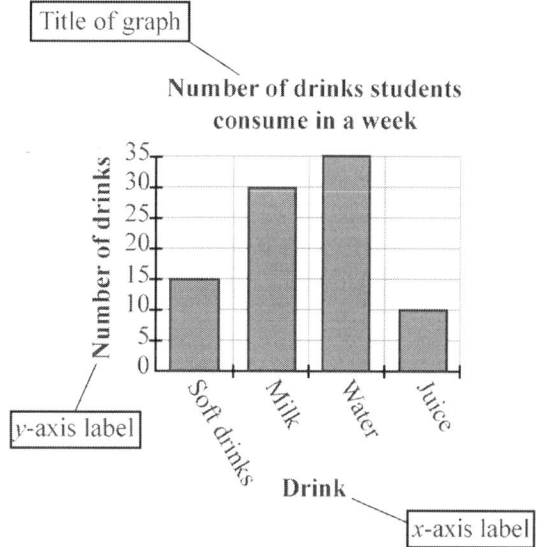

Above is the final chart showing the results of the experiment. The data displayed shows a title, properly labelled axes, and increments. From the results of this graph, you can interpret that water was the most consumed drink in that week, milk was second, soft drinks was third, and juice was the fourth.

This was an example of collecting **primary data**. It is information that you collect on your own. Secondary data is information that is not collected directly by you. Therefore, you would go to a source that has the data you need. For example, obtaining class lists from the school's office to compare the female population with the male population of the school would be an example of gathering **secondary data**. The data has already been collected by another person and then provided to you.

Use the following information to answer the next question.

Number of Medals Won in Different Sports	Number of Medals Won by Girls	Number of Medals Won by Boys
7 gold	5 gold	2 gold
11 silver	3 silver	8 silver
20 bronze	11 bronze	9 bronze

3. Which of the following double bar graphs correctly displays the given data?

A.

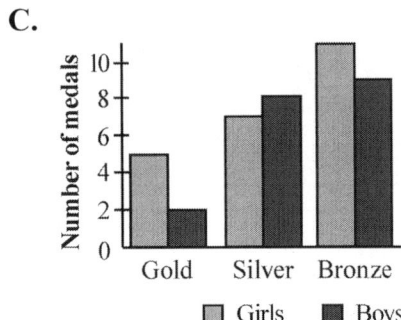

B.

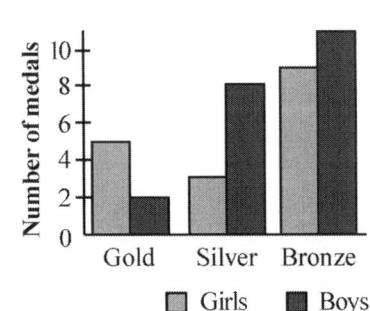

C.

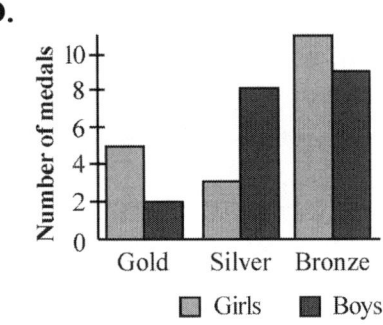

D.

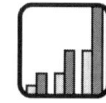

Use the following information to answer the next question.

Each student in Roberto's Grade 6 class read a book for 25 minutes on Monday. They increased their reading time by 5 minutes each day until Friday.

Open Response

4. Make a table to show the amount of reading Roberto's class did each day for a week and display the information on a line graph.

6m72 select an appropriate type of graph to represent a set of data, graph the data using technology, and justify the choice of graph (i.e., from types of graphs already studied, such as pictographs, horizontal or vertical bar graphs, stem-and-leaf plots, double bar graphs, broken-line graphs, and continuous line graphs)

SELECTING A GRAPH TO DISPLAY DATA

Data can be easier to understand and read if it is organized and presented in charts, tables, or graphs. A **graph** is a visual representation of data. Graphs are used to show a relationship between variables or to see if there is a relationship between variables. Usually, a graph depicts the relationship between numbers and amounts. Although different types of graphs can be used to represent the same data differently, one graph is often more appropriate to display certain data.

TYPES OF GRAPHS

You have already learned about **pictographs, bar graphs**, and **double bar graphs** in an earlier grade.

A **stem-and-leaf plot** is another method of displaying and organizing data to easily make comparisons. In a stem-and-leaf plot, the tens digit can be shown as the stem and the ones digit as the leaf.

In a stem-and-leaf plot of the numbers 31, 33, and 35, the stem is 3 and the leaves are 1, 3, and 5.

Stem	Leaves
3	1 3 5

A **broken-line graph** is a graph that shows the shape of the relationship between the values on the x- and y-axes with broken lines or line segments connecting the dots. Broken line graphs are often used to show changes over a period of time.

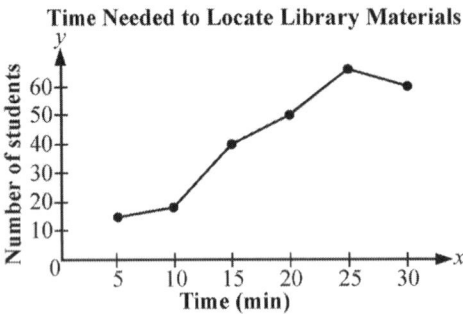

A **continuous line graph** is a graph that shows the relationship of two items as a continuous line. There are no broken segments to this line. Continuous line graphs are often used to display continuous data such as weather patterns or temperatures.

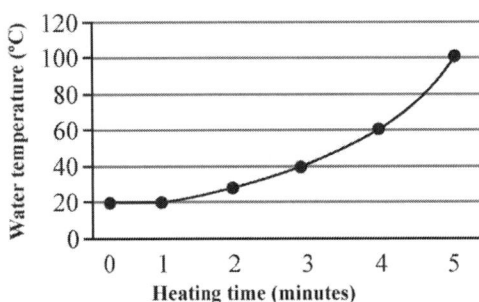

A **circle graph**, or pie chart, is a graph that is made by dividing a circle into sectors that represent parts of a whole. Usually, the amounts in each sector are represented in percent, so that all of the amounts total 100%.

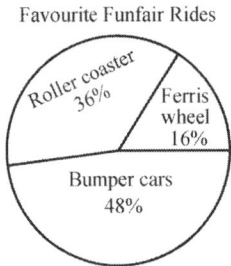

Data is easier to understand if it is organized and presented appropriately. All the graphs detailed above can be used to display collected data. Make sure to choose the appropriate type of graph to display your data when you have conducted an experiment.

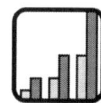

Use the following information to answer the next question.

The table shows the amount of snowfall in the town of Glendon for a period of 4 weeks.

Week	Snowfall (cm)
1	28
2	30
3	29
4	32

5. Which of the following types of graphs would **best** display the given data?

A. A Line Plot   **B.** A Venn Diagram

C. A Broken-Line Graph   **D.** A Stem-and-Leaf Plot

Use the following information to answer the next question.

Anand did a survey of his class to find out everyone's favourite colour.

Favourite Colour	Number of Students
Red	8
Blue	5
Purple	4
Orange	2
Yellow	6

Open Response

6. Make a graph to display this data and explain your choice of graph. Remember to include all titles and labels.

Draw and label the graph properly.

of the method that was used to collect the data

6m73 determine, through investigation, how well a set of data represents a population, on the basis of the method that was used to collect the data

SAMPLING DATA

Once you have formulated a survey question for investigation and chosen the method that you will use to gather the data, you need to decide whether it is appropriate to take a sample of a population or gather data from the entire population. The **population** refers to the entire group being discussed. A population could refer to all the students in a school or the all the people that live in a city.

Since the whole population is usually too large of a group to survey, a smaller group from the population is chosen. This smaller group is called a sample. Samples of the populations above could be one or two grades in the school or the people over age 50 who live in a city.

In order for a sample to be representative of a larger population, a sample needs to be sufficiently large, random, and unbiased. The number of people being sampled should be a large number to get a range of data. Making sure the sample is random will ensure that people from various interests and backgrounds will give data that is well balanced. Finally, the sample should be unbiased—the question should not influence a person's answer.

Example
If you were inquiring about the favourite sports of all Grade 6 students in your community, you could survey a sample of 50 students. Try to make sure your sample represents the entire population. Survey only Grade 6 students. If your population includes males and females of all ages, be sure your sample does as well. Remember, if your population is more limited, your sample should also be limited.

---

7. Bina is doing a survey to determine the type of drink preferred by adults. Which of the following methods of gathering data will **most likely** give him a representative sample?
    A. Doing a random telephone survey

    B. Polling the spectators at a basketball game

    C. Surveying all the employees in an office building

    D. Polling the students and teachers at a local high school

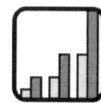

Use the following information to answer the next question.

A survey is conducted to test people's reaction to a new diet coffee that is being introduced into the market place. Patrons in a mall are offered a taste of the coffee and are asked to fill out a short questionnaire about the beverage.

8. Which of the following groups of people would most likely **not** represent the population targeted by the survey?

   A. Customers in a sporting goods store   **B.** Customers in a coffee shop

   C. High school students   **D.** Children

6m74 read, interpret, and draw conclusions from primary data and from secondary data, presented in charts, tables, and graphs (including continuous line graphs)

INTERPRETING PRIMARY AND SECONDARY DATA

INTERPRETING PRIMARY DATA

Remember that primary data is information that you collect on your own. Once you have collected and displayed your data, you can read, interpret, and draw conclusions from your data.

Example

   Lawrence is curious to find out the number and colour of cars that drive by his house on a Saturday between 10 A.M. and 12 P.M.

   Lawrence gathers the information and creates a graph to display the data he collected from his observations.

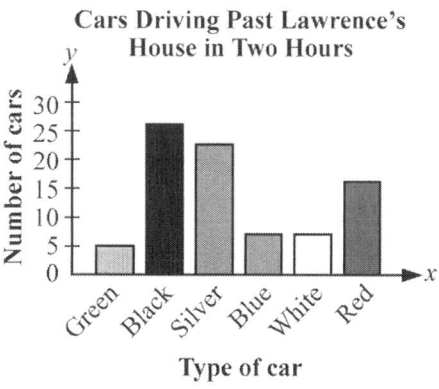

What is the **most popular** type of car in Lawrence's neighbourhood?

Solution

The bar that represents black cars is the highest. This means that black cars pass by Lawrence's house the most during this time period.

You can then draw conclusions about the data. You could conclude that black cars are the most popular in Lawrence's neighbourhood, while green cars are the least popular.

INTERPRETING SECONDARY DATA

Remember that secondary data is information that comes from another source. The data may come from the Internet, a newspaper, or a magazine. Sometimes secondary data is given as a chart or table, and other people make a graph of the data so that it is easier to interpret what the data means.

Example

Julia was reading the Sunday newspaper with her dad. She was very interested in topics related to population growth. She read an article that showed the population growth of Ontario from 2003 to 2007. The article included the graph shown below.

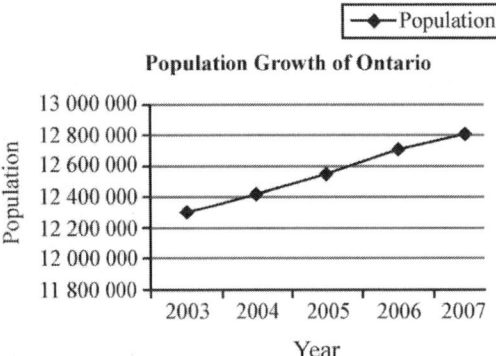

Julie can interpret and draw conclusions about the data. Julie can see from the continuous line graph that the population of Ontario has had a steady increase from 2003 to 2007. The largest increase occurred between 2003 and 2004. The smallest increase occurred between 2006 and 2007. By looking at the graph, Julie can also infer that the population is likely to continue growing over the next year.

By collecting and displaying data, you are able to see the information more clearly and draw conclusions about the information that you may not have been able to notice from observations alone.

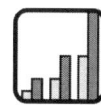

To train for a race, Ahmad runs 10 metres every second after a 2 second start.

9. Which of the following graphs describes the distance that Ahmad ran in each second of his training run?

A.

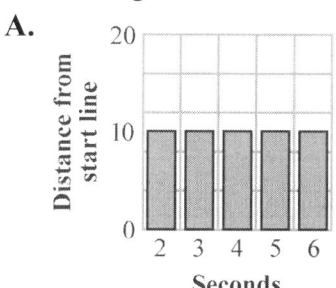

B.

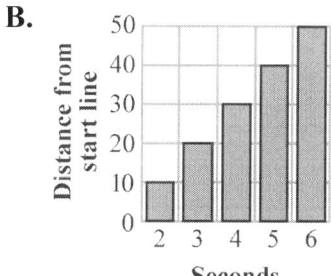

C.

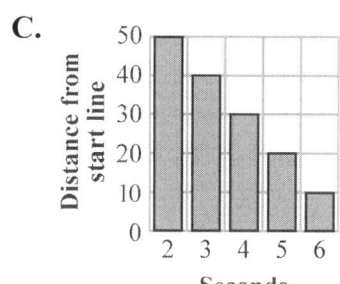

D.

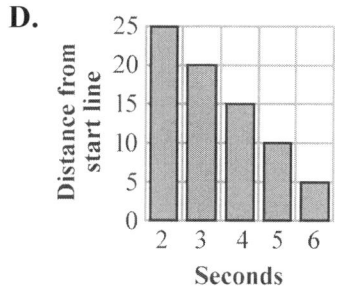

Use the following information to answer the next question.

Bob made a stem-and-leaf plot to show the weights, in kilograms, of some of the students in his class.

Stem	Leaves
2	4 6
3	8 9 9 9
4	1 2 4
5	0

10. From the given data, it can be assumed that most of the students' weights are in the

A. 20 kg range   **B.** 30 kg range

C. 40 kg range   **D.** 50 kg range

6m75 compare, through investigation, different graphical representations of the same data

COMPARING DIFFERENT GRAPHS THAT DISPLAY THE SAME DATA

You have been introduced to various types of graphs and charts. When you have conducted an experiment and want to record the data, make sure to choose the graph that best represents your data. Each type of graph and chart has its own advantages and disadvantages. When you are thinking about how to display your data, you must think about what you want to show, who will be using your graph, and what might affect the appearance of your graph.

Example
Below are three different types of graphs showing the same data. Notice what benefits and limitations each type of graph has.

As a **horizontal bar graph**:

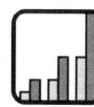

As a **pictograph**:

As a **circle graph, or pie chart**:

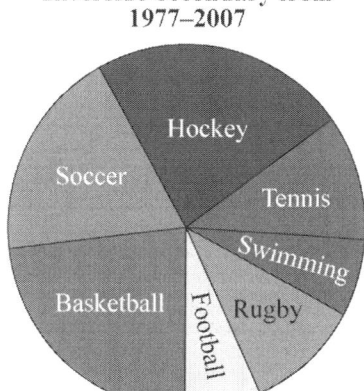

Now that you have taken a look at these three different graphs, you can see that they can all represent the same set of data.

There are some similarities and differences between the three graphs.

How the graphs are the same	How the graphs are different
Graphs give the same information	Easier to see which sport had the most wins on the horizontal graph or circle graph
Graphs are easy to read and understand	Need to calculate wins on the pictograph
Graphs are visually appealing	Circle graph shows most wins by size of section, but does not show numbers

Use the following information to answer the next question.

Aruna asked the students in her class, "What type of music do you like listening to?" Aruna used their answers to make the following picture graph. One CD represents one student vote.

Favourite Type of Music	Number of Students
Rock	🗂🗂🗂🗂🗂🗂🗂🗂
Country	🗂🗂🗂🗂🗂
Pop	🗂🗂🗂🗂🗂🗂
Jazz	🗂🗂🗂🗂

11. Which of the following tally charts shows the same information as the picture graph?

A.

Favourite Type of Music	
Rock	卌 |||
Country	卌
Pop	卌	
Jazz	||||

B.

Favourite Type of Music	
Rock	卌 ||
Country	卌
Pop	卌	
Jazz	||||

C.

Favourite Type of Music	
Rock	卌 |||
Country	||||
Pop	卌	
Jazz	||||

D.

Favourite Type of Music	
Rock	卌 |||
Country	||||
Pop	卌	
Jazz	|||

Use the following information to answer the next question.

Danny trains for the Iron Man competition by riding his bike for 6 hours per day. The bar graph shown illustrates his average speed per hour for each of the 6 hours.

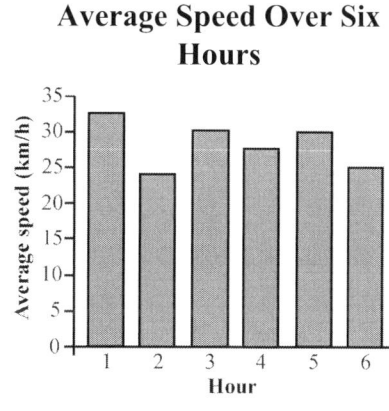

Average Speed Over Six Hours

12. Which of the following broken-line graphs represents the same data as in the given bar graph?

A.

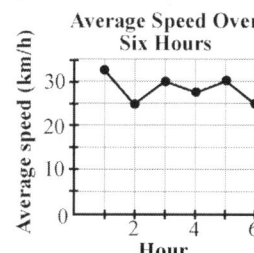

B.

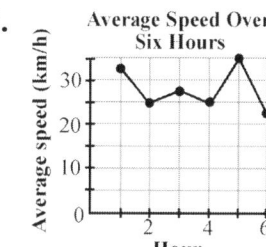

C.

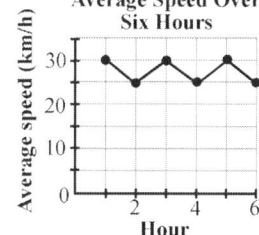

D.

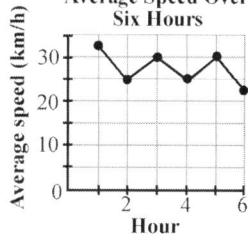

6m76 explain how different scales used on graphs can influence conclusions drawn from the data

UNDERSTANDING SCALES ON GRAPHS

A **scale** is a series of marks on a graph at set intervals that allow the reader to easily judge the value of a variable. On a graph, a scale is shown with a sequence of markers.

Example

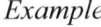

Here, you can see that each number has a marker on the line. This line can be either on the *x*-axis or *y*-axis. The numbers are in increasing order. The pattern of increase of the numbers depends on the data being recorded. The value of the numbers could increase by ones, fives, tens, hundreds, or any other number that is appropriate for the graph. The markers do not always have to be numbers; they can also be days of the week, months, or any other variable that is not a number.

Range is the span from the lowest number to the highest number in a set of data. When selecting a scale, it is always important to choose a scale that is appropriate to the range of your data. For example, if you are dealing with numbers from 12 000 to 15 000 in your data, you would likely use increments of 500 or 1 000. Choosing the right scale is most important to ensure that your data is properly displayed on the graph.

Example

Florian decided to take a survey of the exercise habits of Grade 4, 5, and 6 students at his elementary school. He wondered how many hours per week each student did some sort of physical activity. He did an email survey and asked the students to respond by email. For each grade, he added up each hour of physical activity done by each student in a week. He created a table to show his results.

Weekly Hours Physical Activity – Sherwood Elementary School Students

Grade	Hours
4	25
5	22
6	14

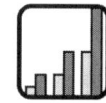

Once Florian had the data, he created a bar graph to show the results of his survey.

Weekly Hours of Physical Activity
- Sherwood Elementary School
Students

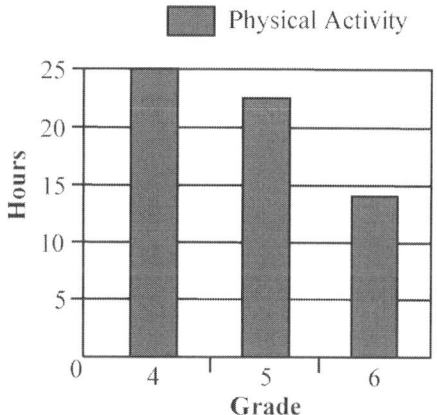

By looking at this graph, you can see the scales are for hours of physical activity and grade. The scale with the numbers shows a range of 0 to 25. This is a perfect range for the data set being displayed. Interpreting this graph, you can see that Grade 4 students are the most active and Grade 5 students are slightly less active. There is a gradual decline in activity from Grade 4 to Grade 6.

What would happen if the scale were different or incorrect?

Weekly Hours of Physical Activity
- Sherwood Elementary School

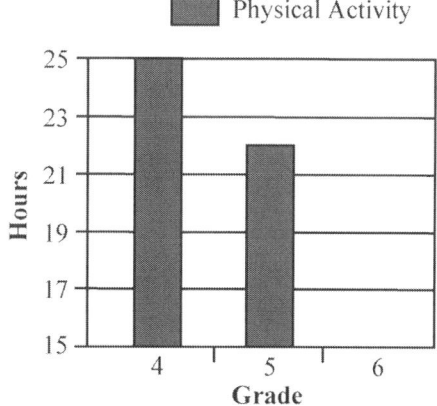

Here the scale ranges from 15 to 25. The scale begins at 15, so Grade 6 is not even on the graph. You can see that by changing the range of the scale, the same data looks very different. The interpretation of this data at first glance could be that Grade 6 does little to no physical activity. Also, the interpretation could be that Grade 4 does a lot more activity than Grade 5, and there is a large decline in activity from Grade 5 to Grade 6.

As you can see, making sure the scale is at an accurate range is the key to making sure your graph will be interpreted correctly and that the graph is an accurate representation of the data set.

Use the following information to answer the next question.

Jose asked all of the students at his school, "What is your favourite Internet activity?" He entered his findings into a table.

Internet activity	Number of people
Chat	134
Surf	225
Games	93
Music	160
Research	78

13. The **most appropriate** scale to represent Jose's findings is to count by

A. 2s   B. 5s

C. 10s   D. 20s

6m77 demonstrate an understanding of mean, and use the mean to compare two sets of related data, with and without the use of technology

DETERMINING THE MEAN OF A DATA SET

The **mean** of a data set is the average number in the data set. You can find the average or mean by adding all the numbers in a set and then dividing this sum by the number of items or numbers in the set.

Example

Find the mean of the following set of numbers:

12, 15, 12, 8, 12, 13

Add up all the numbers:

$12 + 15 + 12 + 8 + 12 + 13 = 72$

Since there are 6 numbers in the set, divide 72 by 6 to get the mean.

The mean is 12.

Example

Ryan and Angela live next door to each other. Ryan rode to school in his father's minivan, and Angela took the bus. They wondered which method of transportation was the fastest to get to school. They timed the journey from home to school for 10 days and recorded their results in the following table.

Ryan and Angela's Journey to School

Days	Bus travel (min)	Van travel (min)
1	25	21
2	22	21
3	21	21
4	25	25
5	30	27
6	27	25
7	23	25
8	20	21
9	22	21
10	25	23

As you can see from the data collected, there are many variations in the times for both methods of travel. Therefore, it is difficult to conclude from the data alone which method of transportation is most effective.

To answer the question, calculate the mean of each method of travel to find the average time it took per day to travel by bus and by van.

To find the average bus travel time, add the length of each trip and then divide by the number of trips.

$$\left(\begin{array}{l} 25 + 22 + 21 + 25 + 30 \\ +27 + 23 + 20 + 22 + 25 \end{array}\right) = 240$$

$$\frac{240}{10} = 24$$

You can conclude that it takes an average of 24 minutes to travel to school by bus.

To find the average van travel time, add the length of each trip and then divide by the number of trips.

$$\left(\begin{array}{l} 21 + 21 + 21 + 25 + 27 \\ +25 + 25 + 21 + 21 + 23 \end{array}\right) = 230$$

$$\frac{230}{10} = 23$$

You can conclude that it takes an average of 23 minutes to travel to school by van.

Overall, the conclusion you can make is that it takes an average of 23 minutes to travel to school by van and 24 minutes by bus. The answer to Ryan and Angela's question is that it is one minute faster to travel by van than bus.

Use the following information to answer the next question.

12 15 10 18 20 14 16

14. What is the mean of the given data?

    A. 10   **B.** 12

    C. 15   **D.** 20

Use the following information to answer the next question.

Ravi received the following marks on his math tests:

85 77 64 77 82

15. What is Ravi's mean math mark?

    A. 67   **B.** 77

    C. 87   **D.** 97

6m78 demonstrate, through investigation, an understanding of how data from charts, tables, and graphs can be used to make inferences and convincing arguments

UNDERSTANDING HOW TO MAKE INFERENCES FROM DATA

By looking at data from charts, tables, and graphs, you can make inferences about the data. An **inference** is a conclusion you reach by using your own background knowledge and reasoning. Being able to read and interpret graphs and charts is a valuable tool in understanding issues in your daily life. You can read, interpret, and use the data to support your thoughts on a topic and make inferences of what might occur beyond the data given. You can also make convincing arguments that support your own ideas.

Example

If you wanted to learn more about the topic of global warming, you could look at a graph from a newspaper or magazine that displays data on global temperatures.

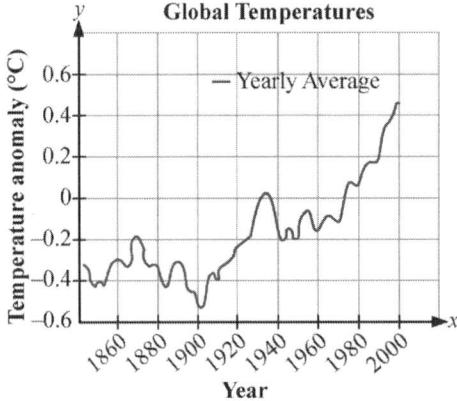

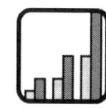

By looking at the graph, you can see that global temperatures have increased over the decades. You can see that the past decade was the hottest of the past 150 years. By making inferences, you may think that temperatures will continue to rise. By drawing conclusions, you may think that global warming is a true occurrence.

Use the following information to answer the next question.

Teen Girl is a magazine that caters to females 13 to 19 years old. Teen Girl recently asked its readers to complete a survey regarding school sports. Of the thousands of respondents, 65% indicated that they were on a school sports team and 70% indicated they played sports outside of school.

16. Which of the following inferences about the teenage population is supported by the survey?

   A. The majority of teenage girls like playing sports.

   B. The majority of teenagers like playing sports.

   C. The majority of teenage girls like school.

   D. The majority of teenagers like school.

6m79 express theoretical probability as a ratio of the number of favourable outcomes to the total number of possible outcomes, where all outcomes are equally likely

Probability is the chance that a particular outcome will occur. It gives information about the likelihood of an event occurring. When you use mathematics to calculate the probability of an event occurring without doing an experiment, it is called theoretical **probability**. **Experimental probabilities** are based on the results of an experiment.

THEORETICAL PROBABILITY

Outcomes can be either favourable or possible. A favourable outcome is the possible number of desired results of an experiment. The total results that can occur in an experiment are called possible outcomes. These two outcomes are usually compared using a ratio sign.

The probability formula states that the chance of an event occurring is the total favourable outcomes divided by the total possible number of outcomes.

$$\text{Theoretical Probability} = \frac{\text{total favourable outcomes}}{\text{total possible number of outcomes}}$$

Example

You could use this formula to determine the probability of rolling a 6 on a six-sided number cube. The number of possible outcomes when you roll a number cube one time is 6 because it has 6 sides. There is only 1 favourable outcome when you want to roll the number 5 because it appears only once on the cube.

The probability of rolling a 5 on a number cube is $\frac{1}{6}$.

Example

Determine the probability of rolling an odd number on a six-sided number cube.

Solution

You must first determine how many favourable outcomes and how many possible outcomes exist. When you roll a six-sided number cube there are 6 possible outcomes because it has 6 sides. There are only 3 odd numbers on a number cube: 1, 3, and 5. Therefore, there are 3 favourable outcomes.

The probability of rolling an odd number on a number cube is $\frac{3}{6}$, which, in lowest terms is $\frac{1}{2}$.

Use the following information to answer the next question.

In a large flower pot, there are 5 red flowers, 3 pink flowers, 4 white flowers, 6 yellow flowers. A bee lands on one of the flowers.

17. What is the probability of the bee landing on a pink or yellow flower?

A. $\frac{1}{6}$

B. $\frac{1}{3}$

C. $\frac{1}{2}$

D. $\frac{5}{9}$

Use the following information to answer the next question.

At Hilltop School, there are 50 students in Grade 7, of which 22 are boys.

18. If a student is chosen at random from the group of 50 students, what is the probability that the student chosen is male?

A. $\frac{1}{25}$

B. $\frac{11}{25}$

C. $\frac{25}{3}$

D. $\frac{25}{11}$

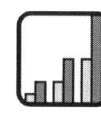

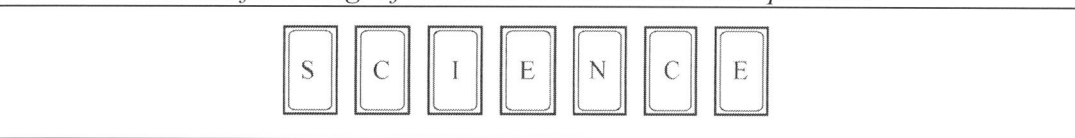

19. Tiles with letters written on them to form the word SCIENCE are placed in a box. Joe randomly chooses a tile from the box. What is the probability that Joe will choose a tile with a vowel on it?

   A. $\dfrac{1}{7}$ B. $\dfrac{2}{7}$

   C. $\dfrac{3}{7}$ D. $\dfrac{5}{7}$

Use the following information to answer the next question.

> Franz's mom bakes cookies for Franz to take to his grandma. She places 3 raisin, 5 spice, 4 bran, and 8 oatmeal cookies in a box.
>
> When Franz gets to his grandma's house, she reaches in the box without looking and takes one cookie.

| Open Response |

20. What is the probability that Franz's grandma will choose an oatmeal cookie? Show your work.

6m80 represent the probability of an event (i.e., the likelihood that the event will occur), using a value from the range of 0 (never happens or impossible) to 1 (always happens or certain)

EXPRESSING PROBABILITIES AS A VALUE FROM 0 TO 1

Probability is the chance that a particular outcome will occur. It is the likelihood of an event occurring. There are events in daily life that are certain and others that are impossible.

All probabilities can be expressed as a decimal number between 0 and 1. These numbers represent the likelihood of an event. The value 0 represents the probability of an impossible event or one that will never happen, such as rolling a 7 on a six-sided number cube. The value 1 represents an event that always happens or is certain, such as the sun rising in the morning.

For example, the probability of tossing a coin once and it landing on heads is $\dfrac{1}{2}$ or 0.5. The number of favourable outcomes—landing on heads—is 1, and the number of possible outcomes—landing on heads or on tails—is 2. Therefore, the probability of landing on heads is $\dfrac{1}{2}$ which is equal to 0.5.

Example

In a bag of 40 marbles, there are equal numbers of red, green, blue, and orange marbles. What is the probability of pulling a green marble out of the bag?

Solution

Since there are 40 marbles and there are equal numbers of each colour of marble, there must be 10 marbles of each colour in the bag (40 marbles ÷ 4 colours = 10 marbles of each colour). The number of favourable outcomes (pulling a green marble out of the bag) is 10, and the number of possible outcomes (pulling any colour of marble out of the bag) is 40. Therefore, the probability of pulling a green marble out of the bag of 40 marbles is $\frac{10}{40}$, which is equal to $\frac{1}{4}$ or 0.25.

You can see that by using the probability range from 0 to 1, you can give an event a numerical representation of its likelihood of occurring. You have learned that something that will always occur and is a certain event will have a numerical representation of 1. The number 0 represents those events that are impossible and will never occur. Everything else falls in between the 0 to 1 range and is in the form of a ratio or a decimal.

21. Janice asks her father to randomly pick a number from 1 to 5. What is the probability that her father will pick an odd number?

A. 0.25   **B.** 0.50

C. 0.60   **D.** 1.00

22. What is the probability of rolling an even number on an eight-sided number cube?

A. 0.25   **B.** 0.50

C. 0.75   **D.** 1.0

6m81 predict the frequency of an outcome of a simple probability experiment or game, by calculating and using the theoretical probability of that outcome.

PREDICTING THE FREQUENCY OF AN OUTCOME

You can use what you now know about theoretical probability to determine the probability of real-life events. You must know how many possible outcomes exist and how many favourable outcomes exist in a given circumstance. You must be sure that the experiment is fair, meaning that each outcome has an equal chance of occurring. If an experiment has a bias, then it is not a fair experiment.

To predict the frequency of an event in a probability experiment, you must calculate the theoretical probability of the outcome occurring once and then multiply the probability by the number of trials.

For example, the probability of tossing a coin and it landing on heads is $\frac{1}{2}$ or 0.5.

To find how many times a coin will land on heads in 20 tosses, multiply the probability of landing on heads by the number of tosses. Since 20 × 0.5 = 10, the number of times you could expect heads to be the result in 20 coin tosses is 10.

Example

If a colour wheel with four equal-sized areas with different colours is spun 100 times, predict how often the spinner will land on the same colour.

Solution

The probability of spinning the wheel and landing on any colour is $\frac{1}{4}$ or 0.25.

To predict how often the spinner will land on the same colour if the wheel is spun 100 times, multiply 0.25 by 100.
$0.25 \times 100 = 25$

If the wheel is spun 100 times, the spinner will land on the same colour about 25 times.

Use the following information to answer the next question.

The spinner shown is divided into 10 equal parts.

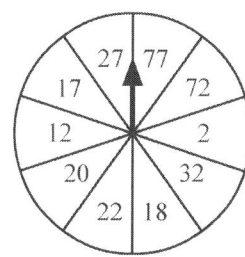

23. If Ron spins the spinner 20 times, how many times should the spinner land on a number that has a 2 in it?

    A. 3   **B.** 7

    C. 14   **D.** 20

24. If Paul tosses a coin 48 times, how many times should he expect it to land heads up?

    A. 2   **B.** 12

    C. 24   **D.** 48

25. If a six-sided number cube is rolled 16 times, how many times should you expect to roll a number greater than 3?

    A. 3   **B.** 4

    C. 8   **D.** 16

Open Response

26. If a six-sided number cube is rolled 50 times, how many times should you expect an even number be rolled?

Explain your thinking.

ANSWERS AND SOLUTIONS
DATA MANAGEMENT AND PROBABILITY

1.	D	7.	A	13.	D	19.	C	25.	C
2.	C	8.	D	14.	C	20.	OR	26.	OR
3.	D	9.	B	15.	B	21.	C		
4.	OR	10.	B	16.	A	22.	B		
5.	C	11.	A	17.	C	23.	C		
6.	OR	12.	A	18.	B	24.	C		

1. D

To find what question Trisha asked, look at the information given on the graph.

The graph lists four different art activities. It also gives a number of students for each activity.

That means that the question had to be about art activities. The numbers could refer to how many students chose each activity.

The survey question that Trisha could have asked is "Which art class activity do you like the most?"

2. C

A This is too time consuming and not realistic for a Grade 6 class.

B The sample size would be too small.

C The best method to find the average size of families in Canada is to obtain the information from Statistics Canada. When a census is conducted, every household is contacted so a fairly exact number can be obtained.

D The sample size is too small and the population may not be a good representation of the average Canadian family size.

3. D

To find the double bar graph that correctly displays the given data, look at how high each bar extends in each graph and compare the numbers with those in the chart. The graph that correctly displays the given data is D.

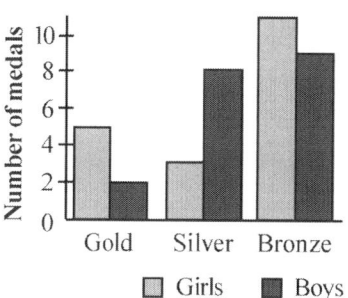

4. OR

Points	Sample Answer
4	To make a table of the amount of reading Roberto's class did each day, start with 25 minutes on Monday and add 5 minutes each day.

Days of the week	Minutes Read
Monday	25
Tuesday	30
Wednesday	35
Thursday	40
Friday	45

Points	Sample Answer
	To graph the information on a line graph, you can use a scale with increments of 5 or 10.

Time spent reading

A line graph titled "Time spent reading" with y-axis "Minutes read" (0 to 50) and x-axis "Day" (M, T, W, Th, F)

Is able to make a table of the given data. Displays the data correctly in a line graph.
Is able to make a table of the given data with minor errors. Displays the data in a line graph with minor errors.
Is somewhat able to make a table of the given data. Displays the data in a line graph with errors.
Is unable to make a table of the given data. Does not display the data in a line graph.

5. C

Step 1

Determine the type of information given in the table.

The information given is the amount of snow that fell over four consecutive weeks in a particular town. The data shows a change over time.

Step 2

Match the type of data given to the kind of graph that best displays that kind of data.

- A line plot is best used to display clusters of data.
- A Venn diagram is best used to display relationships among sets of things.
- A broken-line graph is best used to display a change over time.
- A stem-and-leaf plot is best used to display data according to place values.

A line graph is usually used to show a change over time, so it would best display the given information.

6. OR

Points	Sample Answer
4	Understands how to make a graph with correct labels and titles. Gives a thorough explanation for the type of graph chosen. A pie chart or a bar graph are the most appropriate graphs to use to shows this information.

A pie chart titled "Favourite Colours" with sections labelled Yellow, Red, Orange, Purple, Blue

A bar graph with y-axis "Number of Students" (1 to 9) and x-axis "Colours" (Red, Blue, Purple, Orange, Yellow)

Points	Sample Answer
3	Understands how to make a graph with correct labels and titles, but with minor errors. Gives a good explanation for the type of graph chosen.
2	Understands somewhat how to make a graph with correct labels and/or titles. Gives a short explanation for the type of graph chosen.
1	Understands somewhat how to make a graph with correct labels and/or titles. Gives no explanation for the type of graph chosen.

7. A

In order to collect accurate data, you must focus on whether your sample is representative of the entire population. Focusing on the spectators at a basketball game or the workers in a building limits your sample to people in certain positions or with certain interests, which could bias your sample. In addition, you must ensure that the participants in your survey match the question you are asking. Your survey asks for the "type of drink adults prefer," and therefore polling high school students is not appropriate. Therefore, doing a random telephone survey (**A**) would provide the most representative sample.

8. D

The population that would strongly misrepresent the population to be targeted by the survey is the most inappropriate or biased sample. Of the populations listed, children are the most inappropriate population to be surveyed. This is because children are not a population that will commonly drink coffee, therefore children will not reflect consumer preferences for coffee.

9. B

Reading a bar graph is very similar to reading a line graph. Start with the *x*-axis and follow the bar to the top. Then, read across to the *y*-axis to find the value that the bar reaches. An increase of 10 metres from the start line for every second of Ahmad's run is shown in B.

10. B

There are four students who have weights in the 30 kg range, which is more than any other range. Therefore, most of the students' weights are in the 30 kg range.

11. A

First, count the number of CDs in the pictograph for each singer or music group.

Rock – 8; Country – 5; Pop – 6; Jazz – 4.

Now, match the tallies with the number of students who chose each type of music.

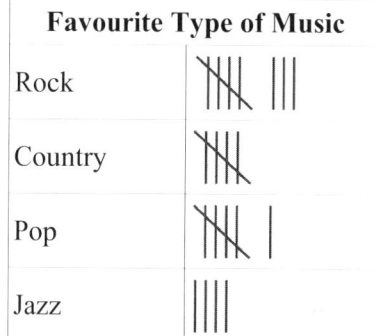

Tally chart A matches the data in the pictograph.

12. A

From the first hour to the sixth, the bar graph represents the following speeds: 33 km/h, 25 km/h, 30 km/h, 27 km/h, 30 km/h, and 25 km/h. The only broken-line graph whose numbers correspond with the bar graph is alternative A.

13. D

To choose a scale for the number of people, look at the range. The lowest number is 78 and the highest number is 225. The range is 225 – 78, or 147. Since the range is so great, it would not be reasonable to count by 2s, 5s or even 10s. Therefore, a scale counting by 20 is most appropriate.

14. C

To find the mean, add up all the numbers and then divide by the number of numbers, which in this case is 7.

$12 + 15 + 10 + 18 + 20 + 14 + 16 = 105$

$\dfrac{105}{7} = 15$

The mean of the given data is 15.

15. B

To find the mean, add up all the numbers and divide by the number of numbers, which in this case is 5.

$85 + 77 + 64 + 77 + 82 = 385$

$\dfrac{385}{5} = 77$

Therefore, Ravi's mean math mark is 77.

16. A

Of the people that responded to the survey, 65% said they were on a school sports team. This means that 35% of the readers were not. Since the sample is drawn from a teenage girl magazine, it is incorrect to infer that both teenage boys and teenage girls like playing sports. The inference that is supported by the survey is that the majority of teenage girls like playing sports.

17. C

There are 18 flowers on which the bee can land: 5 red flowers + 3 pink flowers + 4 white flowers +6 yellow flowers.

There are 9 favourable flowers on which the bee can land: 3 pink flowers + 6 yellow flowers.

Therefore, the probability of the bee landing on a pink or yellow flower is $\dfrac{9}{18}$ or, in lowest terms, $\dfrac{1}{2}$.

18. B

There are 50 students to choose from, so there are 50 possible outcomes.

There are 22 boys to choose from, so there are 20 favourable outcomes.

Therefore, the probability that the student chosen is male is $\dfrac{22}{50}$ or, in lowest terms, $\dfrac{11}{25}$.

19. C

There are 7 possible outcomes because there are 7 letters.

There are 3 favourable outcomes because there are 3 vowels.

Therefore, the probability that Joe will choose a tile with a vowel on it is $\dfrac{3}{7}$.

20. OR

Points	Sample Answer
4	Understands how to calculate theoretical probability and does so correctly.

There are 20 possible outcomes because there are 20 cookies in total.

There are 8 favourable outcomes because there are 8 oatmeal cookies.

The probability that Matt's grandma will choose an oatmeal cookie is $\dfrac{8}{20}$, or in lowest terms, $\dfrac{2}{5}$.

Points	Sample Answer
3	Understands how to calculate theoretical probability and does so correctly but with minor errors.
2	Understands somewhat how to calculate theoretical probability and does so with errors.
1	Limited ability calculating theoretical probability.

21. C

There are 5 possible outcomes: 1, 2, 3, 4, and 5. There are 3 favourable outcomes: 1, 3, and 5. Therefore, the probability that Janice's father will pick an odd number is $\dfrac{3}{5}$ or 0.60.

22. B

There are 8 possible outcomes when rolling a six-sided number cube: 1, 2, 3, 4, 5, 6, 7, or 8.

There are 4 favourable outcomes of rolling an even number: 2, 4, 6, or 8.

Therefore, the probability of rolling an even number is $\frac{1}{2}$, or 0.50.

23. C

Since 7 of the 10 numbers on the spinner contain a 2, the probability of the spinner landing on a number with a 2 is $\frac{7}{10}$.

To find out how many times the spinner will land on a number containing a 2, multiply the probability of landing on a number containing 2 by the number of spins.

$$\frac{7}{10} \times 20 = 14$$

The number of times that the spinner will land on a number containing the number 2 in 20 spins is 14.

24. C

To find the frequency of an outcome, find the probability of an event and multiply it by the number of times the event occurred.

There are 2 possible outcomes: landing heads up or landing tails up. There is 1 favourable outcome: landing heads up. Therefore, the probability of the coin landing heads up is $\frac{1}{2}$.

To find the frequency of the outcome, multiply the probability $\left(\frac{1}{2}\right)$ by the number of times Paul tossed the coin (48).

$$\frac{1}{2} \times 48 = 24$$

Therefore, Paul can expect the coin to land heads up 24 times.

25. C

There are 6 possible outcomes: 1, 2, 3, 4, 5, and 6. There are 3 favourable outcomes: 4, 5, and 6.

The probability of rolling a number greater than 3 is $\frac{1}{2}$.

To predict the frequency of a number greater than 3 being rolled when a number cube is rolled 16 times, multiply the probability of rolling a number greater than 3 by 16.

$$\frac{1}{2} \times 16 = 8$$

Therefore, if a number cube is rolled 16 times, it should land on a number greater than three, 8 times.

26. OR

Points	Sample Answer
4	Can predict the frequency of an outcome.
	Since there are six sides on a number cube, there are 6 possible outcomes.
	The total number of favourable outcomes of rolling an even number (2, 4, or 6) is 3.
	The probability of rolling an even number is $\frac{3}{6}$, which in lowest terms is $\frac{1}{2}$.
	To find the number of times an even number would be rolled if a number cube is rolled 50 times, multiply $\frac{1}{2}$ by 50.
	$\frac{1}{2} \times 50 = \frac{50}{2} = 25$.
	Therefore, if a number cube is rolled 50 times, an even number will be rolled about 25 times.
3	Can predict the frequency of an outcome with minor errors.
2	Can somewhat predict the frequency of an outcome.

Points	Sample Answer
1	Limited ability predicting the frequency of an outcome.

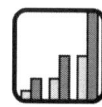

UNIT TEST — DATA MANAGEMENT AND PROBABILITY

1. Which of the following questions is the **best** question for a survey about what brand of cars students prefer?

   A. Do you prefer cars or trucks?

   B. Which is your favourite brand of car?

   C. Which is your favourite colour for a car?

   D. What types of cars do your parents drive?

Use the following information to answer the next question.

Aruna follows five steps to conduct a survey and collect data. The steps are not in order.

1. Add up the results of the tally and make a chart.
2. Write a survey question with four choices for answers.
3. Read the survey question to the class and ask students to raise their hands for their choice.
4. Count the raised hands for each choice and write the number of hands or make a tally of that number beside each choice.

2. Which of the following sets of steps are in the order that Aruna should follow?

   A. 2, 4, 3, 1   **B.** 1, 2, 3, 4

   C. 2, 3, 4, 1   **D.** 1, 3, 4, 2

Use the following information to answer the next question.

An organization studying population growth in a town conducted a survey in various years. The annual percentage population growth from the year 1998 to 2002 is shown.

Year	1998	1999	2000	2001	2002
Growth %	8	10	13	15	20

3. Which of the following graphs is the **best** representation of the data in the table?

A.

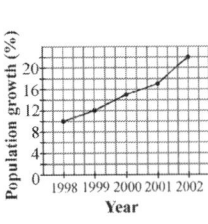

B.

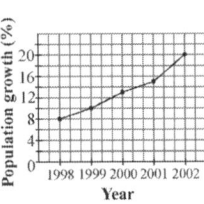

C.

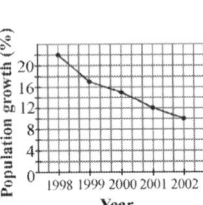

D.

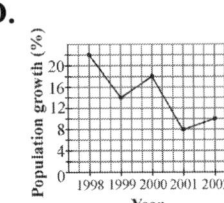

Use the following information to answer the next question.

The following table shows the average weight of twelve boys and girls at various ages.

	Boys	**Girls**
Age 5	23 kg	25 kg
Age 6	26 kg	28 kg
Age 7	32 kg	31 kg
Age 8	34 kg	33 kg
Age 9	37 kg	36 kg
Age 10	39 kg	38 kg

4. Which of the following methods of displaying will **best** present this information?

   A. Pie chart   **B.** Pictogram

   C. Line graph   **D.** Double-bar graph

5. Safi claims that European cars are better made than American cars. Which of the following sources would **most likely** be a source of unbiased accurate information?

   A. A survey of the members of the Canadian Car Maker's Association

   B. A survey of people in a German automaker's Internet chat group

   C. A recent Consumer Reports magazine's ratings of various cars

   D. An article in a car magazine that mentions various cars

6. The owner of a hockey team wants to find out if the fans would like live music played by an organist or recorded music played over the public address system. Which sampling procedure would be the **most** biased?

   A. Ask 100 fans from 25 sections throughout the arena.

   B. Survey every sixth fan of the 15 000 who attend the game.

   C. Survey the first 2 500 fans that go through the concession lines.

   D. Ask fans in seat numbers with the digits 1 or 2, until a total of 2 500 surveys have been collected.

Use the following information to answer the next question.

The Grade 5 students at Midtown School were surveyed to see how they get to school. The results are shown in the given graph.

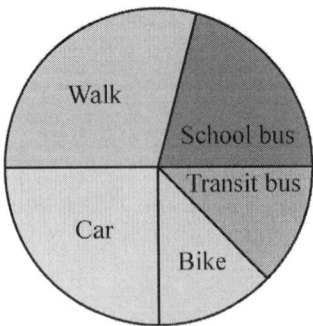

May, Melody, Deborah, and Amy each wrote two conclusions based on the data in the graph. They then indicated if their conclusions were true or false.

7. Which of the students correctly indicated if their conclusions were true or false?

A.   **May**

The number of students riding in cars is the same as the number of students riding the school bus.	True
The number of students riding in cars is the same as the number of students biking and taking the transit bus together.	False

B.   **Melody**

Half of the students walk or take the school bus.	False
There are more students taking the transit bus than the school bus.	True

C.   **Deborah**

There are more students taking the transit bus than the school bus.	False
The number of students riding in cars is the same as the number of students biking and taking the transit bus together.	False

D.   **Amy**

More than half of the students walk or take the school bus.	False
The number of students riding in cars is the same as the number of students biking and taking the transit bus together.	True

Use the following information to answer the next question.

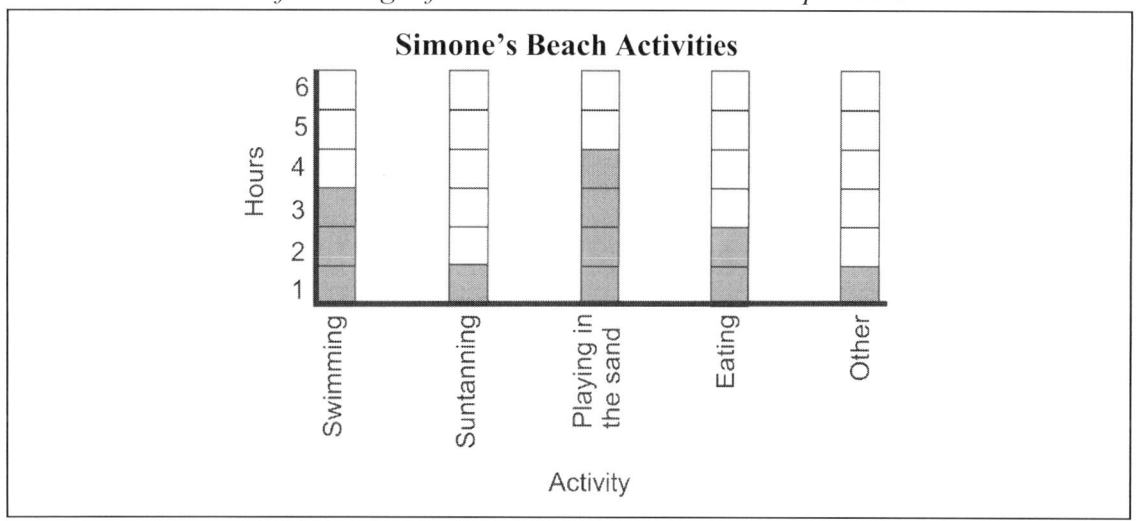

Simone's Beach Activities

8. Which of the following bar graphs displays the data from the given graph?

A.

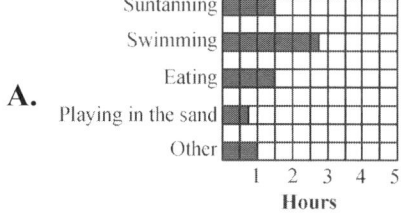

B.

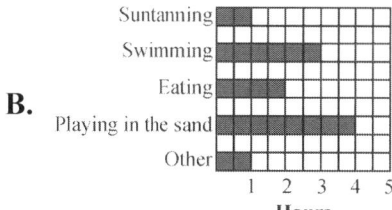

C.

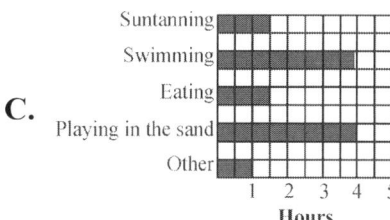

D.

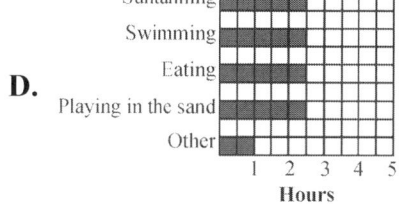

Use the following information to answer the next question.

Neva makes a line plot of the different numbers that come up on a spinner.

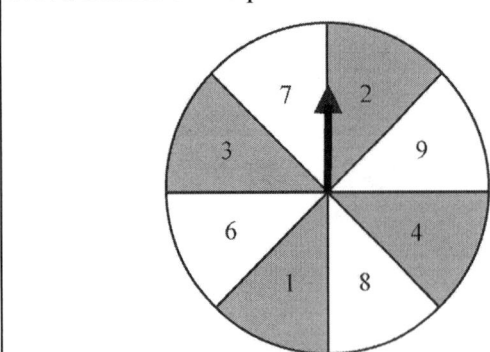

9. Which of the following bar graphs shows the same data as the line plot?

A.

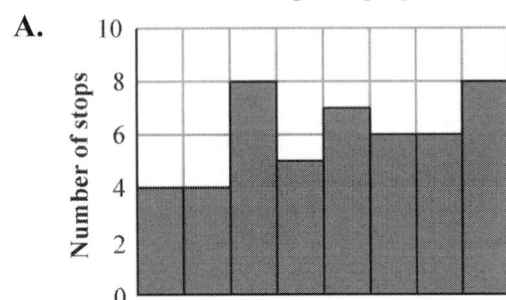

B.

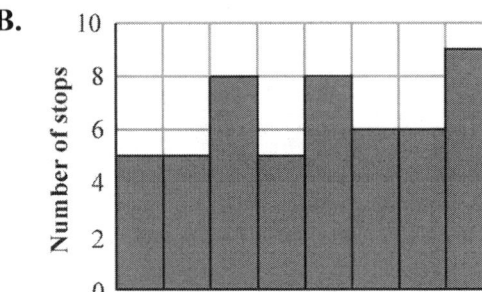

C.

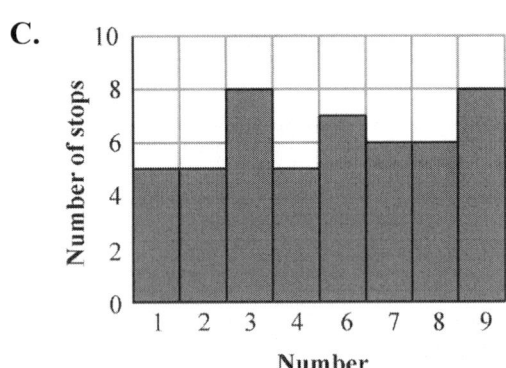

D.

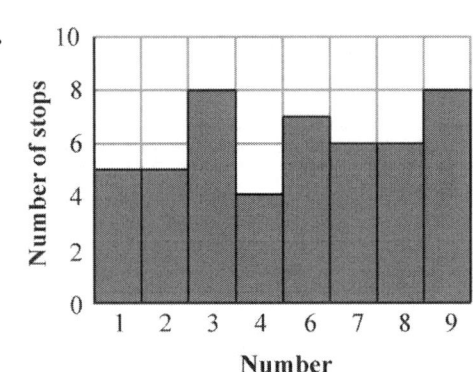

Use the following information to answer the next question.

16, 17, 18, 15, 20, 19, 21

10. What is the mean of the given data?

A. 16   B. 18

C. 24   D. 126

Use the following information to answer the next question.

Method of Transportation	Percentage of Students(%)
Walk	58.5
Bicycle	22.9
Bus	10.8
Driven by Parent	7.8

A survey question is given to Grade 10 students to find out how they get to school. The data collected is summarized in the table below.

11. Given the information in the table, which of the following inferences can be made?
A. Grade 10 students prefer to walk to school.
B. Grade 10 students do not take the bus to school.
C. The majority of Grade 10 students do not own bicycles.
D. Grade 10 students do not want their parents to drive them to school.

Use the following information to answer the next question.

Without looking, Fiona reaches into a dresser drawer to pull out a pair of socks. She has 1 pair of white, 2 pairs of striped, 3 pairs of pink, and 4 pairs of black socks in the drawer.

12. What is the probability that Fiona will select a pair of striped socks?
A. $\frac{1}{5}$
B. $\frac{2}{5}$
C. $\frac{3}{5}$
D. $\frac{4}{5}$

Use the following information to answer the next question.

There are 5 red flowers, 4 white flowers, 3 pink flowers, and 2 yellow flowers in a flower pot in front of a house. A butterfly lands on one flower.

13. What is the probability that the butterfly landed on a white or yellow flower?
A. $\frac{3}{4}$
B. $\frac{2}{5}$
C. $\frac{2}{7}$
D. $\frac{3}{7}$

14. When two regular coins are tossed, what is the probability of obtaining two heads?
A. 0.25
B. 0.50
C. 0.75
D. 1.0

15. A carton contains 200 electric bulbs, of which 6 are defective. If one bulb is taken out at random from the carton, what is the probability that the chosen bulb is **not** defective?

A. 0.03   B. 0.30

C. 0.94   D. 0.97

16. The faces of a 10-sided number cube are numbered from 1 to 10. If Seema rolls the number cube 100 times, how many times could she expect to roll a prime number?

A. 25   B. 40

C. 50   D. 100

Use the following information to answer the next question.

Denise had a bag filled with 20 different coloured markers. She had 4 purple, 3 pink, 7 red, and 6 yellow markers.

Open Response

17. If Denise asks her friend to pick a marker out of the bag 10 times (putting the markers back in the bag each time), how many times will a purple marker be picked?

Explain your thinking.

ANSWERS AND SOLUTIONS — UNIT TEST

1. **B**	6. **C**	11. **A**	16. **B**
2. **C**	7. **D**	12. **A**	17. **OR**
3. **B**	8. **B**	13. **D**	
4. **D**	9. **C**	14. **A**	
5. **C**	10. **B**	15. **D**	

1. B

If the survey is being conducted to find out which brand of cars people like best, the survey question has to be "Which is your favourite brand of car?"

Asking, "Do you prefer cars or trucks?" is unrelated to brands of cars.

Asking, "Which is your favourite colour for a car?" is related to cars, but it does not find out which brand of cars people like best.

Asking, "What types of cars do your parents drive?" does not ask information about the brand of car the students like, only the brand that their parents drive.

2. C

The correct order of the steps that Aruna should take to conduct a survey and collect data is:

2. Write a survey question with four choices for answers.

3. Read the survey question to the class and ask students to raise their hands for their choice.

4. Count the raised hands for each choice and write the number of hands or make a tally of that number beside each choice.

1. Add up the results of the tally and make a chart.

3. B

The plotted points represent data presented as pairs of numbers. Find the coordinates of the points on the graph of each option and verify with the data in the given table.

A The y-coordinate of the point (1998, 9) is 9. This means that the growth percent in 1998 was 9. But in the table, the growth percent in 1998 is 8. Therefore, the graph in A is incorrect.

B The line graph in B plots the points (1998, 8), (1999, 10), (2000, 13), (2001, 15), and (2002, 20), which are the same as the data given in table.

C22C

D22D

4. D

A double-bar graph is the best method for presenting this information because a double-bar graph is a comparison of two factors, in this case boys' weight and girls' weight.

Pie charts, pictograms, and line graphs are not the best graphs to present a comparison of two factors.

5. C

A Surveying an association of Canadian car makers would probably give results biased toward North American cars.

B Surveying individuals in a German automaker's Internet chat room would probably give results biased toward European cars.

C This is the best choice out of the ones presented because Consumer Reports does not build cars. It provides a rating of many cars. All cars are judged on the same criteria. Consumer Report collects data firsthand and publishes it for their readers.

D An article in a car magazine may be biased depending on who wrote the article and may not offer an evaluation of the cars in question.

6. C

The sampling procedure that would produce the most biased sample is the sampling method where the population is least fairly represented.

In A, sampling 100 fans from 25 sections ensures that 2 500 fans are surveyed. This would be a fairly random sample.

B is a random sample of the fans who attend the game.

In C, 2 500 fans are surveyed, but only fans that purchase concession items would be represented. This may result in a biased sample as not all fans may buy items from the concessions. This is the most biased because it only samples the segment of the population that goes through the concession lines.

D randomly samples fans from all over the arena, so the sample should be unbiased.

7. D

Amy is the student who correctly indicated that her conclusions were true or false. A circle graph represents information as parts of a whole. Usually, the amounts in each sector are represented in percentages so that all amounts total 100%. The inferences that were made from the circle graph were correct. Half of the students walk or take the school bus. One fourth of the students riding bikes and taking the transit bus is equivalent to one fourth of the students riding cars.

8. B

The graph titled "Simone's Beach Activities" shows that Simone went swimming for 3 hours, suntanned for 1 hour, played in the sand for 4 hours, ate for 2 hours, and did other activities for 1hour.

The activities on the bar graphs are not given in the same order as they were on the titled graph, and each square on the bar graph represents one half hour, not one hour.

Bar graph B displays the same information as the titled graph.

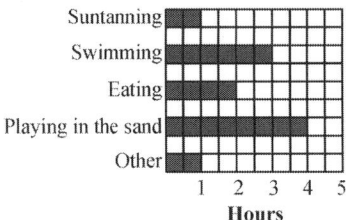

9. C

Match the number of stops recorded on the line plot with the number of stops on the bottom of the bar graph. The *X*s on the line plot and the length of the bars are the number of times the spinner stopped on each number.

The number of stops on the line plot is the same as the number of stops on the bar graph in C.

10. B

To find the mean of the given data, add up the numbers and then divide by the number of numbers, which is 7 in this case.

$16 + 17 + 18 + 15 + 20 + 19 + 21 = 126$

$\dfrac{126}{7} = 18$

The mean of the data is 18.

11. A

A The highest number is 58.5. It can be inferred that students prefer walking to school over the other alternatives. This is the correct answer.

B About 1 in 10 Grade 10 students takes the bus, which means that some students do take the bus.

C There is only data given about who rides a bike to school. There is no data on who owns a bike.

D There is no information given that indicates the students do not want a ride from their parents. There is only information given on who is driven to school.

12. A

There are 10 possible outcomes because there are 10 pairs of socks.

There are 2 favourable outcomes because there are 2 pairs of striped socks.

Therefore, the probability that Fiona will select a striped pair of socks is $\frac{2}{10}$ or, in lowest terms, $\frac{1}{5}$.

13. D

There are a total of 14 flowers, so there are 14 possible outcomes.

There are 6 flowers that are either white or yellow.

Therefore, the probability of the bee landing on a white or a yellow flower is $\frac{6}{14}$ or, in lowest terms, $\frac{3}{7}$.

14. A

There are four possible outcomes from flipping two coins: tails and tails, tails and heads, heads and tails, and heads and heads.

Only one of those outcomes is favourable: heads and heads.

So, the probability of getting two heads is $\frac{1}{4}$ or 0.25.

15. D

Since there are 6 defective bulbs in the carton, the total number of non-defective bulbs is 194.

$200 - 6 = 194$

Therefore, the probability of getting a non-defective bulb is $\frac{194}{200}$.

To find the probability of selecting a non-defective bulb as a decimal between 0 and 1, change the probability to a fraction and then into a decimal.

$\frac{194}{200} = \frac{97}{100} = 0.97$

The probability of selecting a non-defective bulb is 97%.

16. B

Because the faces of the number cube are numbered from 1 to 10, the total number of outcomes is 10.

The prime numbers between 1 and 10 are 2, 3, 5 and 7. So, the number of favourable outcomes is 4.

The probability of an event is $\dfrac{\text{number of favourable outcomes}}{\text{number of possible outcomes}}$

The probability that the number is prime is $\frac{4}{10} = \frac{2}{5}$.

To predict the expected number of times a prime number could be rolled if the number cube is rolled a total of 100 times, multiply the probability of the event by the number of times the event occurred.

$\frac{2}{5} \times 100 = 40$

Therefore, if Seema rolls a 10-sided number cube 100 times, she could expect to roll a prime number about 40 times.

17. OR

Points	Sample Answer
4	Can predict the frequency of an outcome. The probability of a purple marker being picked out of the bag is $\frac{4}{20}$, which in lowest terms is $\frac{1}{5}$. To find the number of times a purple marker will be picked out of the bag if Denise's friend picks a marker out of the bag 10 times, multiply $\frac{1}{5}$ by 10. $\frac{1}{5} \times 10 = \frac{10}{5} = 2$ If Denise's friend picks a marker out of the bag 10 times, a purple marker should be picked about 2 times.
3	Can predict the frequency of an outcome with minor errors.

Points	Sample Answer
2	Can somewhat predict the frequency of an outcome.
1	Limited ability in predicting the frequency of an outcome.

Key Strategies for Success on Tests

KEY STRATEGIES FOR SUCCESS ON TESTS

THINGS TO CONSIDER WHEN TAKING A TEST

It is normal to feel anxious before you write a test. You can manage this anxiety by using the following strategies:

- Think positive thoughts. Imagine yourself doing well on the test.

- Make a conscious effort to relax by taking several slow, deep, controlled breaths. Concentrate on the air going in and out of your body.

- Before you begin the test, ask questions if you are unsure of anything.

- Jot down key words or phrases from any instructions your teacher gives you.

- Look over the entire test to find out the number and kinds of questions on the test.

- Read each question closely, and reread if necessary.

- Pay close attention to key vocabulary words. Sometimes, these words are **bolded** or *italicized*, and they are usually important words in the question.

- If you are putting your answers on an answer sheet, mark your answers carefully. Always print clearly. If you wish to change an answer, erase the mark completely, and ensure that your final answer is darker than the one you have erased.

- Use highlighting to note directions, key words, and vocabulary that you find confusing or that are important to answering the question.

- Double-check to make sure you have answered everything before handing in your test.

- When taking tests, students often overlook the easy words. Failure to pay close attention to these words can result in an incorrect answer. One way to avoid this is to be aware of these words and to underline, circle, or highlight them while you are taking the test.

- Even though some words are easy to understand, they can change the meaning of the entire question, so it is important that you pay attention to them. Here are some examples.

all	always	most likely	probably	best	not
difference	usually	except	most	unlikely	likely

Example

1. Which of the following expressions is **incorrect**?

    A. $3 + 2 \geq 5$

    B. $4 - 3 < 2$

    C. $5 \times 4 < 15$

    D. $6 \times 3 \geq 18$

TEST PREPARATION AND TEST-TAKING SKILLS

HELPFUL STRATEGIES FOR ANSWERING MULTIPLE-CHOICE QUESTIONS

A multiple-choice question gives you some information and then asks you to select an answer from four choices. Each question has one correct answer. The other choices are distractors, which are incorrect.

The following strategies can help you when answering multiple-choice questions:

- Quickly skim through the entire test. Find out how many questions there are, and plan your time accordingly.

- Read and reread questions carefully. Underline key words, and try to think of an answer before looking at the choices.

- If there is a graphic, look at the graphic, read the question, and go back to the graphic. Then, you may want to underline the important information from the question.

- Carefully read the choices. Read the question first and then each choice that goes with it.

- When choosing an answer, try to eliminate those choices that are clearly wrong or do not make sense.

- Some questions may ask you to select the best answer. These questions will always include words like *best*, *most appropriate*, or *most likely*. All of the choices will be correct to some degree, but one of the choices will be better than the others in some way. Carefully read all four choices before choosing the answer you think is the best.

- If you do not know the answer, or if the question does not make sense to you, it is better to guess than to leave it blank.

- Do not spend too much time on any one question. Make a mark (*) beside a difficult question, and come back to it later. If you are leaving a question to come back to later, make sure you also leave the space on the answer sheet, if you are using one.

- Remember to go back to the difficult questions at the end of the test; sometimes, clues are given throughout the test that will provide you with answers.

- Note any negative words like *no* or *not*, and be sure your answer fits the question.

- Before changing an answer, be sure you have a very good reason to do so.

- Do not look for patterns on your answer sheet, if you are using one.

HELPFUL STRATEGIES FOR ANSWERING WRITTEN-RESPONSE QUESTIONS

A written response requires you to respond to a question or directive indicated by words such as explain, predict, list, describe, show your work, solve, or calculate. The following strategies can help you when answering written-response questions:

- Read and reread the question carefully.

- Recognize and pay close attention to directing words such as *explain*, *show your work*, and *describe*.

- Underline key words and phrases that indicate what is required in your answer, such as *explain*, *estimate*, *answer*, *calculate*, or *show your work*.

- Write down rough, point-form notes regarding the information you want to include in your answer.

- Think about what you want to say, and organize information and ideas in a coherent and concise manner within the time limit you have for the question.

- Be sure to answer every part of the question that is asked.

- Include as much information as you can when you are asked to explain your thinking.

- Include a picture or diagram if it will help to explain your thinking.

- Try to put your final answer to a problem in a complete sentence to be sure it is reasonable.

- Reread your response to ensure you have answered the question.

- Ask yourself if your answer makes sense.

- Ask yourself if your answer sounds right.

- Use appropriate subject vocabulary and terms in your response.

ABOUT MATHEMATICS TESTS

WHAT YOU NEED TO KNOW ABOUT MATHEMATICS TESTS

To do well on a mathematics test, you need to understand and apply your knowledge of mathematical concepts. Reading skills can also make a difference in how well you perform. Reading skills can help you follow instructions and find key words, as well as read graphs, diagrams, and tables. They can also help you solve mathematics problems.

Mathematics tests usually have two types of questions: questions that ask for understanding of mathematics ideas and questions that test how well you can solve mathematics problems.

HOW YOU CAN PREPARE FOR MATHEMATICS TESTS

The following strategies are particular to preparing for and writing mathematics tests:

- Know how to use your calculator, and, if it is allowed, use your own for the test.

- Note taking is a good way to review and study important information from your class notes and textbook.

- Sketch a picture of the problem, procedure, or term. Drawing is helpful for learning and remembering concepts.

- Check your answer to practice questions by working backward to the beginning. You can find the beginning by going step by step in reverse order.

- Use the following steps when answering questions with graphics (pictures, diagrams, tables, or graphs):

  1. Read the title of the graphic and any key words.

  2. Read the test question carefully to figure out what information you need to find in the graphic.

  3. Go back to the graphic to find the information you need.

  4. Decide which operation is needed.

- Always pay close attention when pressing the keys on your calculator. Repeat the procedure a second time to be sure you pressed the correct keys.

TEST PREPARATION COUNTDOWN

If you develop a plan for studying and test preparation, you will perform well on tests.

Here is a general plan to follow seven days before you write a test.

COUNTDOWN: 7 DAYS BEFORE THE TEST

1. Use "Finding Out about the Test" to help you make your own personal test preparation plan.

2. Review the following information:

   – Areas to be included on the test

   – Types of test items

   – General and specific test tips

3. Start preparing for the test at least seven days before the test. Develop your test preparation plan, and set time aside to prepare and study.

COUNTDOWN: 6, 5, 4, 3, 2 DAYS BEFORE THE TEST

1. Review old homework assignments, quizzes, and tests.

2. Rework problems on quizzes and tests to make sure you still know how to solve them.

3. Correct any errors made on quizzes and tests.

4. Review key concepts, processes, formulas, and vocabulary.

5. Create practice test questions for yourself, and answer them. Work out many sample problems.

COUNTDOWN: THE NIGHT BEFORE THE TEST

1. Use the night before the test for final preparation, which includes reviewing and gathering materials needed for the test before going to bed.

2. Most importantly, get a good night's rest, and know you have done everything possible to do well on the test.

TEST DAY

1. Eat a healthy and nutritious breakfast.

2. Ensure you have all the necessary materials.

3. Think positive thoughts, such as "I can do this," "I am ready," and "I know I can do well."

4. Arrive at your school early, so you are not rushing, which can cause you anxiety and stress.

SUMMARY OF HOW TO BE SUCCESSFUL DURING A TEST

You may find some of the following strategies useful for writing a test:

- Take two or three deep breaths to help you relax.

- Read the directions carefully, and underline, circle, or highlight any important words.

- Look over the entire test to understand what you will need to do.

- Budget your time.

- Begin with an easy question or a question you know you can answer correctly rather than follow the numerical question order of the test.

- If you cannot remember how to answer a question, try repeating the deep breathing and physical relaxation activities. Then, move on to visualization and positive self-talk to get yourself going.

- When answering questions with graphics (pictures, diagrams, tables, or graphs), look at the question carefully, and use the following steps:

  1. Read the title of the graphic and any key words.

  2. Read the test question carefully to figure out what information you need to find in the graphic.

  3. Go back to the graphic to find the information you need.

- Write down anything you remember about the subject on the reverse side of your test paper. This activity sometimes helps to remind you that you do know something and are capable of writing the test.

- Look over your test when you have finished, and double-check your answers to be sure you did not forget anything.

NOTES

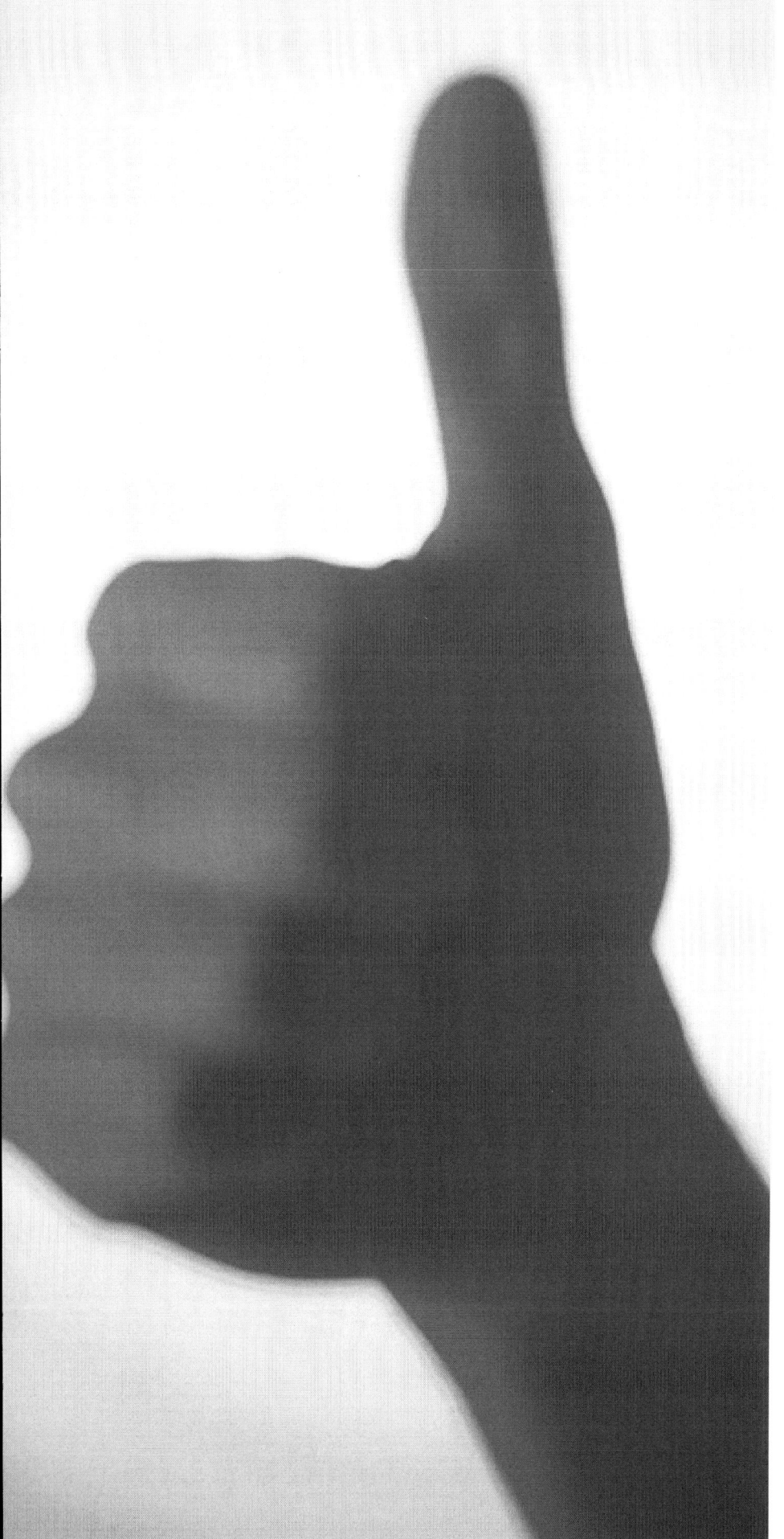

Practice Tests

PRACTICE TEST 1

Use the following information to answer the next question.

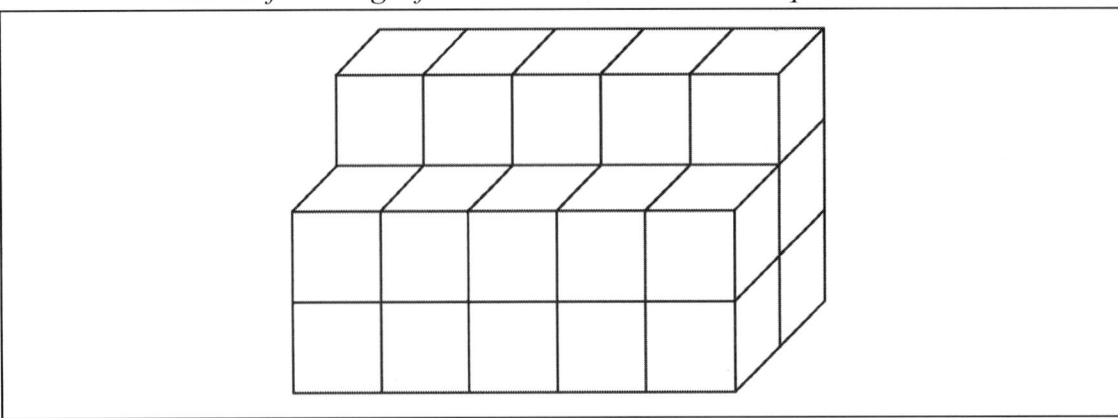

Open Response

1. Sketch the front, side, and top views of the given figure.

Use the following information to answer the next question.

A juice carton is shown.

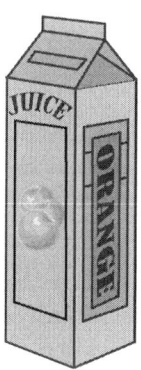

2. What is the **best** estimate of the capacity of the juice carton?
   A. 10 millilitres   B. 100 millilitres

   C. 1 litre   D. 10 litres

3. Which of the following units is **most appropriate** for measuring the height of a flag pole?
   A. millimetres   B. centimetres

   C. metres   D. kilometres

4. If a toy weighs 2 kg, how many grams does it weigh?
   A. 2 g   B. 20 g

   C. 200 g   D. 2 000 g

Use the following information to answer the next question.

At a party, each of the 20 party guests drank two 400 mL glasses of pop.

5. How many litres of pop did the guests drink in total?
   A. 10 L   B. 14 L

   C. 16 L   D. 18 L

Use the following information to answer the next question.

Farrah has a wire that is 42 cm long. She bends the wire and makes a rectangle.

6. Which dimensions could the rectangle have?
   A. 7 cm × 6 cm   B. 12 cm × 9 cm

   C. 18 cm × 6 cm   D. 20 cm × 2 cm

Use the following information to answer the next question.

Advertising posters for a school play will be drawn on posterboard. A large piece of posterboard measures 3.0 m × 1.2 m, and the size of each poster will be 60 cm × 80 cm.

Open Response

7. What is the greatest number of posters that can be drawn on one piece of posterboard? Show your work.

8. Mary is refinishing the cushions on her couch. In order to buy the fabric for the cushions, she needs to find the surface area of each cushion.
   If the dimensions of each cushion are 22 cm by 24 cm by 5 cm, what is the surface area of each cushion?

   A. 51 cm^2 **B.** 528 cm^2

   C. 1 516 cm^2 **D.** 2 640 cm^2

Use the following information to answer the next question.

The triangular prism shown below has a volume of 92 cm^3 and a height of 6 cm.

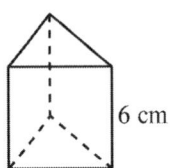

6 cm

9. Which of the following areas represents the best estimate for the area of the base of the prism?

   A. 15 cm^2 **B.** 30 cm^2

   C. 40 cm^2 **D.** 50 cm^2

10. Which graph shows the point $P(2, 7)$ plotted correctly?

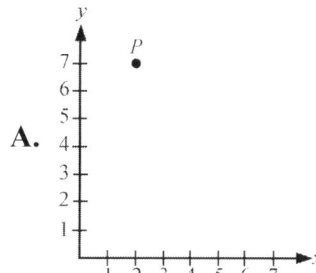

A.

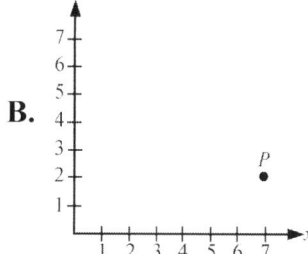

B.

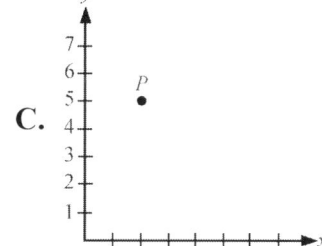

C.

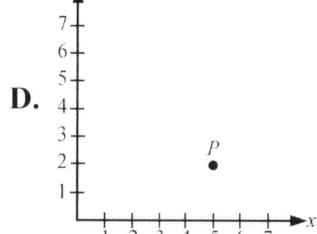

D.

11. Which design is an example of a 90 ° clockwise rotation?

A.
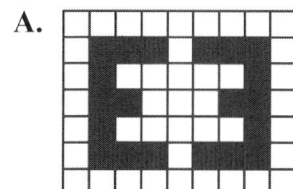

B.

C.
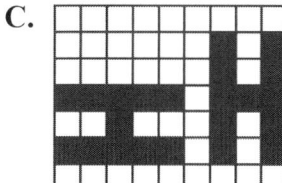

D.

Use the following information to answer the next question.

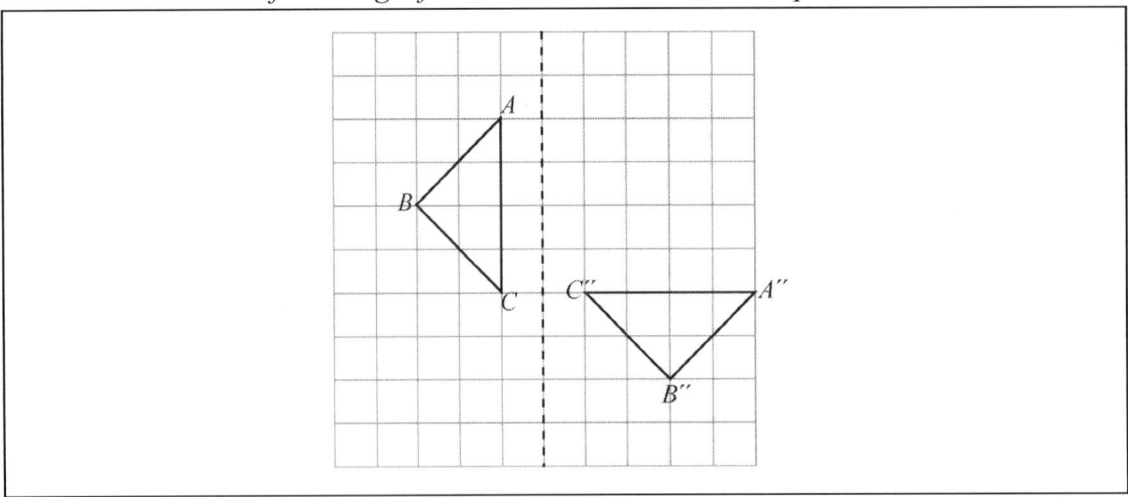

Open Response

12. Explain which two transformations have occurred to figure *ABC* to get the new figure *A″B″C″*.

13. Which of the following fractions is equivalent to 64 %?

  A. $\dfrac{14}{25}$ B. $\dfrac{15}{25}$

  C. $\dfrac{16}{25}$ D. $\dfrac{17}{25}$

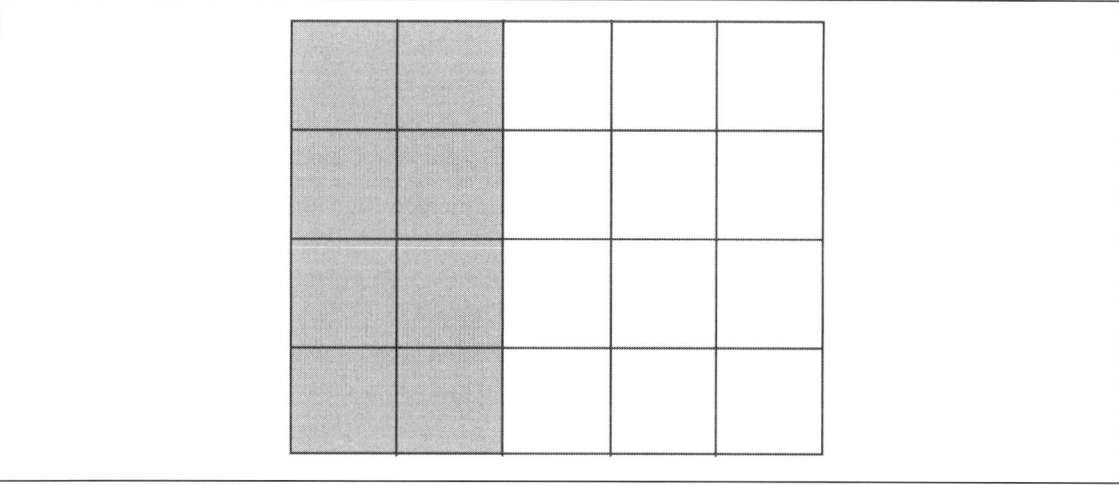

Open Response

14. Determine the part of the diagram that is shaded. Write your answer as a decimal, fraction, and percent. Show your work.

Use the following information to answer the next question.

Mr. Rajan writes this pattern rule on the board.
"The ones digit decreases by 1. The hundreds digit increases by 1."
He asks his students to write a set of numbers that show this rule.

15. Which set of numbers is an example of the pattern rule?
    A. 423, 524, 625, 726   **B.** 265, 364, 463, 562
    C. 664, 675, 686, 697   **D.** 955, 854, 753, 652

Use the following information to answer the next question.

Felipe's hourly wage over five years is shown in the table.

Year	Felipe's Wage
2004	$11.83
2005	$11.98
2006	$12.18
2007	$12.43
2008	$12.73

16. If the pattern continues, what will Felipe's wage be in 2009?

A. $13.03

B. $13.08

C. $13.33

D. $13.48

Use the following information to answer the next question.

The following graph shows the amount of rainfall in four hours.

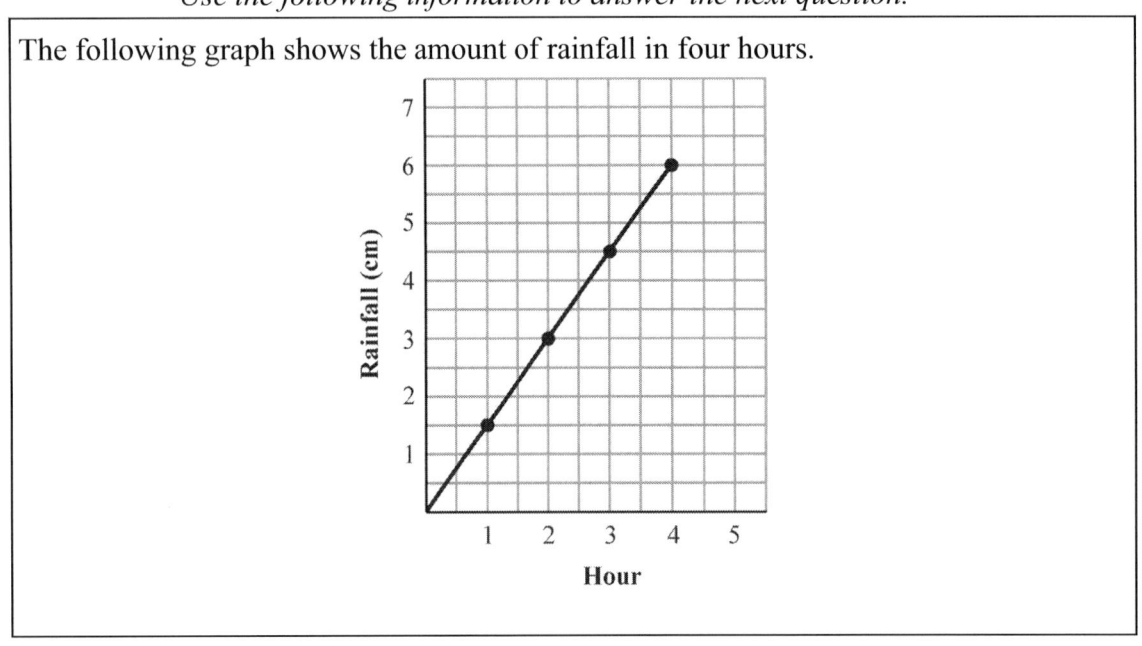

17. If the rain continues falling at the same rate, what will the total rainfall be at the fifth hour?

A. 1.5 cm

B. 4.5 cm

C. 7.5 cm

D. 12.0 cm

Use the following information to answer the next question.

Nina makes a number pattern by using a rule. The pattern is 7 776, 1 296, 216, 36.

18. Which of the following rules could be used to make Nina's pattern?

A. Subtract 6 480 from each successive number.

B. Subtract 1 80 from each successive number.

C. Multiply every succeeding number by 6.

D. Divide every succeeding number by 6.

Use the following information to answer the next question.

Kate and four friends play a game. To start the game, Kate follows a pattern and gives a different number of toothpicks to each person.
Carl…6 toothpicks
Matt…13 toothpicks
Sari…27 toothpicks
Minn…55 toothpicks
Kate…? toothpicks

19. According to the pattern, how many toothpicks will Kate receive?

A. 56   B. 57

C. 110   D. 111

Open Response

20. For the pattern 1 600, 1 425, 1 250, 1 75, 900, …, find the tenth term.

Explain your thinking.

21. Mr. Owens owns x number of cars. Mr. Willis owns 3 cars less than twice the number of cars that Mr. Owens owns.

Which of the following expressions represents the number of cars that Mr. Willis owns?

A. $2x + 3$ **B.** $2x - 3$

C. $3x + 2$ **D.** $3x - 2$

22. Sophie wanted to find out how many hours a day students in her Grade 6 class spent watching television. She also wanted to know how many hours each student spent studying. How could Sophie **most effectively** collect this data?

　　A. Designing and conducting an experiment.

　　B. Using electronic networks, such as the Internet.

　　C. Designing and using a structured questionnaire.

　　D. Making observations and charting the information.

Use the following information to answer the next question.

Sylvia saved up her allowance for one month to give to the Food Bank as a donation. Sylvia did a survey of the students in her class to see how much weekly allowance they received, hoping that she could convince them to do a monthly donation as a class to the Food Bank.

- Students who received $0.00 (no allowance): 5 students
- Students who received $1.00 – $5.00: 9 students
- Students who received $6.00 – $10.00: 8 students
- Students who received $11.00 – $15.00: 3 students
- Students who received more than $15.00: 2 students

Open Response

23. Display the information Sylvia collected in an appropriate graph and explain your choice of graph. Remember to include all titles and labels.

Use the following information to answer the next question.

A publishing company mailed 5 000 questionnaires to an average, middle-class neighbourhood, asking people to select the magazine they would most likely read. The company published the table below showing the reading preferences of the 2 000 people who completed the survey.

	Sports Digest	News Weekly	Fashion Patrol	Wilderness Magazine	Woodworking Wonders
Males under 18	115	32	16	67	20
Females under 18	41	26	124	77	7
Males 18 and over	207	167	89	114	108
Females 18 and over	91	156	338	162	43
Totals	454	381	567	420	178

24. Which of the following conclusions can be drawn from the data?

   A. Wilderness Magazine is the most popular magazine.

   B. More people prefer News Weekly over Sports Digest.

   C. More males prefer to read Sports Digest than News Weekly.

   D. Woodworking Wonders is the magazine preferred by most people.

Use the following information to answer the next question.

The weights of 5 apples were recorded, as shown below.

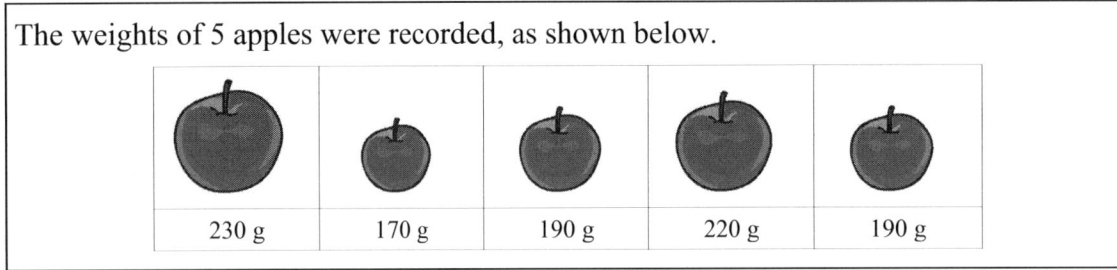

25. What is the mean mass of the apples?

   A. 180 g   **B.** 190 g

   C. 200 g   **D.** 220 g

Use the following information to answer the next question.

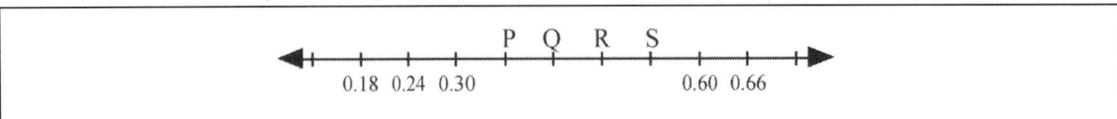

26. Which of the following points represents a value of 0.48 on the given number line?

   A. *P*   **B.** *Q*

   C. *R*   **D.** *S*

Open Response

27. How many days do 1 000 000 minutes make up? Show your work.

28. What are the prime factors of 28?

   A. 1, 2   **B.** 2, 7

   C. 1, 2, 7   **D.** 1, 2, 4, 7, 14, 28

29. What is the value of the expression $2 \times 14 \times 5$?

   A. 10   **B.** 14

   C. 100   **D.** 140

30. One edition of Mark Twain's book *The Adventures of Tom Sawyer* has 310 pages. If there are approximately 190 words per page, what is the **best** estimate for the total number of words in the book?

   A. 45 000   **B.** 56 900

   C. 60 000   **D.** 70 000

31. Anisha bought a hot chocolate for $2.55 with the $10 bill she received as her weekly allowance. How much money will she have left for the rest of the week?

   A. $6.55   **B.** $7.45

   C. $8.45   **D.** $12.55

32. In a raffle for one prize, 2 000 tickets are sold. If Derrick buys 6 tickets, what is the probability that he will win the prize?

   A. $\dfrac{1}{2\ 000}$ **B.** $\dfrac{1}{10}$

   C. $\dfrac{3}{1\ 000}$ **D.** $\dfrac{1}{6}$

33. If 10 people each flip a coin 10 times, then what is the **most probable** number of times that the coins will land showing heads?

A. 5   B. 10

C. 50   D. 100

| Open Response |

34. Juan likes to play baseball. On average, he hits the ball 7 times for every 10 swings. If Juan takes 30 swings in a season, how many times can he expect to hit the ball each season? Explain your thinking.

Use the following information to answer the next question.

Ryan made a riddle about a quadrilateral. These are the clues he gave.

- I have 2 sets of parallel lines.
- Not all of my sides are equal in length.
- I am made up of 2 greater than right angles.
- I am also made up of 2 less than right angles.

35. Ryan's riddle is about which quadrilateral?

A.

Square

B.

Rectangle

C.

Trapezoid

D.

Parallelogram

Use the following information to answer the next question.

The figure below displays lines of symmetry.

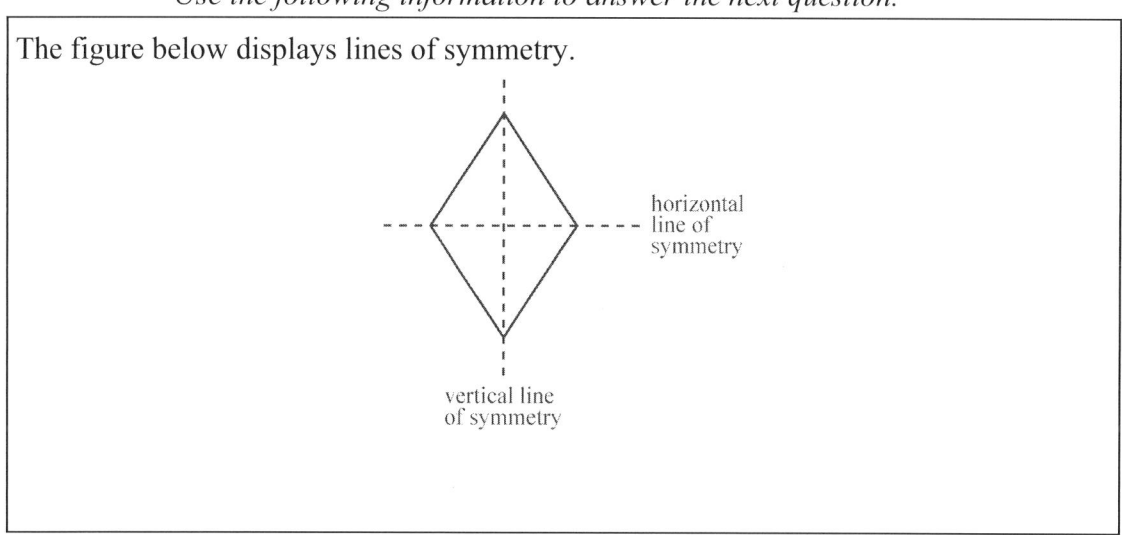

horizontal line of symmetry

vertical line of symmetry

36. Which figure has the same number of lines of symmetry as the one shown above?

A.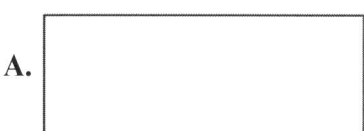

B.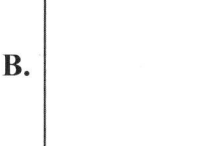

C.

D.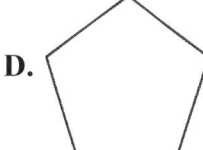

PRACTICE TEST 2

Use the following information to answer the next question.

An outdoor swimming pool is surrounded by tiles, as illustrated in the figure below.

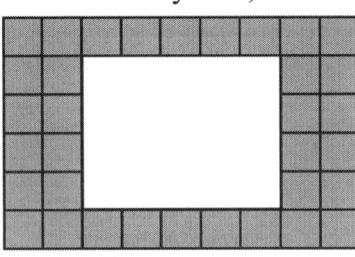

1. If the area of each tile is one square metre, what is the total area covered by the tiles?

   A. 20 m^2 **B.** 34 m^2

   C. 36 m^2 **D.** 54 m^2

2. In a race, Harry ran 925 m and Eri ran 1 025 m. Harry, Eri, and Alex together ran 3 km. How far did Alex run?

   A. 925 m   **B.** 1 025 m

   C. 1 050 m   **D.** 1 950 m

Use the following information to answer the next question.

Triangle *ABC* has a base, *BC*, 10 cm long and a height, *AB*, of 6 cm.

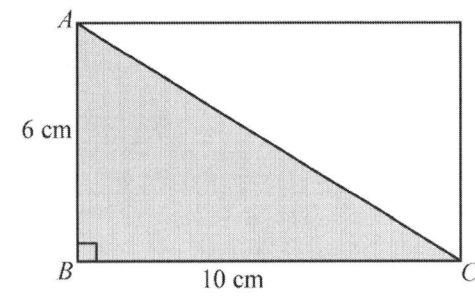

3. If two triangles identical to *ABC* were put together to form a rectangle, what would the area of the rectangle be?

   A. 20 cm^2 **B.** 30 cm^2

   C. 50 cm^2 **D.** 60 cm^2

Use the following information to answer the next question.

In the figure, *AB* is parallel to *CD*, and *BD* is perpendicular to *CD*.

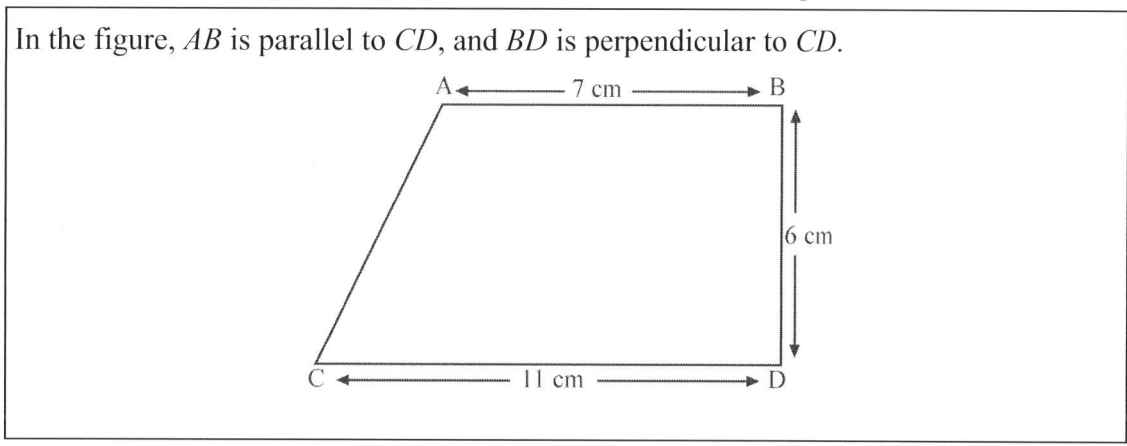

A ◄──── 7 cm ────► B

6 cm

C ◄──── 11 cm ────► D

Open Response

4. What is the area of figure *ABCD*? Explain your answer.

5. If a parallelogram has a base that is 5 m long and a height of 10 m, what is its area?
   A. 15 m^2
   B. 40 m^2
   C. 50 m^2
   D. 150 m^2

6. Written in centimetres, what is the area of a rectangle with sides of 3 m and 2 m?
   A. 30 000 cm^2
   B. 48 000 cm^2
   C. 60 000 cm^2
   D. 64 000 cm^2

Use the following information to answer the next question.

A covered box is 25 cm long, 10 cm wide, and 8 cm high.

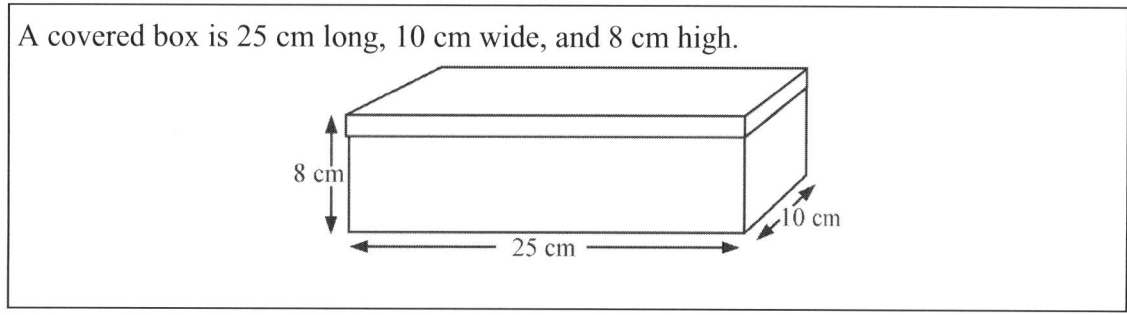

8 cm

25 cm

10 cm

7. What is the surface area of the covered box?
   A. 530 cm^2
   B. 710 cm^2
   C. 810 cm^2
   D. 1 60 cm^2

8. Which prism has the greatest volume?

A.

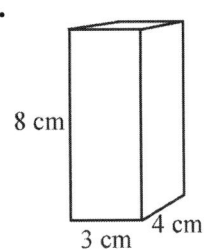

8 cm

3 cm   4 cm

B.

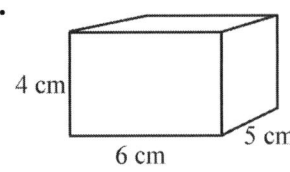

4 cm

6 cm   5 cm

C.

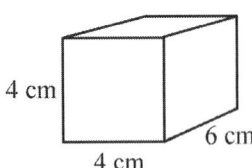

4 cm

4 cm   6 cm

D.

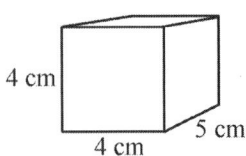

4 cm

4 cm   5 cm

Open Response

9. Move figure *ABC* 5 units to the right. Draw the new figure and write the coordinates of the new figure.

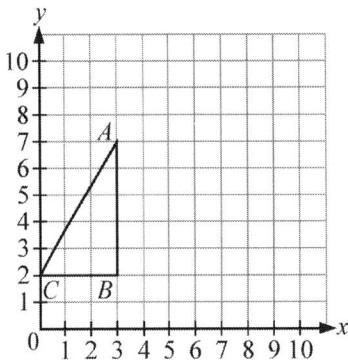

The new coordinates are _____.

The figure below is used in a transformation.

10. Which figure is formed by rotating the given figure clockwise 90°?

A.

B.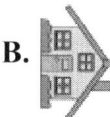

C.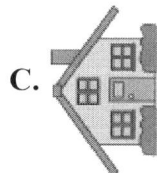

D.

Use the following information to answer the next question.

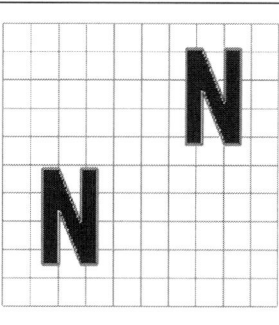

11. Which type of transformation is represented in the diagram?

A. rotation

B. translation

C. reflection across a vertical line

D. reflection across a horizontal line

Use the following information to answer the next question.

Ginny invited 32 of her friends over for a party. Of her total group of invited friends, 20 were girls, and the rest were boys.

12. What is the ratio of boys to the total number of friends at the party?

A. 3:8

B. 3:5

C. 5:8

D. 8:3

13. Jackson spends $306 to purchase 17 cans of paint to finish the interior of his house.
What is the price per can of paint?

A. $10/can

B. $17/can

C. $18/can

D. $23/can

Use the following information to answer the next question.

Pam makes a pattern using stickers.

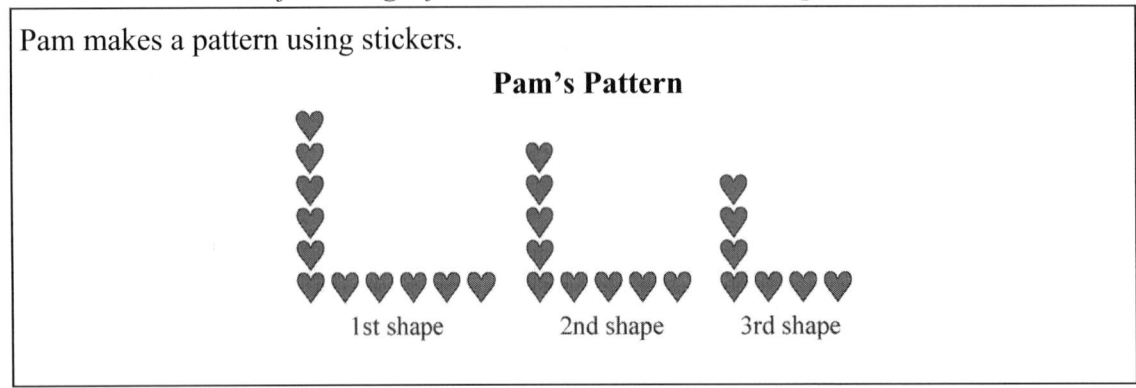

14. How many hearts would be in the next three shapes in Pam's pattern?

A. 5, 3, and 1

B. 5, 4, and 3

C. 6, 4, and 2

D. 7, 5, and 3

Open Response

15. Use the pattern rule, *double each term and subtract 1*, to list the ordered pairs in the table below.

Term Number	Term Value
2	

Plot the ordered pairs on the grid below.

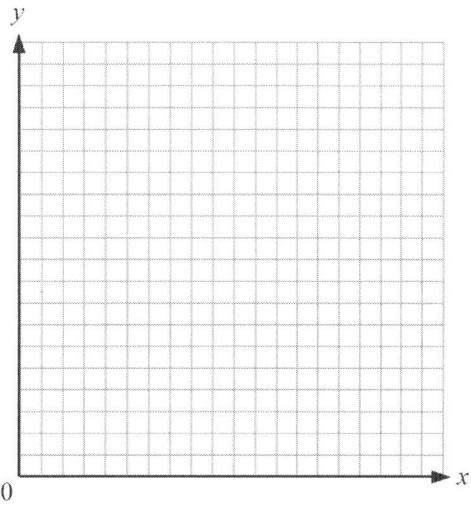

Use the following information to answer the next question.

Rhea works in a bakery. She uses this chart to help her plan how much flour and icing she needs for each set of trays of cinnamon buns that she makes.

Number of Trays	Cups of Flour	Cups of Icing
6	10	3
12	15	6
18	20	9
24	25	12

16. How many cups of icing will Rhea need for 42 trays of cinnamon buns?

A. 18   **B.** 21

C. 24   **D.** 40

Use the following information to answer the next question.

Jim makes the pattern below.

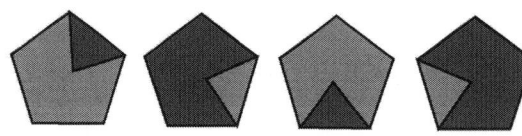

17. Which figure is next in Jim's pattern?

A.    **B.**

C. 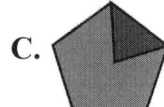   **D.**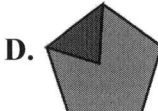

18. What are the variables in the expression $x + 2y - 4$?

A. $-1, x$ **B.** $3, y$

C. x, y **D.** $2, y$

19. Which situation **most likely** exhibits a constant rate?

A. a person's income

B. the wind speed over an area

C. the sale of books over a period of one week

D. the time taken by the moon to complete one revolution around Earth

20. If $x = 1$ and $y = 2$, what is the value of the expression $10x + 4y$?

    A. 16   **B.** 17

    C. 18   **D.** 19

Use the following information to answer the next question.

Mark's elementary school has a bake sale every year. For next year, the school would like to know which items were best sellers. Mark conducted a survey of item sales for 2007 and compared it with a list of the sales from 2006, which he found in the school office.

School's Bake Sale Results for 2007				
Baked Goods	Muffins	Pies	Cookies	Tarts
Amount Sold in 2007	35	40	49	22

School's Bake Sale Results for 2006				
Baked Goods	Muffins	Pies	Cookies	Tarts
Amount Sold in 2006	50	45	42	29

Open Response

21. Display only the primary data results in a bar graph. Remember to include all titles and labels.

Use the following information to answer the next question.

Mr. Takada surveyed a group of Grade 4 students to find out which foreign languages they would like to learn. The chart below shows the percentages of his finding.

Languages	Percentage
Mandarin Chinese	25
Spanish	50
French	15
Italian	10

22. Which graph **best** shows the data that Mr. Takada collected?

A.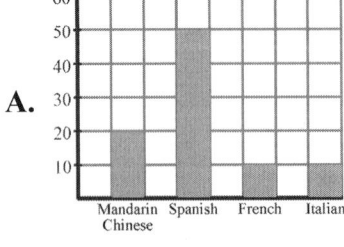

B.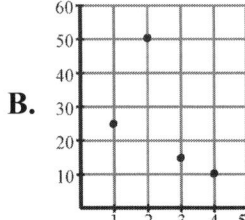

C.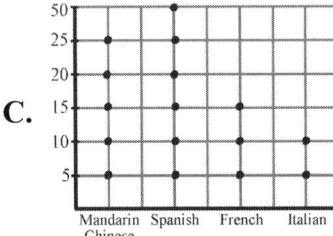

D.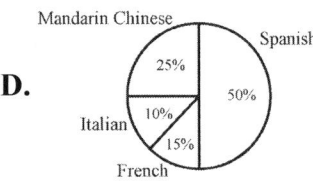

23. The sports department of a school wants to know which sport is the most popular among the students. Which group would prove **most** useful for the survey?

A. A group of 15 teenage girls

B. A group of 15 teenage boys

C. A group of 15 kindergarten children

D. A group of 15 boys and girls of all ages

Use the following information to answer the next question.

Ari is training for an Iron Man competition. He rode his bike for 6 hours one day. This graph shows his average speed per hour for each of the 6 hours.

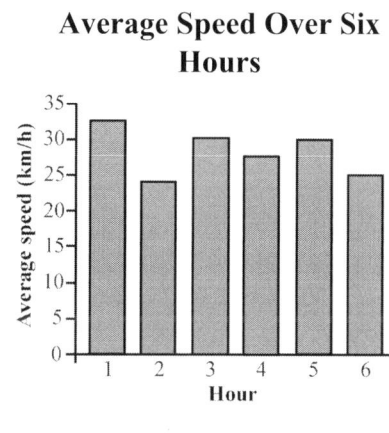

24. Which broken-line graph represents the same data as the bar graph?

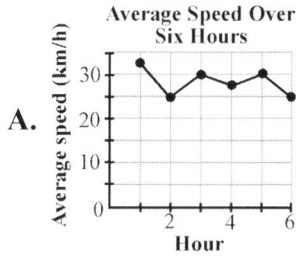

A.

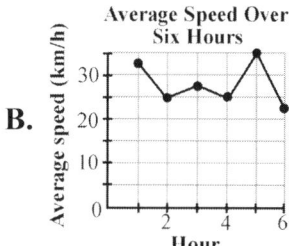

B.

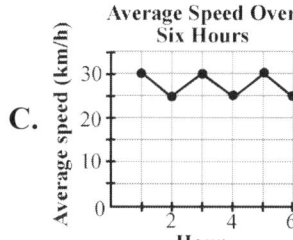

C.

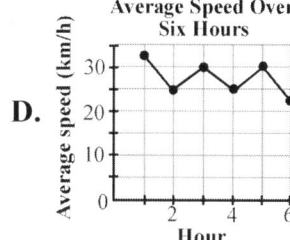

D.

25. What is the place value position of the digit 2 in the number 143.329?

    A. Hundredths place   **B.** Tenths place

    C. Tens place   **D.** Hundreds place

Open Response

26. Write the fractions $2\frac{1}{2}$, $\frac{3}{8}$, $\frac{6}{4}$, and $\frac{7}{12}$ in order from least to greatest. Explain your thinking

27. Which of the following sets of fractions is correctly ordered from least to greatest?

A. $\frac{1}{2}$, $\frac{3}{4}$, $\frac{11}{2}$, $\frac{16}{5}$

B. $\frac{11}{2}$, $\frac{16}{5}$, $\frac{3}{4}$, $\frac{1}{2}$

C. $\frac{1}{2}$, $\frac{3}{4}$, $\frac{16}{5}$, $\frac{11}{2}$

D. $\frac{3}{4}$, $\frac{11}{2}$, $\frac{16}{5}$, $\frac{1}{2}$

28. Kam cut a 45.60 m long rope into 15 equal segments. What is the length of each segment?

A. 2.04 m

B. 2.40 m

C. 3.04 m

D. 3.40 m

29. Dave received $40 for doing chores. Then, he spent $27.87 on a video game. About how much money does Dave have left?

A. $10.00

B. $11.00

C. $12.00

D. $13.00

Use the following information to answer the next question.

Jasjit solves the following question:

$3 + 2 \times 4 - 5$

$= 5 \times 4 - 5$

$= 20 - 5$

$= 15$

Open Response

30. Is Jasjit's answer correct? Why or why not? Explain your thinking.

Use the following information to answer the next question.

Rolf bought a bag of candy that had a mixture of gummy bears, jellybeans, and mints. He counted the number of different candies and the colour of each type of candy. Then, he made the following chart.

	Red	Yellow	Green
Gummy Bears	5	4	3
Jellybeans	1	5	6
Mints	8	2	2

Rolf decides to pick a candy out of the bag, return it to the bag, and pick a candy out again. He plans to do this five times.

Open Response

31. What is the probability of Rolf choosing a green gummy bear on his last pick? Show your work.

Use the following information to answer the next question.

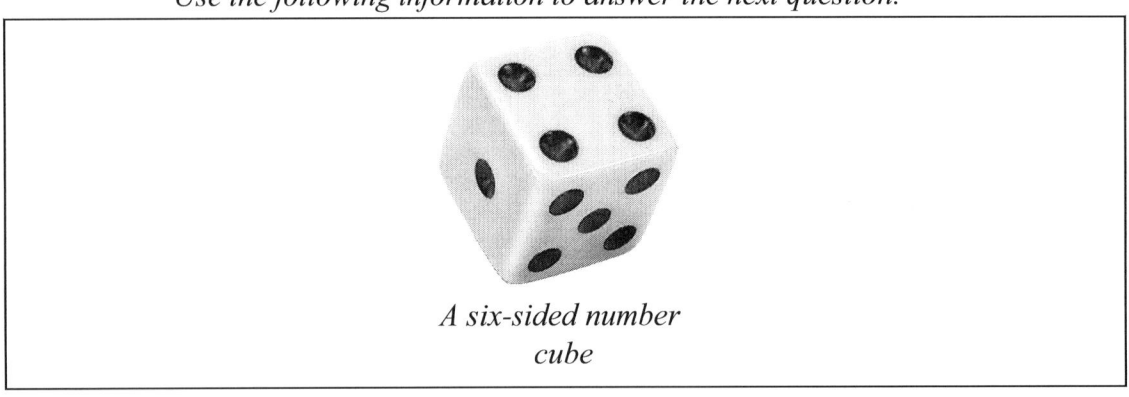

A six-sided number cube

32. On a six-sided number cube, what is the probability of rolling a number greater than 3?

A. 0.25   B. 0.50

C. 0.60   D. 0.75

33. The probability of rolling a 4 on a number cube is $\frac{1}{6}$. If a number cube is rolled 60 times, how many times would 4 be rolled?

    A. 4   **B.** 10

    C. 40   **D.** 60

Use the following information to answer the next question.

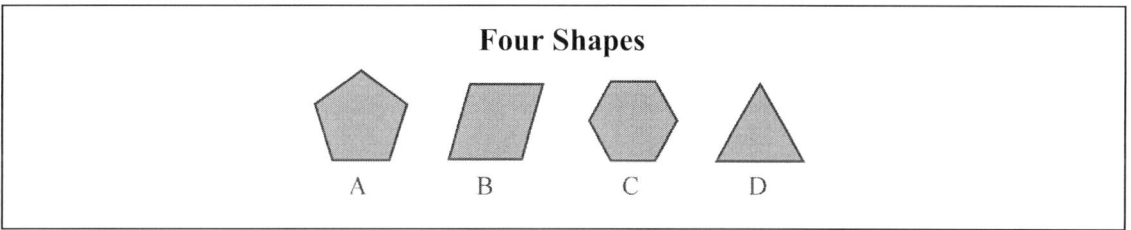

Four Shapes

34. What is the correct order of the shapes from the shape with the most lines of symmetry to the shape with the fewest lines of symmetry?

    A. C, A, D, and B   **B.** C, A, B, and D

    C. A, C, B, and D   **D.** A, C, D, and B

35. Which pizza slice shows an angle that is approximately 45 degrees?

    A. 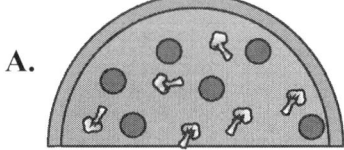   **B.**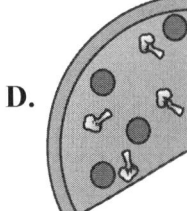

    C.    **D.**

Use the following information to answer the next question.

Using a ruler and a protractor, construct a quadrilateral with:

- 2 angles measuring 45° each
- 2 angles measuring 135° each
- 2 parallel sides measuring 6 cm each
- 2 parallel sides measuring 4 cm each

Open Response

36. What is the name of the quadrilateral?

ANSWERS AND SOLUTIONS — PRACTICE TEST 1

1. OR	9. A	17. C	25. C	33. C
2. C	10. A	18. D	26. C	34. OR
3. C	11. C	19. D	27. OR	35. D
4. D	12. OR	20. OR	28. B	36. A
5. C	13. C	21. B	29. D	
6. B	14. OR	22. C	30. C	
7. OR	15. B	23. OR	31. B	
8. C	16. B	24. C	32. C	

1. OR

Points	Sample Answer
4	Thorough ability in sketching the different views of a 3-D figure.

The 3-D figure shows that the front view is three levels high, the side view is two levels wide with two levels high on the front and three levels high on the back, and the top view is two levels wide.

Each view would look like this:

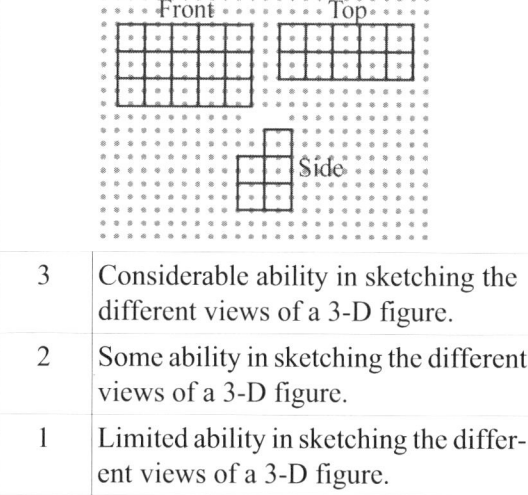

3	Considerable ability in sketching the different views of a 3-D figure.
2	Some ability in sketching the different views of a 3-D figure.
1	Limited ability in sketching the different views of a 3-D figure.

2. C

Both 10 millilitres and 100 millilitres are too low, while 10 litres is too high. The best estimate of the capacity of the juice carton is 1 litre.

3. C

Since $\begin{array}{l} 1\ 000\ \text{mm} = 1\ \text{m} \\ 100\ \text{cm} = 1\ \text{m} \end{array}$, millimetres and centimetres are too small to measure the height of a flag pole.

Since 1 000 m = 1 km, kilometres are too large to measure the height of a flag pole.

The most appropriate unit to use is the metre.

4. D

To convert kilograms into grams, remember that 1 kg is equal to 1 000 g.

Since the toy weighs 2 kg, it should be multiplied by 1 000 to obtain the weight in grams.

$2 \times 1\ 000 = 2\ 000$

Therefore, the toy weighs 2 000 g.

5. C

To find the total litres of pop the guests drank, first find out how many total millilitres the guests drank.

Each guest drank two 400 mL glasses of pop.

$2 \times 400 = 800$ mL

Each guest drank 800 mL of pop.

20 guests × 800 mL = 160 mL

The guests drank a total of 16 0 mL of pop.

To convert millilitres into litres, remember that 1 0 mL = 1 L.

$160 \div 1\ 0 = 16$ L

Therefore, the total litres of pop the guests drank was 16 L. Alternative C is correct.

6. B

Farrah bends the wire into a rectangle, which means that the length of the wire is the same as the perimeter of the rectangle.

The perimeter of the rectangle is 42, so the length of each side must be found:

perimeter of a rectangle

$= $ side $+$ side $+$ side $+$ side

$= 2 \times$ length $+ 2 \times$ width

If the rectangle's dimensions were 7 cm $\times$ 6 cm, the perimeter would be $7 + 7 + 6 + 6 = 26$ cm, which does not match the length of Farrah's wire.

If the rectangle's dimensions were 12 cm $\times$ 9 cm, the perimeter would be B

If the rectangle's dimensions were 18 cm $\times$ 6 cm, the perimeter would be C

If the rectangle's dimensions were 20 cm $\times$ 2 cm, the perimeter would be D

Therefore, the dimensions of the rectangle could be 12 cm $\times$ 9 cm.

7. OR

Points	Sample Answer
4	Thorough ability in calculating the area of a rectangle. Is able to convert square metres to square centimetres.

To determine the greatest number of posters that can be drawn on one piece of posterboard, find the area of the large piece of posterboard and the area of each poster.

Area of posterboard

$= 3.0$ m $\times 1.2$ m $= 3.6$ m^2

Area of each poster

$= 60$ cm $\times 80$ cm $= 4800$ cm^2

Because the area of the posterboard and the area of each poster are in different units, convert both to the same unit.

Points	Sample Answer
	There are 10 0 cm^2 in 1 m^2.
	$3.6 \times 100 = 360$ cm^2
	To find out what is the greatest number of posters that can be drawn on one piece of posterboard, divide the area of the posterboard by the area of each poster.
	360 cm^2 $\div 4800$ cm^2 $= 7.5$ cm^2
	Therefore the greatest number of posters that can be drawn on one piece of posterboard is 7.
3	Considerable ability in calculating the area of a rectangle and demonstrates a considerable ability to convert square metres to square centimetres with minor errors.
2	Some ability in calculating the area of a rectangle and/or is somewhat able to convert square metres to square centimetres.
1	Limited ability in calculating the area of a rectangle and/or is not able to convert square metres to square centimetres.

8. C

To find the surface area of the cushion, use the formula: $SA = 2B + pH$, where B is the area of the base, p is the perimeter of the base, and H is the height.

$B = $ length $\times$ width

$B = 22$ cm $\times 24$ cm

$B = 528$ cm^2

$p = $ side $+$ side $+$ side $+$ side

$p = (22 + 22 + 24 + 24)$ cm

$p = 92$ cm

$H = 5$

$SA = (2 \times 528 \text{ cm}^2) + (92 \text{ cm} \times 5 \text{ cm})$

$SA = 156$ cm$^2 + 460$ cm^2

$SA = 1516$ cm^2

Therefore, the surface area of each cushion is 1 516 cm^2.

The correct alternative is C.

9. A

The volume V of a prism is $B \times h$, where B is the area of the base of the prism, and h is the height of the prism.

This prism has a triangular base. Therefore, to find the area of the shaded region, we have to find the area of the triangle.

The volume of the triangular prism is 92 cm³, and the height of the prism is 6 cm.

$V = B \times h$
$92 = B \times 6$
$B = \dfrac{92}{6}$
$\approx 15.3 \text{ cm}^2$

The best choice is 15 cm².

10. A

To plot point $P(2, 7)$ on a graph, move 2 units right from the origin on the x-axis and then 7 units up.

The correct graph, A, is shown below.

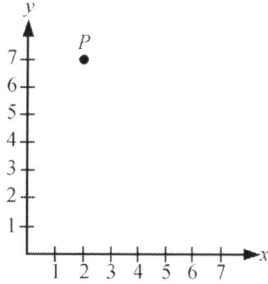

11. C

The diagram in choice A shows an example of a reflection. The two images are mirror reflections meaning that they are the same shape and size just facing opposite directions. They have not been rotated.

The diagram in choice B shows an example of a translation. The two images are the same shape and size and are facing the same direction. They have not been rotated.

The diagram in choice C shows an example of a 90 ° C rotation. The image on the right side shows a 90 degree C clockwise rotation. They are still the same shape and size but are now in different directions without producing a mirror image.

The diagram in choice D shows an example of a reflection. The two images are mirror reflections meaning that they are the same shape and size just facing opposite directions. They have not been rotated.

12. OR

Points	Sample Answer
4	Thorough understanding of transformations and is able to explain which transformations have occurred.

Figure ABC has been reflected across Line 2 and rotated clockwise 90° about point C.

Figure ABC could also have been translate 6 units to the right and then rotated counter-clockwise 90° about point C.

3	Considerable understanding of transformations and is able to explain which transformations have occurred.
2	Some understanding of transformations and is somewhat able to explain which transformations have occurred.
1	Limited understanding of transformations and is not able to explain which transformations have occurred.

13. C

To change a percent to a fraction, put 64 over 100: $\dfrac{64}{100}$

You can see that the denominator in all the fractions is 25, so you must change $\dfrac{64}{100}$ to a fraction with denominator 25.

Since $100 \div 25$ is 4, you must divide both the numerator and denominator by 4:

$\dfrac{64 \div 4}{100 \div 4} = \dfrac{16}{25}$

The fraction that is equivalent to 64 % is $\dfrac{16}{25}$.

Therefore, alternative C is correct.

14. OR

Points	Sample Answer
4	Demonstrates an understanding of fractions and demonstrates a thorough understanding of how to convert fractions into decimals and percents.

By looking at the diagram, you can see that there are 20 squares and that 8 of them are shaded.

As a fraction, this is written as $\frac{8}{20}$. The fraction means that 8 out of the 20 equal parts are shaded.

To change a fraction into a decimal, divide 8 by 20 on a calculator. $\frac{8}{20} = 0.40$.

To change a decimal into a percent, 0.40 is 40 hundredths and is therefore equal to 40% because 40% is 40 out of 100.

Therefore, the shaded part of the diagram can be written as $\frac{8}{20}$, 0.40, or 40%.

3	Demonstrates an understanding of fractions and demonstrates a considerable understanding of how to convert fractions into decimals and percents.
2	Demonstrates some understanding of fractions and demonstrates some understanding of how to convert fractions into decimals and percents.
1	Demonstrates a limited understanding of fractions and demonstrates a limited understanding of how to convert fractions into decimals and percents.

15. B

In the set 423, 524, 625, 726, the hundreds digit increases by 1, but the ones digit also increases by 1.

In the set 664, 675, 686, 697, the hundreds digit is the same in all the numbers, and the ones digit increases by 1.

In the set 955, 854, 753, 652, the hundreds digit decreases by 1, and the ones digit decreases by 1.

In the set 265, 364, 463, 562, the hundreds digit increases by 1, and the ones digit decreases by 1.

16. B

The difference in Felipe's wages shows that his first wage increased by $0.15, his second increased by $0.20, his third increased by $0.25, and his fourth increased by $0.30. The number that is being added to his wage is increasing by 0.05 each time. Therefore, his next wage increase (for the year 2009) is found by adding $0.35 to his previous wage (the year 2008).

$12.73 + $0.35 = $13.08

Felipe's wage in 2009 will be $13.08.

17. C

The graph shows that the rainfall increases by 1.5 cm every hour. After 4 hours, there is total of 6.0 cm of rainfall. If the pattern continues, by the fifth hour, there should be 7.5 cm of rainfall.

6.0 + 1.5 = 7.5 cm of rainfall.

The correct answer is C.

18. D

Pattern rule A, 7 776 − 6 480 = 1 296, 1 296 − 6 480 = −5184, is incorrect.

Pattern rule B, 7 776 − 1 080 = 6 696, is incorrect.

Pattern rule C, 7 776 × 6 = 46 656, is incorrect.

Pattern rule D, 7 776 ÷ 6 = 1 296D 1 296 ÷ 6 = 216, 216 ÷ 6 = 36, is correct.

19. D

The numbers in the pattern increase by multiplying each number with 2 and adding 1.

6 × 2 + 1 = 13, 13 × 2 + 1 = 27, 27 × 2 + 1 = 55, 55 × 2 + 1 = 111

Therefore, the next number in the pattern is 111. Kate will receive 111 toothpicks.

20. OR

Points	Sample Answer
4	Thoroughly understands how to determine a pattern rule and extend a pattern.
	To find the next terms in the pattern, find the difference between each term.
	$1600 - 1425 = 175$
	$1425 - 1250 = 175$
	$1250 - 175 = 175$
	$175 - 900 = 175$
	The pattern rule is to subtract 175 from each term.
	To find the tenth term, extend the pattern.
	6th term: $900 - 175 = 725$
	7th term: $725 - 175 = 550$
	8th term: $550 - 175 = 375$
	9th term: $375 - 175 = 200$
	10th term: $200 - 175 = 25$
	The 10th term in the pattern is 25.
3	Shows considerable understanding in how to determine a pattern rule and extend a pattern with minor errors.
2	Shows some understanding in how to determine a pattern rule and extend a pattern.
1	Shows limited understanding in how to determine a pattern rule and extend a pattern.

21. B

Let the number of cars that Mr. Owens has be x. The number of cars owned by Mr. Willis is 3 less than twice the number of cars owned by Mr. Owens.

Twice the number of cars owned by Mr. Owens is equal to $2x$. Three less than that is $2x - 3$.

Therefore, the number of cars owned by Mr. Wills is $2x - 3$.

22. C

Sophie wants to find out how many hours a day students in her Grade 6 class spent watching television and how many hours they spent studying. In order to gather data for her project, she must decide which method of collecting the information will best suit her needs.

A Designing an experiment to collect such data is not appropriate because an experiment could not provide the information needed.

B This information would not be found on the Internet.

C The best method for Nicole to gather the information she needs would be for her to design and use a structured questionnaire.

D It would be very difficult to gather this information through observation.

23. OR

Points	Sample Answer
4	Displays the given data in an appropriate graph and gives a thorough explanation for the type of graph chosen.

The best way to display the information would be on a pictograph or bar graph because the amounts of allowance are all within particular ranges.

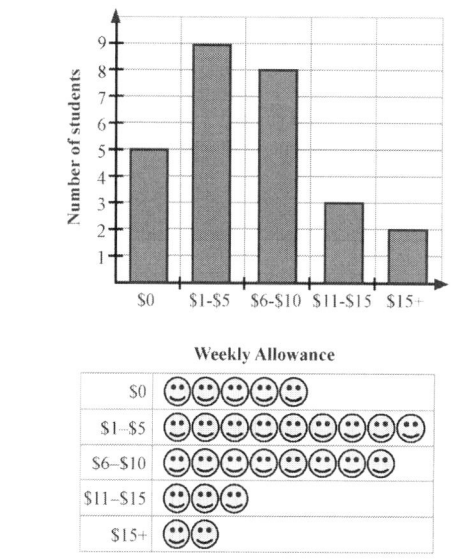

Points	Sample Answer
3	Displays the given data in an inappropriate graph and gives an explanation for the type of graph chosen.
2	Displays the given data in an inappropriate graph and gives an explanation for the type of graph chosen.
1	Displays the given data in an inappropriate graph gives no explanation for the type of graph chosen.

24. C

A Wilderness Magazine is not the most popular, as 567 people preferred Fashion Patrol magazine, while only 420 preferred Wilderness Magazine. This alternative is incorrect.

B News Weekly is preferred by 381 people, but 454 people prefer Sports Digest. This alternative is incorrect.

C Sports Digest is preferred by 322 males, while only 199 males prefer News Weekly. This alternative is correct.

D Woodworking is not preferred by most people, as only 178 out of 2 000 people who responded said they preferred it. This alternative is incorrect.

25. C

To find the mean mass of the apples, add the mass of all the apples together and divide by the number of apples, which is 5.

$230 + 170 + 190 + 220 + 190 = 1\ 000$

$$\frac{1\ 000}{5} = 200$$

Therefore, the mean mass of the apples is 200 g.

26. C

The given number line starts with 0.18 and increases by 0.06 at each consecutive mark. The number 0.48 lies between 0.30 and 0.60. There are four points between 0.30 and 0.60. The first point represents $0.30 + 0.06 = 0.36$, the second point represents $0.36 + 0.06 = 0.42$, and the third point represents $0.42 + 0.06 = 0.48$. Therefore, point R represents 0.48.

27. OR

Points	Sample Answer
4	Thorough understanding of large whole numbers and how to convert days into minutes.

To determine how many days are equal to 1 000 000 minutes, you must first find out how many hours are equal to 1 000 000 minutes.

There are 60 minutes in an hour, so to find out how many hours are equal to 1 000 000 minutes, divide 1 000 000 by 60.

$\frac{1\ 000\ 000}{60}$ is about 16 667 hours.

There are 24 hours in a day, so to find out how many days are equal to 1 000 000 minutes, you must divide 16 667 by 24.

$\frac{16\ 667}{24}$ is about 694 days.

Therefore, about 694 days are equal to 1 000 000 minutes.

3	Considerable understanding of large whole numbers and how to convert days into minutes (e.g., makes a calculation error when dividing in any step).
2	Some understanding of large whole numbers and how to convert days into minutes (e.g., misses a step).
1	Limited understanding of large whole numbers and how to convert days into minutes (e.g., does not understand the relationship of multiples 60 × 60).

28. B

To find the prime factors of 28, use a tree diagram.

28
$= 14 \times 2$
$= 7 \times 2 \times 2$

The prime factors of 28 are 2 and 7.

Therefore, alternative B is correct.

29. D

Using the commutative property, change the order of the numbers to make it easier to multiply.

$2 \times 14 \times 5$ becomes $2 \times 5 \times 14$

$2 \times 5 \times 14$

$= 10 \times 14$

$= 140$

The correct answer is D.

30. C

There are approximately 190 words per page and 310 pages in the book.

First, round 190 up to 200, because the 9 in the tens place is greater than 5.

Then, round 310 down to 300, because the 1 in the tens place is less than 5.

Multiply 200 by 300 for a quick estimate of the number of words in the book ($200 \times 300 = 60\ 000$).

Therefore, there are approximately 60 000 words in *The Adventures of Tom Sawyer*.

31. B

To find out how much money Anisha has left, subtract the amount she spent from the amount she had to begin with.

$10.00
$-$ $2.55
$7.45

Therefore, Anisha has $7.45 left for the rest of the week.

The correct answer is B.

32. C

Derrick has 6 chances to win the prize because he has 6 tickets. There are 2 000 possible outcomes because 2 000 tickets are sold.

Therefore, the probability of winning the prize is $\dfrac{6}{2\ 000}$ or, in lowest terms, $\dfrac{3}{1\ 000}$.

33. C

To predict how many times the coins will land heads up, first find the probability of one coin landing heads up, then multiply it by the number of times the coin is flipped.

There are 2 possible outcomes: heads up or tails up. There is 1 favourable outcome: heads up.

Therefore, the probability of a coin landing heads up is $\dfrac{1}{2}$.

If 10 people flip a coin 10 times, multiply the probability of the coin landing heads up by the number of times the coin is being flipped, then multiply that by the number of people flipping the coins. Since 10 people flipping a coin 10 times is equal to 100 flips, multiply $\dfrac{1}{2}$ by 100.

$\dfrac{1}{2} \times 100 = 50$

Therefore, if 10 people each flip a coin 10 times, you could expect the coins to land heads up about 50 times.

34. OR

Points	Sample Answer
4	Demonstrates a thorough understanding of how to predict the frequency of an outcome.

If Juan hits the ball 7 times out of 10, the probability that he will hit the ball is $\dfrac{7}{10}$.

If he takes 30 swings, he will likely hit the ball $\dfrac{7}{10} \times 30$ times.

$\dfrac{7}{10} \times 30 = \dfrac{210}{10} = 21$.

Each season, Juan can expect to hit the ball 21 times.

3	Demonstrates a considerable understanding of how to predict the frequency of an outcome.
2	Demonstrates some understanding of how to predict the frequency of an outcome.

Points	Sample Answer
1	Demonstrates a limited understanding of how to predict the frequency of an outcome.

35. D

Step 1

Consider the characteristics of each given quadrilateral.

- AA square has 4 sides that are of equal length and 4 right angles.
- BA rectangle has 2 sets of parallel lines, 2 sets of equal side lengths, and 4 right angles.
- CA trapezoid has 1 set of parallel lines. It could have no equal side lengths or it could have one set of equal side lengths. It could have any type of angles (right, greater than right, less than right).
- DA parallelogram has 2 sets of parallel lines, 2 sets of equal side lengths, 2 angles greater than right angles, and 2 angles less than right angles.

Step 2

Identify the quadrilateral that meets all the clues that Ryan gave.

The parallelogram meets all the clues that Ryan gave.

Parallelogram

36. A

The figure shown has 2 lines of symmetry.

A The rectangle has 2 lines of symmetry

B The square has 4 lines of symmetry

C The equilateral (all sides of equal length) triangle has 3 lines of symmetry

A The pentagon (all sides equal) has 5 lines of symmetry

Choice A, the rectangle, has the same number of lines of symmetry as the figure shown.

ANSWERS AND SOLUTIONS — PRACTICE TEST 2

1. B	9. OR	17. D	25. A	33. B
2. C	10. B	18. C	26. OR	34. A
3. D	11. B	19. D	27. C	35. C
4. OR	12. A	20. C	28. C	36. OR
5. C	13. C	21. OR	29. C	
6. C	14. A	22. D	30. OR	
7. D	15. OR	23. D	31. OR	
8. B	16. B	24. A	32. B	

1. B

One way to measure the area covered by the tiles is to count the number of shaded squares. There are 12 tiles in the two vertical columns on the left, 12 tiles in the two vertical columns on the right, and 10 tiles in both the top and bottom rows, for a total of

$12 + 12 + 10 = 34$ tiles.

Each tile has an area of 1 m², so the total area covered by tiles is 34 m².

2. C

To find out how far Alex ran, subtract the distance that Harry and Eri ran from 3 km.

First, you must convert 3 km into metres.

To convert kilometres into metres, remember that 1 km is equal to 1 000 m.

$3 \times 1\ 000 = 3\ 000$ m

$3\ 000$ m $- 925$ m $- 1\ 025$ m $= 1\ 050$ m

Therefore, Alex ran 1 050 m.

3. D

Area of a triangle $= \dfrac{1}{2} \times$ base $\times$ height

The area of the rectangle is twice the area of each triangle.

Area of the rectangle $= 2 \times \dfrac{1}{2} \times b \times h$

Area of the rectangle $= b \times h$

Area of the rectangle $= 10$ cm $\times 6$ cm

Area of the rectangle $= 60$ cm²

Therefore, the area of the rectangle would be 60 cm².

4. OR

Points	Sample Answer
4	Thorough understanding of how to divide a quadrilateral into a triangle and rectangle. Is able to calculate the area of a rectangle and the area of a triangle.

In order to find the area of figure *ABCD*, divide the figure into two shapes (a rectangle and a triangle) find the areas of the two shapes, and add them together.

Figure *ABCD* can be divided into a rectangle and a triangle.

The rectangle has a height of 6 cm and a base of 7 cm.

The triangle has a height of 6 cm and a base of 4 cm(11 cm − 7 cm).

Area of the rectangle
$= 7$ cm $\times 6$ cm $= 42$ cm²

Area of the triangle
$= \dfrac{1}{2} \times 4 \times 6 = 2$ cm $\times 6$ cm $= 12$ cm²

Add the area of the rectangle and the area of the triangle.

42 cm² $+ 12$ cm² $= 54$ cm²

Therefore, the area of figure *ABCD* is 54 cm².

3	Considerable understanding of how to divide a quadrilateral into a triangle and rectangle. Is able to calculate the area of a rectangle and the area of a triangle with minor errors.

Points	Sample Answer
2	Some understanding of how to divide a quadrilateral into a triangle and rectangle. Is somewhat able to calculate the area of a rectangle and/or the area of a triangle.
1	Limited understanding of how to divide a quadrilateral into a triangle and rectangle. Is somewhat able or not able to calculate the area of a rectangle and/or the area of a triangle.

5. C

To find the area of a parallelogram, use the formula:

Area of a parallelogram = base × height

$A = 5 \text{ m} \times 10 \text{ m}$

$A = 50 \text{ m}^2$

6. C

To find the area of a rectangle, use the formula:
$A = \text{length} \times \text{width}$

$A = 3 \text{ m} \times 2 \text{ m}$

$A = 6 \text{ m}^2$

To convert m^2 into cm^2, remember that $1 \text{ m}^2 = 100 \text{ cm}^2$.

$6 \text{ m}^2 = 6 \times 10\ 000 \text{ cm}^2$

$6 \text{ m}^2 = 60\ 000 \text{ cm}^2$

Therefore, the area of the rectangle, in centimetres, is $60\ 000 \text{ cm}^2$.

7. D

To find the surface area of the covered box, use the formula: $SA = 2B + pH$, where B is the area of the base, p is the perimeter of the base, and H is the height of the prism.

$B = \text{length} \times \text{width}$

$B = 25 \text{ cm} \times 10 \text{ cm}$

$B = 250 \text{ cm}^2$

$p = \text{side} + \text{side} + \text{side} + \text{side}$

$p = (25 + 25 + 10 + 10) \text{ cm}$

$p = 70 \text{ cm}$

$H = 8$

$SA = (2 \times 250 \text{ cm}^2) + (70 \text{ cm} \times 8 \text{ cm})$

$SA = 500 \text{ cm}^2 + 560 \text{ cm}^2$

$SA = 160 \text{ cm}^2$

8. B

To calculate the volume of each prism, use the formula $V = l \times w \times h$.

A is $8 \text{ cm} \times 3 \text{ cm} \times 4 \text{ cm} = 96 \text{ cm}^3$

B is $4 \text{ cm} \times 5 \text{ cm} \times 6 \text{ cm} = 120 \text{ cm}^3$

C is $4 \text{ cm} \times 6 \text{ cm} \times 4 \text{ cm} = 96 \text{ cm}^3$

D is $4 \text{ cm} \times 5 \text{ cm} \times 4 \text{ cm} = 80 \text{ cm}^3$

The prism with the greatest volume is prism B.

9. OR

Points	Sample Answer
4	Thorough ability in translating a figure on a coordinate plane and able to write the new coordinates.

Points	Sample Answer
	The coordinates of *ABC* are *A*(3,7), *B*(3, 2), *C*(0, 2).
	If each coordinate is moved to the right 5 units, the *x*-coordinate values increase by 5.
	The new coordinates become *A*(8, 7), *B*(8, 2), *C*(5, 2).
	The new figure should look like this: 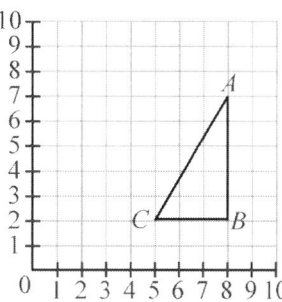
3	Considerable ability in translating a figure on a coordinate plane and is able to write the new coordinates.
2	Some ability in translating a figure on a coordinate plane and/or is somewhat able to write the new coordinates.
1	Limited ability in translating a figure on a coordinate plane and/or is not able to write the new coordinates.

10. B

A figure and its rotated image have the same shape and size, but may have different orientations.

The figure shown in B has been rotated clockwise 90°.

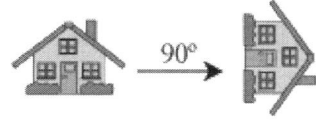

11. B

The figure on the left is translated 5 units right and 4 units up to get the figure on the right. Therefore, B is the correct answer.

12. A

The number of boys invited to the party can be found by subtracting the number of girls invited to the party from the total number of friends invited to the party.

$32 - 20 = 12$. The ratio of boys to the total number of friends is 12:32 or $\frac{12}{32}$.

Both numbers are divisible by 4, so in lowest terms, the ratio can be written as 3:8.

$$\frac{12}{32} \div \frac{4}{4} = \frac{3}{8}$$

Remember to write the number of boys first and the total number of friends second (3:8).

13. C

Since Jackson spent $306 for 17 cans of paint, divide 306 by 17 to get the unit rate per can.

$306 \div 17 = \$18/\text{can}$

Therefore, each can of paint costs $18.

14. A

To find the next three shapes in Pam's pattern, first look carefully at her pattern. Her pattern decreases by two hearts in each new shape. Find the three shapes that continue this pattern and count how many hearts would be in each shape.

To continue the pattern numerically, decrease each term by 2:
$11 - 2, 9 - 2, 7 - 2, 5 - 2, 3 - 2$.

So, the next three terms are 5, 3, and 1.

15. OR

Points	Sample Answer
4	Able to extend a pattern, given the pattern rule, and plot the ordered pairs.

The pattern rule is *double each term and subtract 1*, and the table starts with the term number 2.
$2 \times 2 - 1 = 3$
$3 \times 2 - 1 = 5$
$5 \times 2 - 1 = 9$
$9 \times 2 - 1 = 17$

Points	Sample Answer	

Term Number:	Term Value:
2	3
3	5
5	9
9	17

The ordered pairs are listed with the term number first, then the term value: (2, 3), (3, 5), (5, 9), (9, 17).

To plot the ordered pairs, plot the term number along the *x*-axis and the term value along the *y*-axis.

3	Able to extend a pattern, given the pattern rule, and plot the ordered pairs with minor errors.
2	Somewhat able to extend a pattern, given the pattern rule, and plot the ordered pairs with errors.
1	Somewhat able to extend a pattern, given the pattern rule, and somewhat plot the ordered pairs with errors.

16. B

The pattern of the number of trays shows that the numbers are multiples of 6, or that each number increases by 6.

The pattern of the cups of flour shows that the numbers are multiples of 5, or that each number increases by 5.

The pattern of the cups of icing, you can see that the numbers are multiples of 3, or that each numbers increases by 3.

To find how many cups of icing Rhea will need for 42 trays of cinnamon buns, continue the pattern (increase each number by 6) until 42 trays are reached. Continue the pattern of cups of icing (increase each number by 3) until the number that matches 42 trays is reached.

Number of Trays	Cups of Flour	Cups of Icing
30	30	15
36	35	18
42	40	21

17. D

The little triangle inside the pentagon is rotating clockwise by one side of the pentagon each time. To follow the pattern, the little triangle would rotate clockwise by one side and would end up on the top left side, as in A or D. However, the pattern also changes between light pentagon to dark pentagon, and to follow the pattern, the next pentagon would be light. Therefore, the pentagon in D is correct.

18. C

Variables are letters or symbols that represent an unknown or changing quantity. In the expression $x + 2y - 4$, there are two unknown quantities, x and y.

19. D

The time taken by the moon to complete one revolution around Earth is 27 days 7 hours 43 minutes. This rate is constant.

20. C

It is given that $x = 1$ and $y = 2$. Substitute 1 for the x variable and 2 for the y variable.
$10x + 4y$
$= (10 \times 1) + (4 \times 2)$
$= 10 + 8$
$= 18$

21. OR

Points	Sample Answer
4	Displays the correct information in a graph. Shows thorough understanding of the difference between primary and secondary data.

Points	Sample Answer
	The data that Mark collected through a survey is primary data because it is information that was collected by Mark himself using observations at the bake sale. The data that Mark collected through research is secondary data because it is information that was collected by someone else at the previous year's bake sale. A bar graph displaying the results of the 2007 bake sale would look like this: 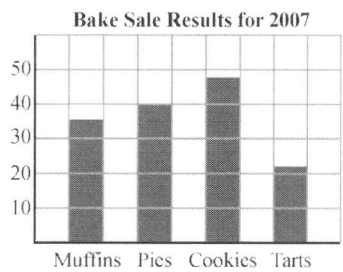 Bake Sale Results for 2007
3	Displays the correct information in a graph with minor errors. Shows considerable understanding of the difference between primary and secondary data.
2	Displays secondary information in a graph with errors. Understands somewhat the difference between primary and secondary data.
1	Does not display either given information in a graph. Shows limited understanding of how to display data.

22. D

In A, the bar graph shows the data incorrectly. For example, the bars for French and Italian are the same height when they should not be. Therefore, graph A does not match the given data.

In B, the numerical coordinates on the *x*-axis do not make sense because they are not matched to any language. Therefore, graph B is incorrect.

In C, there is a jump on the *y*-axis from 25 to 50. Also, it is unclear why there is more than one point graphed for each language. Therefore, graph C is incorrect.

The graph in D is the most appropriate graph for the given data. Circle graphs are best for representing data in percentages. Therefore, the best graph to represent the data in the table is D.

23. D

The best way to judge the most popular sport in the school is to survey boys and girls of all ages.

A This alternative does not consider boys or younger students.

B This alternative does not consider girls or younger students.

C This alternative does not consider students in other grades.

D This alternative is correct because it considers boys and girls of all ages.

The correct answer is D.

24. A

The graph in A is the only broken-line graph with numbers that correspond with the bar graph: 33, 25, 30, 27, 30, 25.

Hour is represented on the *x*-axis and average speed is represented on the *y*-axis. The ordered pairs are $(1, 33)$, $(2, 25)$, $(3, 30)$, $(4, 27)$, $(5, 30)$, and $(6, 25)$.

25. A

To determine the place value of the digit 2 in the number 143.329, use a place value chart.

Ones			.	Parts of a Whole		
H	T	O	.	Tth	Hth	Thth
1	4	3	.	3	2	9

The digit 2 is in the hundredths place, which is two places to the right of the decimal.

26. OR

Points	Sample Answer
4	Thorough understanding of mixed and improper fractions, how to find equivalent fractions, and how to order fractions.

Points	Sample Answer
	When comparing or ordering fractions, there are several methods that can be used, such as benchmarks and equivalent fractions, number lines, and changing fractions to decimals.

One method is to use equivalent fractions.

First, change any mixed numbers into improper fractions.

$2\frac{1}{2} = \frac{5}{2}$ (to find the numerator, $2 \times 2 + 1$, and the denominator stays the same)

Then, find a common denominator for each fraction. The denominator 24 is the lowest common denominator that can be used.

Remember, Whatever is done to the denominator, must also be done to the numerator.

The denominator, 2, must be multiplied by 12 to get the new denominator of 24.
$\frac{5 \times 12}{2 \times 12} = \frac{60}{24}$.

The denominator, 8, must be multiplied by 3 to get the new denominator of 24. $\frac{3 \times 3}{8 \times 3} = \frac{9}{24}$.

The denominator, 4, must be multiplied by 6 to get the new denominator of 24. $\frac{6 \times 6}{4 \times 6} = \frac{36}{24}$.

The denominator, 12, must be multiplied by 2 to get the new denominator of 24.
$\frac{7 \times 2}{12 \times 2} = \frac{14}{24}$.

So, with the same denominator of 24, the new fractions become

$\frac{60}{24}, \frac{9}{24}, \frac{36}{24}, \frac{14}{24}$

Now, order them from least to greatest by looking at the numerator.

$\frac{9}{24}, \frac{14}{24}, \frac{36}{24}, \frac{60}{24}$

In their original form, the fractions ordered from least to greatest are:

$\frac{3}{8}, \frac{7}{12}, \frac{6}{4}, 2\frac{1}{2}$.

Points	Sample Answer
3	Considerable understanding of mixed and improper fractions, how to find equivalent fractions, and how to order fractions (e.g., changes the improper fractions correctly to mixed numbers but makes an error when calculating the equivalency of one fraction).
2	Some understanding of mixed and improper fractions, how to find equivalent fractions, and how to order fractions (e.g., makes an error when changing an improper fraction to a mixed number or does not show understanding of equivalent fractions).
1	Limited understanding of mixed and improper fractions, how to find equivalent fractions, and how to order fractions (e.g., does not show understanding of improper fractions or equivalent fractions).

27. C

When comparing improper fractions, the best strategy is to find common denominators.

The lowest common denominator is 20 because:

$2 \times 10 = 20, \quad 4 \times 5 = 20, \quad \text{and } 5 \times 4 = 20$

$\frac{1}{2} \times \frac{10}{10} = \frac{10}{20}, \frac{3}{4} \times \frac{5}{5} = \frac{15}{20},$

$\frac{11}{2} \times \frac{10}{10} = \frac{110}{20}, \text{ and } \frac{16}{5} \times \frac{4}{4} = \frac{64}{20}.$

The ascending order (least to greatest) of the fractions is $\frac{1}{2}, \frac{3}{4}, \frac{16}{5}, \frac{11}{2}$

28. C

To find out the length of each segment of rope, divide the total length of rope by how many segments Kam cut the rope into.

45.60 m ÷ 15 = 3.04 m

Therefore, each piece of rope is 3.04 m long.

29. C

To estimate how much money Dave has left, round the decimal to a whole number and subtract it from $40.

The number 27.87 is rounded up to 28 because the digit 8 is greater than 5.

$40 - 28 = 12$

Therefore, Dave has about $12.00 left.

30. OR

Points	Sample Answer
4	Demonstrates an understanding of order of operations and is able to apply it with a high degree of effectiveness.

To determine if Jasjit's answer is correct, solve the equation using the rules for order of operations.

Remember to multiply or divide first, then add or subtract.
$3 + 2 \times 4 - 5$

Multiply 2×4 first (Jasjit added first and then multiplied, which is incorrect).
$= 3 + 8 - 5$
$= 11 - 5$
$= 6$

Therefore, Jasjit did not follow the rules for order of operations and did not answer the question correctly.

Points	Sample Answer
3	Demonstrates an understanding of order of operations and is able to apply it with a considerable degree of effectiveness.
2	Demonstrates an understanding of order of operations and is able to apply it with some degree of effectiveness.
1	Demonstrates an understanding of order of operations and is able to apply it with a limited degree of effectiveness.

31. OR

Points	Sample Answer
4	Understands how to calculate theoretical probability and does so correctly.

To find the total number of possible outcomes, add together all of the candies.

The total number of possible outcomes is 36.

To find the total number of favorable outcomes, find the number of green gummy bears.

The total number of favorable outcomes is 3.

To find the probability of Rolf choosing a green gummy bear on his last pick, use the formula for theoretical probability: favourable outcomes/possible outcomes.

The probability of Rolf choosing a green gummy bear is $\frac{3}{36}$, or in lowest terms, $\frac{1}{12}$.

3	Understands how to calculate theoretical probability and does so correctly but with minor errors.
2	Understands somewhat how to calculate theoretical probability and does so with errors.
1	Limited ability in calculating theoretical probability.

32. B

There are 6 possible outcomes when rolling a 6-sided number cube: 1, 2, 3, 4, 5, or 6.

In this case, there are 3 favourable outcomes: 4, 5, or 6.

$$\text{Probability} = \frac{\text{total favourable outcomes}}{\text{total possible number of outcomes}}$$

The theoretical probability of rolling a number greater than 3 on a 6-sided number cube is $\frac{3}{6}$.

Simplify the fraction $\frac{3}{6}$ by dividing both the numerator and the denominator by 3.

This fraction in simplest form is $\frac{1}{2}$.

The probability expressed as a number between 0 and 1 can be found by converting the fraction to a decimal fraction. To do this, divide the numerator by the denominator to obtain 0.50.

33. B

To predict the frequency of a 4 being rolled on a number cube that is rolled 60 times, multiply the probability of rolling a 4 by the total number of times the number cube is rolled.

$$\frac{1}{6} \times 60 = 10$$

Therefore, if a number cube is rolled 60 times, a 4 could be expected to be rolled 10 times.

34. A

Listed in order from the shape with the most lines of symmetry to the shape with the fewest lines of symmetry, the shapes are C, A, D, and B.

Shape A is a regular pentagon and has 5 lines of symmetry.

Shape B is a rhombus and has 2 lines of symmetry.

Shape C is a regular hexagon and has 6 lines of symmetry.

Shape D is an equilateral triangle and has 3 lines of symmetry.

35. C

A The pizza is sliced at an angle of 180°.

B The pizza is sliced at an angle of 90°.

C The pizza is sliced at an angle that is approximately 45°.

D The pizza is sliced at an angle greater than 90°.

The correct answer is C.

36. OR

Points	Sample Answer
4	Thorough ability in constructing a quadrilateral, given instructions.

Because there are no right angles in this quadrilateral, it is not a square or a rectangle, and because there are two sets of parallel sides, this figure is most likely a parallelogram.

Points	Sample Answer
	Use a ruler to draw a line measuring 6 cm.
	At one end of the line, use a protractor to draw an angle of 45°.
	Use a ruler to draw this line measuring 4 cm.
	At the other end of the line measuring 6 cm, draw an angle of 135°.
	Use a ruler to draw this line measuring 4 cm (because it is parallel to the other line measuring 4 cm).
	Connect the lines with a ruler, making sure this last line measures 6 cm (because it is parallel to the other line measuring 6 cm).
	The other two angles should measure 45° and 135°.
3	Considerable ability in constructing a quadrilateral with minor errors, given instructions.
2	Some ability in constructing a quadrilateral, given instructions.
1	Limited ability in constructing a quadrilateral, given instructions.

NOTES

NOTES

NOTES

SOLARO Study Guides
Ordering Information

The SOLARO Study Guides are specifically designed to assist students in preparing for unit tests, final exams, and provincial assessments.

SOLARO Study Guide—$29.95 each plus applicable sales tax

SOLARO
Study Guides

Ontario SOLARO Titles

Mathematics 12, Advanced Functions, University Prep (MHF4U)	Civics 10, (CHV2O)
Mathematics 12, Calculus and Vectors, University Prep (MCV4U)	English 10, Academic (ENG2D)
Mathematics 12, Mathematics of Data Management, University Prep (MDM4U)	OSSLT, Ontario Secondary School Literacy Test
Physics 12, University Prep (SPH4U)	Mathematics 9, Academic, Principles of Mathematics (MPM1D)
Biology 12, University Prep (SBI4U)	Mathematics 9, Applied, Foundations of Mathematics (MFM1P)
Canadian and World Politics 12, University Prep (CPW4U)	Science 9, Academic (SNC1D)
Chemistry 12, University Prep (SCH4U)	Science 9, Applied (SNC2P)
English 12, University Prep (ENG4U)	Geography of Canada 9, Academic (CGC1D)
English 12, College Prep (ENG4C)	English 9, Academic (ENG1D)
World History 12, University Prep (CHY4U)	Science 8
Mathematics 11, Foundations for College Mathematics (MBF3C)	Mathematics 7
Mathematics 11, Functions and Applications, U/C Prep (MCF3M)	Science 7
Mathematics 11, Functions, University Prep (MCR3U)	Mathematics 6
Biology 11, University Prep (SBI3U)	Science 6
Chemistry 11, University Prep (SCH3U)	Language 6
English 11, University Prep (ENG3U)	Mathematics 5
World History 11, University/College Prep (CHW3M)	Science 5
Mathematics 10, Academic, Principles of Mathematics (MPM2D)	Mathematics 4
Mathematics 10, Applied, Foundations of Mathematics (MFM2P)	Science 4
Science 10, Applied (SNC1P)	Mathematics 3
Science 10, Academic (SNC2D)	Science 3
Canadian History 10, Academic (CHC2D)	Language 3
Canadian History 10, Applied (CHC2P)	

To order books, please visit
castlerockresearch.com or call
1.800.840.6224
Volume pricing is available. Contact us at
orders@castlerockresearch.com

Student Notes and Problems
Workbook
Ordering Information

Student Notes and Problems (SNAP) Workbooks contain complete explanations of curriculum concepts, including examples and practice exercises

SNAP Workbook—$29.95 each plus applicable sales tax

Ontario SNAP Titles
Physics 12, University Preparation (SPH4U)
Physics 11, University Preparation (SPH3U)
Math 10, Academic, Principles of Mathematics (MPM2D)
Math 9, Academic, Principles of Mathematics (MPM1D)
Math 9, Applied, Foundations of Mathematics (MFM1P)

Total Cost

SOLARO Study Guides Ordered _____

SNAP Books Ordered _____

Cost Subtotal _____

Shipping and Handling
Please call for current rates _____

GST _____

Order Total _____

Payment and Shipping Information

Name _____
School _____
Telephone _____

SHIP TO:
School Code _____
School Name _____
Address _____
City: _____
Postal Code: _____

PAYMENT OPTIONS:
☐ By Credit Care VISA/MC
Name on Card: _____
Number: _____
Expirely Date: _____

☐ By Enclosed Cheque

☐ Invoice School
PO Number: _____

To order books, please visit
www.castlerockresearch.com

Volume pricing is available. Contact us at
orders@castlerockresearch.com